THE QUEER
TICS OF
ON

READING CONTEMPORARY TELEVISION

Series Editors: Kim Akass and Janet McCabe
janetandkim@hotmail.com

The **Reading Contemporary Television** series offers a varied, intellectually groundbreaking and often polemical response to what is happening in television today. This series is distinct in that it sets out to immediately comment upon the TV *zeitgeist* while providing an intellectual and creative platform for thinking differently and ingeniously writing about contemporary television culture. The books in the series seek to establish a critical space where new voices are heard and fresh perspectives offered. Innovation is encouraged and intellectual curiosity demanded.

THE QUEER POLITICS OF TELEVISION

Samuel A. Chambers

I.B. TAURIS

LONDON · NEW YORK

Published in 2009 by I.B.Tauris & Co Ltd
6 Salem Road, London W2 4BU
175 Fifth Avenue, New York NY 10010
www.ibtauris.com

Distributed in the United States and Canada Exclusively
by Palgrave Macmillan
175 Fifth Avenue, New York NY 10010

ISBN: 978 1 84511 681 1

A full CIP record for this book is available from the British Library
A full CIP record is available from the Library of Congress

Library of Congress Catalog Card Number: available

Typeset in Chaparral Pro by Sara Millington, Editorial and
    Design Services
Printed and bound in India by Thomson Press (India) Limited.

FOR VIRGINIA AND YVETTE

CONTENTS

PREFACE

et me begin with a claim that many readers will refuse to believe: I do not watch very much television. *Really*. I make this statement not as a denial of the significance of television as a cultural artefact. Indeed, one of the indirect aims of this book is to argue strongly for the importance of what I call 'the cultural politics of television'. Instead, I begin with this statement as a confession of ignorance: I have very little 'expert knowledge' on television. But more than that, I have no academic training in film studies, no degree in cultural studies, and no background in literature. I am a political theorist. My graduate 'training' (if it makes sense to call PhD work by that name) falls within the history of political thought and contemporary political theory. My previous work has focused on debates within contemporary social and political thought – debates over the relation between language and politics, the meaning of rights, and the conceptions of time and history that underwrite modern and contemporary politics and political subjectivity. Here I want, briefly, to tell the story of how a political theorist comes to write a book on TV.

That tale starts with a television show that plays no role in this book. *Sports Night* (ABC, 1998–2000), created and exclusively written by Aaron Sorkin, first aired on US television in 1998. It immediately garnered the attention of anyone who could appreciate smart writing, clever wordplay, and sophisticated, intelligent dialogue. Sorkin would later become famous for his 'snippets' – very short scenes marked by a writing style that, when combined with Thomas

Schlamme's Steadicam° directing, created something altogether new on television (Smith 2003). *Sports Night* was the only network television show I watched at the time, but I did not just watch it: I devoured it as a fan, and I also *read it* in much the same way I would read a text in political theory. That is, Sorkin's writing, in terms of both plot and dialogue, gave *Sports Night* a textual richness rarely seen on television (certainly not on US network television), and it made possible, for me at least, a different sort of engaged viewing.

These viewing practices continued over the next year to include not only *Sports Night* but also Aaron Sorkin's second, and soon to be much more famous, series *The West Wing* (NBC, 1999–2006). And it was in the middle of the first season of this new series – well before the show had begun to earn top ratings and awards – that I encountered a 'Call for papers' for panels devoted to *The West Wing*. At first, I dismissed the idea of submitting an abstract of a paper for the conference, and did so for the very reasons listed above – television was not my area of inquiry. But the open secret of abstracts is that it proves much easier to come up with 300 words telling your reader what your paper *would do*, were you invited to write it, than it is to actually write the 7000 words or more that make up the paper. Thus began my first foray into writing about television.

When it came time to write the paper, I did what I already knew how to do: I constructed an argument concerning the relationship between language and politics. Specifically I claimed, as I had done before, that particular theoretical conceptions of language encouraged certain understandings and practices of democracy (while ruling out others). The only difference was that I used an episode of *The West Wing* to help me carry out this work in political theory (Chambers 2003b). In other words, I treated the episode in question as a contribution to an ongoing debate in political theory, while I used the terms of that debate to help me explicate the episode, in particular, and the show, in general. In the process I discovered that this method proved surprisingly effective: (1) it advanced the current dialogue in contemporary political theory (by moving past certain impasses in the debate), (2) it shed a potentially new and different light on the study of television, and (3) it provided a particularly helpful frame for showing students (and others) the relevance and political salience of both television and political theory.

This book takes up the very same methodology that I stumbled upon in my first work on television. However, it does so, I hope, in a more sophisticated and self-conscious manner, as it makes an explicit attempt to bring political theory directly into dialogue with television studies. The medium for carrying out this dialogue is queer theory; the salience of this medium emerged when, in the summer of 2001, I first watched *Six Feet Under* (HBO, 2001–05). On viewing the first few episodes, I felt an immediate urge to write about the show precisely because of the opportunities I saw to read the show with and through queer theory. I recognised that *Six Feet Under* was conveying a number of the most fundamental insights of the founding texts of queer theory, and I saw that I could use the show in an effort to explicate those concepts in clear and accessible language. Simultaneously, I could put the show to work so as to *make a contribution to* the field of queer theory – to do queer theory through television.

Having finished this project I realised that a certain approach to television might help me as a political theorist to overcome a number of the most trenchant dilemmas of my field. These dilemmas usually circulate under the title 'theory and practice', and they often emerge whenever one thinks of theory as something 'abstract', 'ideal', or disconnected from the so-called 'real' world. It is easy to tell when theory is being conceived in this way because with this understanding comes the language of *applying* or *using* theory. To think about or to describe theory as if it were something that one dreams up in isolation and then attempts to 'apply' to real-world problems is to treat 'theory' like some sort of disembodied tool. This tool named 'theory' lies inert in an unspecified, unrooted location, and it only takes on importance if one can find something to fix with it. Thinking of theory in this way creates an obvious problem, as it consistently raises questions such as the following: What are we going *to do* with theory? How will we use it? What problems can it solve? The theory/practice dilemma comes about – and is generally irresolvable – whenever we understand theory to lie beyond practice and whenever we take daily life practices as having nothing to do with theory.

The theory/practice dilemma does not need solving, however. It can be avoided completely by conceiving of theory in an entirely different manner. Theory, I contend, is not something to be applied (see Brown 2002; Norton 2004). Theory, as the Greek *theoria* powerfully expresses, is a way of seeing; it is a way of grasping the world, of configuring it, of remaking it. Theory is not something that one would oppose to 'practice', since theory is precisely something that one practises. Theory is therefore also always a way of *doing*. One of the things that theory does is to clarify concepts, to provide a different language through which one finds meaning in the world around us. This book, then, certainly aims at conceptual clarity. It seeks to make some sense of the political phenomena that circulate around, and more importantly *in*, television. The book clarifies some of the terms of queer theory through the medium of television, just as it throws light on television through the language of queer theory.

While conceptual analysis has a central role to play here, as a work of political theory this book centres on politics. Yet it does not analyse events that would already be deemed to fall under the category of 'politics', but instead explores the very formation and configuration of that category of 'the political' in the first place. Indeed, despite certain appearances (e.g. the supposed frivolity of writing about TV), the political importance and stakes of this book prove higher than much of what I might contribute to mainstream political theory. Let me elaborate that claim. If political theory is seeing, if it is perception and perspective, then the political importance of this book lies precisely in the potential 'seeing' that it makes possible. Theorists not only seek to see the world but to make it visible in new ways for others. But in the field of contemporary political theory those 'others' are often reducible to other professional political theorists, and perhaps a few students. That is to say that only those already versed in the terms of political theory will be capable of reading works in contemporary political thought in such a way as to have that reading illuminate the world in a fundamentally different way. Powerful work, for example, on Heidegger's conception of Being-in-the-World really *can* help one to think of political community, rationality, political agency, and history in radically different ways. But, needless to say, it is not an easy task. And no matter the extent to which political theorists commit themselves to a vision of radical democracy, Heidegger will still remain inaccessible to most.

This is no reason not to read Heidegger or, for that matter, other difficult and even obscure thinkers. It is no reason not to teach these thinkers to students. A complex world demands complex texts, and *thinking*, as Heidegger himself would say, can never and should never be reduced to a simple, straightforward, or mechanistic process. But there must also be a space for helping 'others' to see the world differently through terms and texts that are both more readily available and more accessible to them. Perhaps television is one such medium. What I do here, then, is no different from any other work of political theory that I might write: I try to discern the world differently – to show it in a new light, from a new angle, and with a different arrangement. As a work of political theory, this book stands out not because it is somehow less rigorous or serious, but merely because it uses different devices – i.e. the texts of US television shows – to accomplish its tasks.

The book makes the argument that the political theory of television circulates within a very important (if not always starkly visible) cultural politics. *Cultural politics* names a way for us to think past the dilemmas and impasses of the theory/practice dichotomy described above. Moreover, cultural politics helps to describe the political significance of television and other cultural artefacts, while it simultaneously lends aid to the project of re-conceptualising 'the political'. This means that cultural politics cannot be reduced to a type of politics, where politics 'itself' does not change. Rather, to theorise cultural politics is to change the meaning of politics, to show that there is no such thing as 'politics itself'. The chapters in this work initiate such a project. The book aims to bring the study of television and culture into dialogue with political theory. At the same time – and as with all political theory that eschews the theory/practice dichotomy (i.e. political theory that allows a space for meaningful cultural politics) – it seeks to re-describe and thereby necessarily change the world.

* * *

My explorations of the politics of television began at the 'Presidency on Film' conference in Los Angeles in 2000. I thank the organiser, Peter Rollins, along with my fellow panellists, especially Heather Hayton, Greg Smith, Ted Atkinson, and Jason Vest. For his support and collaboration in pursuit of projects on cultural politics, I am especially grateful to Patrick Finn, whom I also first met at this conference. This is not quite the book that he and I were going to write (but never did), yet this work would not have come about without the thinking that went into our project. My writing on the cultural politics of television has always served as a helpful bridge between research and the classroom and thus I acknowledge my students over the years to whom I subjected my readings of various shows. I am particularly grateful to students at Saint Mary's College of Maryland, in the USA, and at Swansea University, in the UK.

Portions of this book were presented to various audiences and earlier versions of some chapters have been previously published; through this process I have gathered a number of debts. I am grateful to the organisers of panels and audience members at the following conferences: Popular Culture Association/American Culture Association, Toronto, 2002; American Comparative Literature Association, San Diego, 2003; American Political Science Association workshops on Political Myth, Rhetoric and Symbolism, Chicago, 2004, Washington DC, 2005; an invited lecture at Goldsmiths College, London, 2007; and a Department Seminar, Politics and International Relations, Swansea University, 2007. In particular, I would like to acknowledge the comments, criticisms, and organisational efforts of Alan Finlayson, George Lawson, and John Nelson. I also wish to acknowledge both the *Journal of American Culture* for permission to use material from an earlier version of chapter 1, and I.B.Tauris for materials in chapters 2–4.

My development of this project over the years has benefited greatly from critical engagement with earlier versions of various bits of what eventually came to be the chapters here. For their readings and responses, and often for discussion afterwards, I am grateful to the following: Asma Abbas, Ted Atkinson, Rebecca Brown, Anne Caldwell, Terrell Carver, Ruth Feingold, Alan Finlayson, Patrick Finn,

Lilly Goren, John Nelson, Charles Phillips, Christopher Robinson, Gregory Weight, and Daniel Williford. I am particularly indebted to Rebecca Brown and Jairus Grove for reading the entirety of the completed manuscript and providing important feedback at a crucial time.

Although this book is authored only by me – and thus, as always, the mistakes are all mine – my work on the politics of television has often been collaborative. Thus I owe deep debts to Patrick Finn, Daniel Williford, and Anne Caldwell for previous co-authored projects – endeavours from which I have grown as both a writer and a thinker. For truly leading the way in television studies and for their outstanding work as editors, I am very grateful to Kim Akass and Janet McCabe. It has been a great pleasure to work with Philippa Brewster at I.B.Tauris and I thank her for efficient and collegial shepherding of this project to fruition.

Others have collaborated with me on this project in very untypical ways, since in taking television as my object of academic study I have expanded my group of colleagues and peers well beyond the academy. For conversations, debates, and arguments about television, all of which have greatly strengthened my work for this book, I thank the following people: Joel Bettridge, Rebecca Brown, Jackie Chambers, Tim Chambers, Kim Evans, Alan Finlayson, Keri Finlayson, Laurie Frankel, George Lawson, Paul Mariz, Liam McCarthy, Charles Phillips, Gregory Weight, and Daniel Williford. I am very lucky to have had such a team of researchers on my side, and to have had such support.

As always, Rebecca Brown served as co-conspirator in this project, and it owes its greatest debt to her support and influence. Much of what I know about how to read television I learned from observing her skills as a peerless interpreter of visual culture, and I suspect that many of 'my' best insights in the book were stolen from her or emerged jointly through our constant conversations and frequent debates about television. This book simply would not have been possible without her.

I dedicate the book to my grandmothers, Virginia Chambers and Yvette Manning. From Ginny I learned the nobility of a life devoted to teaching and the love of bridge; from Yvette I learned about dignity and inner strength. And although neither set out to teach me such a lesson, from both I learned something of the politics of norms and family that this book explores.

INTRODUCTION
Queer Theory and the Cultural Politics of Television

While giving the keynote address at a recent conference, William Connolly, a prominent North American political theorist, put out an unexpected call to arms (of sorts). He made an impassioned plea, calling on every political theorist under the age of 35 to become as well trained in the reading and analysis of visual culture – particularly television, film, and TV news – as they are in the interpretation of texts within the history of political thought. Connolly went on to clarify that he was invoking no mere dilettantism: he insisted that the reading of television shows[1] will prove to be as important to politics in this century as the study of philosophical texts has been in the past (Connolly 2007). Although this book devotes its first two chapters to *Six Feet Under*[2] – one of the shows that Connolly lists as doing significant political work – my project here does not constitute an explicit response to Connolly's charge. Indeed, all six chapters of this work were drafted well before Connolly called on his colleagues to pay attention to the politics of television. Nevertheless, *The Queer Politics of Television* takes Connolly's contentions very seriously. It can be read as an illustration of his argument about the powerful and constitutive relationship between political theory and television.

Put simply, this book brings together political theory and television studies. Such 'bringing together' means, first of all, that the project must carry out the genuinely interdisciplinary work of developing the terrain created when two fields overlap. More than this, however, this book seeks to mobilise readings of television shows in order to theorise the political, and it tries to grasp the cultural phenomena of television using the conceptual tools of political thought. In other words, the book does political theory by way of television; it treats television shows as serious, important texts that demand rigorous readings from political theorists. At the same time, it develops television studies through the frameworks provided by political theory; it thereby suggests that the hermeneutic tools developed through the history of political thought can be called on effectively within the study of television shows.[3] In general, the book draws freely from the broad field of contemporary political theory, but I focus in particular on the smaller interdisciplinary area of queer theory. In this context I have three main aims: to elucidate the relationship between queer theory and political theory; to advance the politics of queer theory; and to make a specific contribution to the growing field of television studies by developing an account of the *cultural politics* of television.

Much like television studies, queer theory has proven to be one of the fastest growing fields in academia over the past decade. Indeed, queer theory's 'history', which I will discuss in brief below, proves terribly short. In 1990, queer theory did not even exist as a term, much less as a field of study. But with the coining of the term by Teresa de Lauretis in a piece published in 1991, and with the impact of seminal works by Eve Sedgwick and Judith Butler a year before, queer theory – developing out of the essential work of lesbian and gay studies scholars of the 1980s – took off in the 1990s, expanding into a rich and fertile field for the variegated study of gender, sex, and sexuality. By the turn of the twenty-first century, disciplines in both the social sciences and humanities were hiring specialists in 'queer theory', whose work not only furthered historical and cultural research but also expanded on the epistemological groundings of those early, now 'canonical' texts.

Compared with its cousins, film and media studies, television studies remains in its infancy (Brunsdon 1996; cf. Wilcox and Lavery 2002). Nonetheless, like queer theory, television studies has not only established itself extremely quickly, but also come to be taken as an 'established field' in surprising fashion. While writing on television as an explicitly academic enterprise would likely have been questioned a mere two decades ago, today 'television' appears as normal an object of study as 'society', 'culture' or 'politics'. Certain television shows (e.g. *Buffy the Vampire Slayer* (The WB Television Network, 1997–2001; UPN 2001–03)) currently have as broad and deep a secondary literature as famous philosophical texts or major historical events. And edited volumes on so-called 'quality television' (particular shows produced in the USA by the Home Box Office Network, HBO) are often in the works well before the first season of a new series is even complete.[4]

Connolly's bold comments notwithstanding, the field of political theory has arrived late on both of these scenes, still wary of the idea of taking television as a *text* or queer theory as a *theory*. Queer theory has thus not been seriously explored – in the way feminist theory has, for example – as a major contributor to political theory itself, and the politics of television have not been seriously considered. Indeed, Connolly may be the first to insist that political theory study TV in earnest, and there are important trends toward further interaction between queer theory and the broader field of contemporary political theory. Moreover, influential political theorists now insist that, to sustain itself, the field needs to draw on diverse resources from outside its boundaries (Brown 2002; see also Chambers 2006). Other important thinkers suggest that political theory must not only allow, but also aid in the re-conceptualisation of 'the political' – demanding that our understandings of the political be contested, challenged, and eventually changed (Arditi and Valentine 1999).

This book exposes and explores the cultural politics of television by reading contemporary television shows *through the lens* of queer theory. This project is designed to accomplish a number of significant goals simultaneously. First, it makes the case for the profound significance of the cultural politics of television, the way in which the text of a television show itself engages with the politics of its day. Put differently, the book argues for the centrality of cultural politics to politics writ large. Second, and most substantively, it offers a detailed engagement with queer theory, exploring precisely the links between queer theory as a newly emerging specialist field and political theory as a broadly conceived and long-standing area of inquiry. That is, it makes the case for queer theory's essential contribution to our thinking of the political. Third, and perhaps primarily, it initiates a larger project of queer television studies, along the same path that queer film studies has already trod. Finally, it offers a concrete and substantive contribution to the field of queer theory, by articulating and investigating many of the central tenets of queer theory through extended readings of television shows.

In this introduction I elaborate on all four of these main points – thus laying out the framework in which the book is positioned. I articulate the very idea of 'cultural politics' by delineating the relationship between culture, theory, method, text, and politics that this formulation identifies. Genuine and rigorous interdisciplinary work demands that one not merely borrow either objects of analysis or methods of approach from one field and then 'apply' them to another. Cultural politics thereby names the phenomena that emerge at the intersection of political theory and television studies, while it also gives direction to the type of scholarly and political work that must go on in this domain. Queer theory – as I sketch its history and describe its general approach here – can be productively construed as a form of cultural politics, just as it provides important tools for carrying out the work of this book. *The Queer Politics of Television* both elucidates and advances queer theory. At the same time, it seeks to identify cultural politics as a general phenomenon, while it explores one particular dimension of this phenomenon in the form of US television shows.

CULTURAL POLITICS

Culture is a complex and multivalent term; it is often severely misunderstood or under-theorised. On the one hand, 'culture' is used frequently in analyses to stand in for numerous concepts and objects that otherwise prove very much distinct from one another, and on the other, 'culture' is invoked in order to mask gaps in the logic of analysis. In other words, culture seems to be able to mean almost anything and function in almost any way. It is the term that covers everything; it is the explanation of last resort. If you don't know what it is, call it culture; if you can't explain it, attribute it to culture. Moreover, culture's relationship to politics proves even more fraught, with some seeing culture as the *opposite* of politics and others seeing culture as *always* political. All of this leads to a particular predicament for my analysis: some readers will wish to know what 'cultural politics' specifically means; a second group will wonder whether 'cultural politics' can possibly exist at all; and yet a third group will take 'cultural politics' for granted as an object of inquiry. In this section I map out a theory of 'cultural politics'. My purpose is not only to specify the meaning of cultural politics but also to articulate a clear set of parameters for grasping the relationship between culture and politics.

To achieve these ends it proves necessary to take a step back in order to see how culture is often conceptualised. Particularly within efforts to grasp the global political order, or in attempts to understand the domestic frictions and tensions caused by globalisation's movement of peoples between and among nation states, 'culture' is frequently invoked today as a catch-all term that elides differences between religion, race, ethnicity, and nationality. That is, political difference, and current or potential future conflict, are thought as having their source in something called 'culture'. Samuel Huntington's 'clash of civilizations' thesis makes this argument most pointedly and polemically, when he famously asserts at the outset of his widely read article that, in the post-cold war era, 'the great divisions among humankind and the dominating source of conflict will be *cultural*' (Huntington 1993: 22, emphasis added). The logic of this claim required Huntington to divide up the world, figuratively but forcefully, into a few distinct 'cultures'. But any reader of Huntington's work can see that 'culture' in his formula both *substitutes* for ethnicity, race, and religion and *collapses* the distinctions between and among them (Huntington 1993). Similarly, in her analysis of the discourse of tolerance – particularly within Western democracies' debates over multiculturalism – Wendy Brown examines the logic by which 'culture' effects a number of 'conflations and slides' between national identity, ethnic identity, religion, race, and sexuality. Culture stands in for all these terms collectively, and, alternatively, it allows one to move freely from one term to the other: for example, from 'Arab American' to 'Muslim' (Brown 2006a: 19). Indeed, the very term 'multiculturalism' as a marker and buzzword for the complex difference of contemporary societies can serve to mask two crucial facts: first, that today's Western societies are multi-religious, multi-ethnic, and multinational, in addition to being 'multicultural', and second, that, historically, no society has been 'mono-cultural'. In either case, 'culture' becomes a broad and temptingly monolithic term, a category not of analysis or critique, but merely of general description and simplification.

I reject this understanding of culture in the strongest terms. In my effort to theorise 'cultural politics' I consistently resist a conceptualisation of 'culture' as a category of reification or homogenisation, and I repeatedly interrupt what Mahmood Mamdani calls 'Culture Talk', which 'assumes that every culture has a tangible essence that defines it, and ... then explains politics as a consequence of that essence' (Mamdani 2005: 17; also quoted in Brown 2006a: 20). This understanding of culture certainly makes culture 'political', but it does so only by misunderstanding culture, language, and power. And it cuts off from the start any possibility of grasping the phenomena of *cultural politics*. Mamdani makes clear that Culture Talk, or what Brown calls 'the culturalization of politics', that is, the effort to reduce politics and politicisation to a confrontation between cultural differences, bears little or no resemblance to 'the culture studied by anthropologists – face-to-face, intimate, local, and *lived*' (Mamdani 2005: 17; Brown 2006a: 20).

In rejecting this common approach to culture and its overly simplistic understanding of the relation between culture and politics, I begin, then, with the long history of anthropologists' work on culture. I start with Anne Norton's thesis: *'culture is a matrix'* (Norton 2004: 1, emphasis added). With this claim Norton means not only to pay homage to the Geertzian definition of culture as 'a network of meaning',[5] but also to take that conceptualisation a step further. Norton insists that culture is not merely symbolic; it is not about meaning alone, as if meaning were only to do with words, and culture were only to do with non-material or somehow trivial elements. On the contrary, culture is very much material. And culture is a *matrix* because while culture is meaningful, meaning cannot exist in isolation. Meaning is always relational, and so is culture; thus, culture is 'something to be triangulated' (Norton 2004: 2). Nothing exists in isolation from the matrix, so culture (like meaning) is held in 'common'. Culture is common because it is a medium. Norton formulates this point in intentionally circular fashion, since to be *in* culture (and we can never *not* be in culture) is to be within a hermeneutic circle, that is, a space in which 'understanding' can only come about through reference to other or previously shared understandings. As she puts it, culture is 'the medium in which we are cultured' (Norton 2004: 2).

If we start with culture as a matrix of meaning and material practices, then we must resist the 'culturalisation of politics', as Brown says, but we must also refute the idea of culture as a variable, one that would somehow have causal explanatory power, as Norton goes on to argue. More importantly, as both Brown and Norton recognise, 'culture is political' (Norton 2004: 9; Brown 2006a: 21). To defend this claim, as Norton and numerous authors within the tradition of cultural studies have shown, means to secure the following corollary theses:

1) Cultural artefacts, cultural practices, and cultural rites and rituals all prove political – hence the prodigious output of cultural studies that analyses these artefacts, often precisely for their political qualities.

2) Sharp distinctions between the domain of politics, on the one hand, and the domain of culture (or economics, or society, etc.), on the other, are themselves ploys of power (i.e. acts of politics) – hence the work of contemporary social and political theorists (among others) who theorise precisely this *political* process of separating politics from its others.

3) 'Culture' is itself a domain of political contestation – hence the political phenomena of 'culture wars'.

4) Politics is always already cultural; political institutions are embedded within the matrix of culture and themselves make up a part of that matrix – hence the work of comparative scholars who reveal and study political institutions *in* their cultural dimension.[6]

Hence, also, the recent work of Wendy Brown. Although her project on tolerance clearly exceeds the scope of my arguments here, we might take Brown to be doing important work within corollary number 4. That is, Brown moves from the general notion that politics is cultural, to a specific historical defence and elaboration of the argument that 'liberalism is cultural' (Brown 2006a: 22). I want to use her particular analysis of liberalism as cultural, and of liberalism's own capacity to obscure this fact, in order to bring into relief the space of cultural politics within which this book works. Brown shows how liberalism tries to separate culture from politics, while her own analysis of liberalism's mechanisms makes clear that this is a structural impossibility. There can never be a thing called culture that is hermetically sealed off from a thing called politics. As I would put it, *cultural politics* is all there is.

Brown shows that liberalism cannot be neutral with regard to culture, since it encourages and nourishes certain forms of culture (Brown mentions individualism and entrepreneurship) while diminishing, denying, or legally excluding others. Moreover, any particular strand of liberalism only emerges within the context of a national culture, and all liberalisms take on the flavour of the nation. Brown then demonstrates that liberalism can never be pure in form; we only ever find 'varieties of it – republican, libertarian, communitarian, and social democratic' (Brown 2006a: 22). These claims add up to a strong case against the separation of politics from culture, but Brown has a much bolder argument in mind.

Brown wishes to demonstrate that culture is 'neither conquered by liberalism nor absent from liberalism' (Brown 2006a: 22–3). Culture is that which liberalism tries to cordon off, vanquish, or circumscribe, but also that which liberalism operates in and through. Liberalism *is* cultural, as Brown emphasises, even while liberalism tries to make culture other to liberal politics. Brown makes the key points as follows:

> The double ruse on which liberalism relies to distinguish itself from culture – on the one hand, casting liberal principles as universal; on the other, juridically privatizing culture – ideologically figures liberalism as untouched by culture and thus incapable of cultural imperialism. In its self-representation as the sole political doctrine that can

harbor culture and religion without being conquered by them, liberalism casts itself as uniquely tolerant of culture from its position above culture. *But liberalism is no more above or outside culture than is any other political form, and culture is not always elsewhere from liberalism* [or any other political form]. (Brown 2006a: 23, emphasis added)

Here Brown demonstrates the significance of liberalism's structural and *necessary* failures with respect to culture. Those very failures can help us see the importance of cultural politics. Culture serves as the conditions of (im)possibility for liberalism. It is the 'limit concept' of liberalism – that which is said to lie outside liberalism's fundamental commitments to universal principles such as secularism and the rule of law – and it is a necessary, constituent ingredient of liberalism – that on which liberalism relies (that which liberalism *is*) in order to function.

In this book I theorise culture as a matrix, while I simultaneously argue that the matrix is riven with the power relations of politics. 'Cultural politics' therefore names not a particular (and perhaps debased, non-scientific) form of politics that is somehow merely cultural. The concept of cultural politics, as I have built it up here, eschews the temptation to hive politics off from culture (or vice versa). Indeed, the efficacy of the phrase 'cultural politics' could lie in its ability to thwart that tendency, to draw our attention to the mutual imbrication of culture with politics, or of politics with culture. Thus, 'cultural politics' also proves much broader than the mere analysis of cultural artefacts for their political dimensions (corollary 1, above). No doubt, culture is political in this way, but to say that culture is political cannot be the end of the analysis. And not *all* cultural artefacts are worthy of study: merely being in the matrix does not mean much when one recognises that everything is in the matrix. Does this mean that everything is political? Perhaps. But we would do better to say that everything has a political *potential*. Anything *might* be political; we can never know from the outset, nor can we predict. In other words, not everything is political in the same way and to the same extent, and not everything merits the same form of critical scrutiny (Chambers 2006). Sometimes a bad pop artist is just a bad pop artist.

The importance of cultural politics must then lie in particular political mobilisations. Such 'mobilisations' may come from politicians' use of cultural artefacts, or from their efforts to participate directly in cultural politics. They may come from within the cultural forms themselves, intentionally placed there by the 'constructors' of those forms. And they can no doubt come from *readings* of cultural texts by consumers of culture and by analysts thereof. In this book I effect political mobilisations by focusing my inquiry in two ways. First, I narrow my study of cultural politics to one specific political and cultural form: US television shows. Second, I circumscribe my analysis of this form by searching mainly (though not, of course, exclusively) for the politics of gender, sexuality, and their normalisation. In other words, I study the cultural politics of television using the tools of queer theory. Thus, before these studies can get under way, I need to say something about the techniques and tactics I am using – and this demands a succinct introduction to the terms and very recent history of queer theory.

QUEER THEORY

From the perspective of cultural politics as I have sketched it above, the move to queer theory is anything but arbitrary. I approach queer theory neither as a narrow field concerned only with lesbian and gay sexuality nor as a mere theoretical technique (a type of reading one would 'apply' to texts). In the first instance, I conceive of queer theory as a form of cultural politics. Queer theory grasps the mutually constitutive relationship of culture and politics, and it tells us something particular about that link. More concretely, we can see that sex, gender, and presumed sexuality – all central foci of queer theory – prove culturally central to any current concept of identity. Finally, queer theory's understanding of identity and its conceptualisation of norms – both of which I will detail below – provide us with a form of theory that refuses the theory/practice dichotomy. This is precisely the type of theory required for the study of cultural politics.

What we today call 'queer theory' would never have been possible without the pioneering, path-breaking, and truly historical work of scholars in the field of lesbian and gay studies – particularly as that field burgeoned in the 1980s. Moreover, many of those scholars contributed directly to queer studies as this field began to take shape in the 1990s, while many of the most important insights of lesbian and gay studies were taken over by writers and thinkers within the new domain of queer theory. Despite all this, one of the clearest and easiest ways to introduce, define, or orient oneself with respect to queer theory is by way of contradistinction with many of the central tenets, approaches, and methodologies of lesbian and gay studies. Thus, I paint a sometimes stark contrast between these two fields, not in order to argue for queer theory's superiority, nor to suggest any sort of rejection of lesbian and gay studies (nor even its supersession by queer theory, since an important space remains for lesbian and gay studies). Rather, I use these distinctions as a heuristic to help draw a more vivid picture of the core insights and central commitments of queer theory.

Thus I begin with lesbian and gay studies, a field that, though it emerged much later, came from the same roots as the gay liberation movement – the pools of blood outside the Stonewall Inn. The Stonewall Riots of 1969, set off when a relatively 'routine' raid on a 'gay bar' in New York's Greenwich Village turned into a three-day confrontation between hundreds of police and thousands of protesters, sparked the emergence of a national and international movement.[7] This originally inchoate movement fought both for what would later be called 'gay liberation' and for radical sexual politics. However, in the 1970s gay liberation quickly became a part of 'identity politics' with the goal of achieving 'gay rights' (D'Emilio 1983). Fighting under this banner, many organisations of lesbians and gay men sought to define homosexuality as an unchanging and immutable characteristic – as it had been characterised, by way of homophobia, before the emergence of movements for gay liberation. However, now homosexuality was to be considered natural, good, and healthy rather than unnatural, bad, and sick.

In other words, the movement for gay rights based its claims on what we know today as the concept of 'sexual orientation', on the idea of a fixed sexual identity and the view that minority rights should be protected. It is essential to stress that other political strands branched out from Stonewall to wage a broader battle –

often in alliance with radical feminist groups, antiwar groups, and others – against normative sexuality, against the hegemony of marriage and the family. Yet the most well-known and dominant strand fell under the banner of gay rights. Why did gay liberation choose this particular political route? Because, as John D'Emilio puts it, recounting this very history:

> the concept of sexual orientation meshed with the reform brand of political action that evolved in the 1970s and 1980s. *It was easier to argue before a city council for civil rights for a fixed social minority than for a capacity inherent in everyone.* (D'Emilio 1992: xxvii, emphasis added)

D'Emilio also underlines the point that this political process (that of demanding rights based upon identity claims) resonated with the practice of coming out – a practice that D'Emilio describes as, the act of 'discovering ... our identities as gay or lesbian political beings' coupled with the choice to 'to burst out of the closet and to come out in a public, uncompromising way' (D'Emilio 1992: xiv). We can conceptualise lesbian and gay studies, as this field began to appear on US university campuses throughout the 1980s, as the continuation of this logic within the academy. If lesbians and gay men possessed a fixed identity based upon their 'sexual orientation', an identity whose rights should be defended politically, then this meant that there was a gay *identity* to be studied by the academy. Such studies should necessarily include a better understanding of this identity, through historical, literary, political, or psychological analysis. This leads to the academic study not merely of gay identity, but additionally of the historical role of homophobia, and what Eve Sedgwick famously named 'the epistemology of the closet' (as I will discuss in detail in Chapter 1). This insight produces a space for classes on gay authors, gay musicians, and other gay historical figures. It entails the creation of gay history, made famous by John Boswell, with which I will engage in Chapter 2. Overall, then, lesbian and gay studies is an academic project centred on a particular understanding of gay *identity* – a relatively fixed and unchanging category of human existence that persists across individual and historical time.

Queer theory, as I have stressed, would not be possible without the work of lesbian and gay studies: it does not leave behind or transcend the scholarship of this earlier field. There is thus something very wrong about the fact that a Wikipedia search for 'Lesbian and Gay Studies' automatically redirects one to the page for 'Queer Studies'.[8] In the first section of this book (Chapters I and II) I make my own, sometimes detailed, explication of key concepts and categories within queer theory, and throughout the book I repeatedly return to readings of some of the central texts that helped to form the field of queer theory. Here, then, my goal is to give readers previously unfamiliar with the field a clearer sense of what is at stake.[9] This is a deceptively difficult task. Search the literature for concise definitions of 'queer theory' and all you find is disclaimers, evasions, and critiques (e.g. Berlant and Warner 1995; Jagose 1996). Thus, I have taken the time to offer a broad sketch of lesbian and gay studies, not only because of the importance of these scholars and scholarship to queer theory, but also because this outline can help us to grasp one of the central and abiding insights of queer theory.

In distinction to lesbian and gay studies' effort to affirm and sometimes reify what it often took as some sort of 'given' – namely gay identity or sexual orientation – *queer theory starts from an impulse to question, problematise, or even disclaim the very idea of a fixed, abiding notion of identity*. A queer approach always insists on a relational understanding of identity, and it customarily asserts the importance of gender and sexuality to that relational conception. Such theory is 'queer' then in the typical senses of the word: both 'odd' and 'gay'. Throughout this book my invocations of and contributions to queer theory rely on this core (though not confining) meaning.

Queer theory emerges when scholars working within lesbian and gay studies begin to query the conception of gay identity upon which parts of gay liberation had been founded. These thinkers wondered whether it even made sense (theoretically, culturally, politically) to consider homosexuality as some sort of transhistorical and universal immutable characteristic. Was not sexuality, they asked, something more polymorphous than the heterosexual/homosexual dichotomy would lead one to believe? And historically, had not countless acts of violence been perpetrated against people based on the idea of the 'naturalness' of race, gender, and sexuality (Halperin 1990)?

These sorts of questions sparked a new wave of scholarship; they led to productive and often heated debate. The most famous of these is perhaps the essentialist/constructivist debate of the early 1990s, which proved central to the formation of queer theory. This dispute hinged on one central question: was 'homosexuality' a natural or at least general category that has existed throughout history (and could therefore be studied through something called 'gay history'), or were sexual forms and identities constructed *within* history and therefore dependent on the particular context in which certain practices, ideas, and beliefs take shape (Weeks 1981; see also Halperin 1990)?

To frame the issue both bluntly and concretely, in the form it sometimes took during this debate, we can look at the example of paederastic relationships in ancient Athens. These relationships existed between 'a free adult Athenian male and an adolescent [male] youth of citizen status' (Halperin 1990: 47). These were relations of mentorship, friendship, and courtship, and they were often, though certainly not always, sexual in nature (see Dover 1989 [1978]). However, the relationships themselves were highly regulated by cultural norms, and thereby had to follow a set of unwritten (but often very explicit) rules:

1) The two males had to be sharply differentiated in terms of social standing and political power. This was an explicit relation of *inequality* (Halperin 1990: 47).

2) The sexual relations themselves had to reflect this inequality, with the dominant partner in social standing playing the dominant sexual role. Only the superior could 'initiate a sexual act, penetrate the body of his partner, and obtain sexual pleasure' (Halperin 1990: 47).

It must also be kept in mind that the dominant partner in such a paederastic relationship would almost certainly have a wife with whom he would regularly have sex, while he would also routinely avail himself of both prostitutes (women and boys) and slaves as objects of his sexual gratification. Moreover, the inferior/younger/ passive partner in the relationship would one day grow into an adult, take a wife of his own, and likely participate as the dominant partner in his own paederastic relationships.

The central question of the essentialist/constructivist debate was a short yet difficult one: can we call this boy/man 'homosexual'?[10] At the risk of oversimplification: the essentialists said yes, the constructivists said no. To say 'yes' meant to affirm a potentially fixed and unchanging, but clearly transhistorical, conception of homosexual identity; such a declaration was therefore a way of affirming a core value of lesbian and gay studies. To say 'no' meant to insist upon the historical specificity of sexuality and to consistently think of gender and sexuality as relational categories; this position in the debate therefore gives shape to one of the key dimensions of a queer approach.

This debate did not go on within a political vacuum, of course. It emerged and was sustained during the AIDS crisis. And it was waged during a time in which queer political activism took centre stage – a queer activism that distanced itself from the mainstream lesbian and gay interest groups. The crisis produced by the AIDS epidemic, and the lack of governmental response to it, produced a need for a non-identity-based response. This was the case because – despite homophobic presumptions to the contrary – AIDS was not affecting only lesbians and gay men. Like most epidemics it impacted broadly on those communities whose members contracted HIV, and the challenges that HIV/AIDS posed – to those who were sick, to those who might become sick, and to family members, co-workers, friends, and lovers – could not be overcome by isolated individuals. ACT-UP (Aids Coalition to Unleash Power) formed in response to the crisis of AIDS. It was one of the first, and certainly remains one of the most important, queer political movements. It was and is, as its name suggests, a genuine coalition of those affected by the AIDS emergency. This coalition obviously includes a large number of gay men, but it also includes significant numbers of straights (parents, friends, those infected by other means and so on). Thus, we witness in these political practices the movement beyond a rigid understanding of 'homosexuality' that the word 'queer' encourages. This move can be justified both by theo-retical/historical arguments, and by political exigencies.

Indeed, the first usage of the word queer in a non-pejorative sense occurred not in the academy, but within activist circles. In 1990, Te-resa de Lauretis coined the phrase 'queer theory' when she borrowed the use of queer from activist friends and used that phrase as the title of a conference she was organising.[11] As David Halperin helpfully points out, de Lauretis employs the phrase 'queer theory' as some-thing of a joke, since she herself saw the pairing of the typically of-fensive word 'queer' with the high minded seriousness of 'theory' as a bit comical. Of course, she had serious intentions as well, even if the seriousness of queer theory would soon leave far behind any of the humour. Writing more recently, Halperin summarises this history:

> ...she had intended the title as a provocation. She wanted specifically to unsettle the complacency of 'lesbian and gay studies' ... which im-plied that the relation of lesbian to gay male topics in this emerging field was equitable, perfectly balanced, and completely understood ... She also wished to challenge the erstwhile domination of the field by the work of empirical social scientists, to open a wider space within it for reflections of a theoretical order, to introduce a problematic of multiple differences into what had tended to be a monolithic, homog-enizing discourse of (homo)sexual difference, and to offer a possible escape from the hegemony of white, male, middle-class models of analysis. Beyond that, she hoped both to make theory queer (that is, to challenge the heterosexist underpinnings and assumptions of what conventionally passed for 'theory' in academic circles) and to queer theory (to call attention to everything that is perverse about the project of theorizing sexual desire and sexual pleasure). Queer theory was thus a placeholder for a hypothetical knowledge-practice not yet in existence, but whose consummation was devoutly to be wished. (Halperin 2003: 340)

This summary comes from a short essay by Halperin entitled 'The normalization of queer theory', in which he argues, a mere 13 years after the coining of the term, that the 'empty placeholder' queer theory was far too quickly *presumed* to be filled with content, even when it was not. The radical potential of queer theory could be lost, Halperin warns, precisely as a result of its institutional successes.

Lauren Berlant and Michael Warner, writing in 1995 (just two years after Warner's edited volume *Fear of a Queer Planet* helped queer theory to go mainstream), voiced their own quasi-disavowal of the term thus: 'the critical mass of queer work is more a matter of perception than of volume. Queer is hot' (Berlant and Warner 1995: 343).

However, many now worry that queer burned too brightly, and thereby burned itself out. Halperin laments both the de-radicalising and de-sexualising of queer. That is, queer can now be used as a theoretical tool like any other: it need not disturb or disrupt the disciplines, and it need not specifically invoke the lives of those whose gender and/or sexuality puts them at risk in today's societies (Halperin 2003: 341–2). Unlike others along the way, who have simply called for the abandonment of queer theory (at least in name if not in principle), Halperin holds out a hope for queer theory's future. His vision looks like this:

> If queer theory is going to have the sort of future worth cherishing, we will have to find ways of renewing its radical potential – and by that I mean not devising some new and more avant-garde theoretical formulation of it but, quite concretely, reinventing its capacity to startle, to surprise, to help us think what has not yet been thought. (Halperin 2003: 343).

In my effort to heed Halperin's call, I conceive of this book as a work within the folds of queer theory. I insist on the specificity of queer theory to revolve around (though therefore not centre upon) fundamental issues of gender and sexuality. This means that queer theory need not be exclusively linked or generally tied to inquiries regarding gender and sexuality. In other words, queer theory is not just about sex, since its resistance to and subversion of the category of the normal has wide-reaching effects. Nevertheless, there must always be some thread that connects 'queer' to gender/sex/sexuality and specifically to those lives rendered unintelligible by the power of heterosexuality when it functions as a disciplinary norm.[12] I mobilise my readings, both of television shows and theoretical texts, in the service of thinking what has not been thought, of seeing – with regard to the queer politics of television – that which has not yet been seen.

Thus, for my purposes here, queer theory poses questions of gender and sexuality not in terms of identities that one might map within a grid, but in terms of relationalities that one would plot along a normal curve. The so-called object that we refer to as 'queer theory' is nothing of the sort (see Berlant and Warner 1995: 343). Queer theory, instead, both refers to an intellectual and methodological orientation toward particular issues concerning subjectivity and politics, and denotes a set of frameworks or tools helpful in analysing both historical and contemporary problematics to do with norms – particularly norms of gender and sexuality. To do theory that is queer, to conceive of a 'queer politics', means to call attention to that which is marginal with respect to dominant norms. Thus, 'queer' should call to mind a vision of the normal bell curve, because norms involve much more than common, typical or average behaviours or practices. Norms must include both the median point on the normal curve and the tails or outer edges of the curve. This is why a norm is not a norm without the marginal and the deviant; outliers are exactly what sustain the norm. Practices and behaviours that 'deviate from the norm' must be conceived as practices and behaviours that make the norm possible, in that they establish the distance between 'the normal' and its other (see Foucault 1978). Thus there is really no such thing as 'outside' the norm; there is only the queer with respect to the norm. I describe the work done in this book as 'queer theory' in precisely this sense.

QUEERING TELEVISION

Before starting that work, I must specify one final but vital dimension of it: television. As the title of this introduction clearly announces, this book is about queer theory and the cultural politics of television. What that entails should now also be clearer: it means using queer theory to illuminate a particular cultural politics, and it relies upon reading the texts of US television shows in order to further queer theoretical and political projects. As noted, Connolly calls television *political* in the most fundamental way. He is not alone in this claim. Others writing in contemporary political theory have not only recognised television as a cultural form, but have also identified it as a particularly 'politically perspicacious' one. This phrase belongs to Michael Shapiro, who goes on to argue that certain 'cultural texts' must be understood to constitute significant 'political interventions' (Shapiro 2001: 5, 14). And, in this context Shapiro suggests that television, given the prominent role of reruns on any daily schedule, produces a powerful 'historical consciousness' (Shapiro 2001: 15). Perhaps ironically, Shapiro makes these repeated references to the political salience of television – to the participation of television in what I am calling cultural politics – within the introduction of a book that then goes on to discuss cinema, not television. And, for his part, Connolly admits that the political work to be done on television must come from a new generation of scholars, not from him. These earlier arguments provide an important point of departure, yet my work here moves beyond the identification of television as a form of cultural politics. This book does more than recognise television's political salience: it assesses and mobilises the cultural politics of television.

My conception of cultural politics and my use of queer theory both serve to circumscribe my methodology with respect to television. That is, while there are a wide variety of ways to study or analyse television, I take up a very particular and focused interpretive methodology. To state the point starkly: I approach the study of television shows in much the same way as I would approach a text in the history of political thought. *I aim to read the show for the politics contained within it.* Here I follow an important tradition within the burgeoning field of television studies: scholars have insisted on the continuity between television as a meaning-making artefact and other literary forms. Fiske and Hartley, who are credited with coining the phrase 'Reading Television' in their 1978 book of that name, insisted on links between television and Shakespeare. More recently, Rhonda Wilcox draws numerous and repeated connections to *Buffy*, using T.S. Eliot, Charles Dickens, and others to tie her analysis to canonical literary works (Wilcox 2005: 31). The title of Wilcox's seminal book on *Buffy* explicitly poses the question *Why Buffy Matters* (2005) while it implicitly asks why television matters. Wilcox's answer lies in showing the literary status of *Buffy* (and by corollary, of other television shows), by demonstrating, as her subtitle declares, that *Buffy* is art. In drawing from this tradition, I insist more on the importance of *reading* a television show like one might read any other text, and focus significantly less on treating television like a great work of literature. This book therefore offers developed readings of particular shows and episodes, designed not to connect television to the 'great works' but to mine television for its political possibilities. Thus, these shows 'matter' not because of their status, but because of the queer politics that can be drawn to light from particular readings of them.

It may well be important to know something of the context surrounding the show in order for these readings to be coherent and successful, and thus I sometimes elucidate controversies surrounding the shows or analyse the political context in which they appear. Nonetheless, my overall concern lies more with the political possibilities of the reading I offer and less with the historical impact that the text may or may not have had upon its original publication (or airing). For this reason, viewer reception of the show is not a chief concern in my analyses; neither is a study of the micro-politics of the self that watching television might enact (Connolly 2002, 2005).[13] Instead, I wish to locate and analyse a queer cultural politics in certain television shows, and to explore in some depth and detail those dimensions of the shows that make such a politics possible. My interest in television lies firmly in exploring possibilities for cultural politics; for this reason I am primarily concerned more with what certain readings of television shows *can tell us about the world*, and less with what experiences of watching television could teach us about ourselves or society writ large.

For these reasons I do not place enormous emphasis on production details, or audience demographics and ratings. It seems important to be very clear about this point: I am by no means dismissing the importance of the fact that *Six Feet Under* aired on a premium cable channel (HBO), *Buffy* appeared on two different minor channels (WB and UPN), and *Desperate Housewives* (2004–) runs on one of the main network channels (ABC). Instead, I am merely suggesting that these differences should not be seen to place burdensome constraints on the potential readings of these shows, any more than the fact that *Hamlet* was first performed at the Globe Theatre would be seen to limit our interpretations of that work – or that Aristotle's *Politics* did not have a wide audience upon its original appearance. While I concentrate on neither the individual psychology of the viewer (micro-politics) nor on the sociological average of all viewers (viewer reception), my critical approach to television still keeps the viewer in mind. That is, I am certainly concerned with the position of the viewer as a structural component of the medium of television. Therefore, although I insist on the analogy of television shows to political texts, I do not wish to elide the difference between the two. The *politics* of television emerges through the interpretations of shows that I offer here, but there is another important dimension to this politics: namely, the force and effects of television as a cultural medium. Television can and should be *read*, but it remains an element of visual culture. Television has a distinct temporality and historicity; it reaches a mass audience; and its serial format has important consequences for the viewer's sense of time and narrative (Feuer 1984; Thompson 1996; Newcomb 1997; Wilcox 2005). All of these dimensions of television have notable political valences. While this book does not make such phenomena its central focus, I see my project here as complementary to past and future efforts to explore them.

Furthermore, in articulating my approach to television I need to place some emphasis on the title of this book. The book is called *The Queer Politics of Television*; it is not called *The Politics of Queer Television*. This latter title would make sense and such a book could certainly be written. But this is not that book. Here, I read the queer politics within television and I do so without labelling the shows I use as either 'queer' or 'gay'. Thus I distinguish my project from an effort to identify an object called 'queer television' and then describe its (possible) politics. It is worth pointing out, however, that 'queer television' as a label would be better named 'gay television', since this identity-based approach fits better with a more static understanding of gay identity. Thought rigorously, 'queer television' would describe television that suggests a relational understanding of (sexual) identity and/or television that resists or subverts normative heterosexuality. 'Gay television', in contrast, would account for shows – as discussed below – with primary gay themes or characters. This also means that genuine *queer television* could not be discovered in advance but would only emerge through a queer reading. It is only in this particular sense that this book is concerned with 'queer television', and therefore to maintain a clear distinction between my approach and that which I eschew, I refer, both in the title and throughout the book, to the queer politics of television.

Undoubtedly 'queer television' could easily be read differently, in the way that it is already used in the very titles of contemporary television programmes. Thus, 'queer television' could conceivably be used to name a category of gay and lesbian themed or focused shows, shows that centre on gay characters, have predominantly gay casts, or consistently explore gay 'issues'. *Queer as Folk* (Showtime Networks, 2000–05), *The L Word* (Showtime Networks, 2004–09), and *Queer Eye for the Straight Guy* (NBC, 2003–07) are just a few shows that come to mind to head up this category (see 'LOGO' 2007). While this book mentions all of these shows, and devotes an entire chapter to one of them, the book itself is not about 'queer television' in this sense. Indeed, I will repeatedly argue that in terms of cultural politics 'gay shows' often turn out to be much less queer than one might otherwise expect. This book uses queer theory to read television shows for their cultural politics, but the shows themselves are chosen not for any particular content of gay identity or themes, but for the way they participate, or can be made to participate, in cultural politics.

It is therefore important to specify some elements of the general context, to describe the matrix that constitutes the cultural politics in which this book participates. As noted above, for reasons of consistency I use US television terminology throughout the book. But this terminological choice must not be taken to reflect politics. As a whole, the book draws on American and non-American political and social contexts, including, especially, examples from the UK (where all of the shows I discuss have aired). In other words, the cultural politics I am describing cannot be confined to an American context, and I interpret these shows in order to describe a politics that always outruns any particular context.

In general, however, the queer politics of television speaks to a set of contemporary political conditions marked heavily by what this book will name *heteronormativity*. Much of the book is devoted to defining and theorising heteronormativity and I will not rehearse that work here. Rather, I merely want to indicate that heteronormativity plays a constitutive political role in the world today: the world we inhabit is structured by the presumption of heterosexuality and partially determined by the dominant norm of heterosexuality. While this phenomenon often proves to be masked, sometimes seems invisible, and is often rendered unintelligible, we can witness it through a variety of cultural and political practices that either prop up the heterosexual norm explicitly or merely presuppose that norm and thereby support it implicitly. These practices constitute the context in which the queer politics of television takes shape.[14] The queer politics of television does not emerge *ex nihilo*. That is, the idea of 'queering television' does not come about for its own sake, but for the potential contribution it might make to cultural politics. Therefore the queer politics of television has a significant role to play, specifically in the frame of contemporary cultural and political practices that stigmatise and marginalise gays, lesbians, and transgender individuals. Moreover, it also has a contribution to make, perhaps a more important one, to a politics of norms that affects all individuals, gay or straight – and does so through disciplinary and normalising powers that have far-reaching political effects.

* * *

To carry out the task of understanding these powers and analysing these effects, the book is divided into three parts, each with two chapters. The book begins with the politics of the closet, one of the most important contributions made by queer theory to an understanding of gender, sexuality, and identity in the late-modern world. Part I explores some of the central insights and core tenets of queer theory through two different readings of the HBO series *Six Feet Under*. In Chapter 1, I use the first season of *Six Feet Under* to elaborate Eve Sedgwick's powerful notion of 'the epistemology of the closet'. This phrase gives a name to the way in which the ostensibly secret knowledge of (homo)sexuality structures and constrains the lives of all lesbians and gay men. The closet is a pervasive feature of the lives of everyone who deviates from the heterosexual norm, but it also has an often invisible impact on the lives of straights as well. In this chapter I argue that *Six Feet Under* not merely shows viewers gay characters: for the first time it reveals the closet to viewers and it gives them a glimpse of how the closet operates. Chapter 2 takes this analysis further by returning to *Six Feet Under*, this time in its third season. Here I contend that the show provides an even more powerful understanding of queer relational identity through its development of a character that refuses both categories of modern sexual identity (gay and straight). With the character of Russell Corwin[15] we have a sexuality that proves almost impossible to render clearly, but precisely this illegibility gives us the starkest sense of the meaning of queer.

Having come to terms with some of the central tenets of queer theory, Part II moves on to investigate the politics of heteronormativity. Both chapters draw from Judith Butler's political theory, particularly as her work can serve to illuminate the power of norms. Chapter 3 calls for a turn toward a queer politics of norms and away from an identity politics that rests on notions of representation. It uses this argument about the importance of norms in order to mobilise a counterintuitive critique of *The L Word* for its unwitting reification of heteronormativity. Despite the plethora of gay characters, *The L Word* offers less than one might expect to queer politics. I pair this critique of an apparently 'progressive' show with a politically productive reading of *Desperate Housewives*. Thus, Chapter 4 works in inverted fashion to make the counterintuitive case that *Desperate Housewives* – despite its severely constrained soap opera context – actually serves to undermine and subvert heteronormativity because it challenges the norm from within.

Finally, Part III closes the book with an investigation of the cultural politics of family. Chapter 5 argues for a radical resignification of family in Joss Whedon's *Buffy the Vampire Slayer*. Here I challenge both conservative defences of the traditional or nuclear family *and* putatively radical calls for 'chosen' families. Instead, I use the family relations on *Buffy* to mount a critique of what I call the *sanguinuptial* model of family (family based on blood and marriage). By rework-

ing and refiguring the very meaning of family, *Buffy* contributes
to a queer politics that proves much more radical than the notion
of 'chosen families'. Chapter 6 advances this argument through an
analysis of one of HBO's more recent shows, *Big Love* (HBO, 2006–).
I argue that within the practice of plural marriage on this show, one
can locate a space and dimension of queer family. This conception
of queer family provides one way of reconfiguring the politics of the
family beyond the sanguinuptial model criticised in Chapter 5. I leverage this conception of queer family in order to make a particular
rejoinder to some of the central debates in queer theory and politics
over the slippery and contentious issue of so-called 'gay marriage'.
Building on what has come before, this section of the book thereby
offers the clearest picture of the queer politics of television because
it answers directly some central questions within queer theory, while
it speaks very concretely to contemporary politics.

Given my understanding, however, of both queer theory and
cultural politics, it should be evident that the queer politics of television names an ongoing and never-complete project. It is for this
reason that I end the book without overarching or totalising synthe-
sis. Queer theory cannot be grand theory – theory that offers com-
prehensive and comprehending explanations. And cultural politics
promises no final victory or telos. My hope, then, is that the book
contributes to both of these projects. More so, this book should spur
further investigations into the pivotal role that queer theory can play
within political thought more generally, and it opens up the crucial
dimension of the cultural politics to be found in television.

NOTES

1   Because this book centres on readings of US television shows, and above
    all for the sake of consistency, I will employ US terminology with re-
    spect to television. Thus, I use 'television shows' rather than 'television
    programmes', I refer to 'seasons' rather than 'series' to describe quasi-
    annual sequences of televised episodes, and I reserve the word 'series'
    to name the entire run of episodes over the life of the show.

2   For production details on all episodes of all shows cited in this book,
    please see the Episode Guide at the back of the book.

3   It seems worth noting at the outset that texts in political theory, on the one hand, and television shows, on the other, have more in common than one might expect. Some (both writers and readers) approach texts in political theory as if they provide nothing but pure, logical arguments, but even a cursory reading of Plato shows us that texts are dramatic constructions (see Carver 2004). They tell stories. To grasp the argument of a text in political theory we must also follow the story. And in this book I demonstrate that one can do the same with television shows: track the story to find the argument.

4   I could provide a long list of examples here of both the rich and deep academic literature of a few of those volumes in production. To do so, however, would be to get ahead of myself, as I engage with a great deal of that literature in this book. Here I wish merely to set the stage.

5   I call this definition 'Geertzian' because, as Norton explains, it is 'variously *attributed* ... to Max Weber and Clifford Geertz' and it remains associated with Geertz's approach to culture; however, neither Geertz himself, nor Weber, ever defined culture so concisely as this (Norton 2004: 2, emphasis added).

6   I intentionally do *not* refer to comparativists who study the 'cultural dimension *of* political institutions', as that formulation would imply that culture and institutions can be somehow separable, that each might form a distinct independent variable that would then be used to explain political phenomena. This example offers one more angle on the approach to culture and politics that I reject. Institutions and culture are not distinct; rather, political institutions are a part of the matrix that is culture. To understand political institutions is to understand culture, that is, to understand that politics is cultural. As Norton explains, this logic leads us to abandon the concept of 'political culture' (Norton 2004: 11–12). I suggest, in turn, that such logic should also lead us to adopt and theorise the notion of *cultural politics*.

7   For the most commonly cited authority on 1960s and 1970s US gay history see D'Emilio (1983), and for the definitive historical account of Stonewall, see Carter (2004).

8   See the entry for 'Queer Studies' at Wikipedia, redirected from a search for 'lesbian and gay studies', available at *http://en.wikipedia.org/wiki/ Lesbian_and_gay_studies*, accessed 27 May 2007.

9   Readers already well versed in queer theory will therefore necessarily find nothing new here, and for my own contributions to the field I point these readers to my specific arguments about queer theory in the first two chapters of the book and in general to my theorisation of heteronormativity over the entirety of the work.

10   I have no intentions here of trying to make a contribution to long-standing debates about classical Greece, nor do I necessarily wish to endorse any of the historiography that I have summarised. I work through this example simply as a heuristic device to help grasp some of the central elements of queer theory, and I do so because this debate proved central to queer theory's emergence as a field.

11   With queer theory, then, just as with Stonewall, we see that not only political transformation but also intellectual change is often wrought by 'ordinary' individuals and their actions. Queer theory, like the broader movements of both gay liberation and queer activism, must be understood as a field that emerges from a confluence of events, many of which far exceed the scope and intentions of academia.

12   This means that the effort to generalise queer theory, to use it in contexts that we might call 'non-sexual', must still, in the final analysis, be capable of being traced back genealogically to sexuality and to the history of queer activism. My own inclination is to expand and broaden the remit of queer theory, but at the same time I very much heed the warnings of Leo Bersani, and later Halperin, concerning the 'despecify[ing] of the lesbian, gay, bisexual, [and] transgender ... content' (Halperin 2003: 341; cf. Bersani 1995).

13   Relatedly, I do not investigate the socio-economic conditions of production for the television shows I interpret. It is doubtless the case that the creation, marketing, and production of these shows participate in the logic of late modern capitalism. Television is a commodity, even as it serves as one of the primary media for selling commodities. I have no desire to deny this important fact, but, for my purposes, to focus on it narrowly or to allow it to take on a determinative dimension in my work would be to make a banal point. The cultural politics of television may far outstrip the capitalist structure within which it operates.

14   Examples of these practices include obvious attempts in the USA to disenfranchise lesbian and gay citizens through Federal and State Defense of Marriage Acts, known as DOMAs (see Chambers 2003a). More importantly for a theory of cultural politics, they extend to seemingly hollow US Presidential declarations like the 'National Defense of Marriage Week' or to President Bush's (again, apparently only 'symbolic') support for a Federal Marriage Amendment (Bush 2003 and 2006; see also Chambers 2006). In the UK, heteronormativity is brought to the fore more obviously in the resistance to the policy that allows lesbians and gays legally to adopt (see 'Gay adoption row', BBC 2007), and, less obviously, through the constant worry over 'mixed-sex' hospital wards – a worry that belies the heteronormative assumption that segregated

hospital wards are somehow better, more 'natural' (see 'Row over mixed-sex wards', BBC 2006). These examples are not determinative, but they suggest some of the flavour of the cultural politics involved.

15   In my approach to TV, I try very hard to resist the tendency to reduce characters to actors. In the texts of the show that I read, it is the character that matters, not the person playing that character. For this reason, and in order not to interrupt the flow of the text, I do not provide actors' names in the main body of the text. For full information on actors, see the Cast List at the back of this volume.

PART I

Closet Politics

1

Telepistemology of the Closet

even to come out does not end anyone's relation to the closet
(Sedgwick 1990: 81)

'I t's not TV; it's HBO.' HBO's now seemingly timeless slogan
first rang true with the storied success of *The Sopranos* (1999–
2007), but it was confirmed by the five-season run of Academy
Award winner Alan Ball's *Six Feet Under*. As with the Mafia violence
of *The Sopranos* and the graphic sexual language (much more graphic
than the sex itself) of *Sex and the City* (HBO, 1998–2004), *Six Feet
Under* has its own share of content that could simply never appear on
US network television. This forbidden subject matter takes the form,
mostly, of naked dead people – some of whom speak. While setting the
show in a funeral home, and weaving each of the episode's numerous
plots in and around death and funerals, certainly makes *Six Feet Under*
unique (and often rather surreal), what makes the show both path-
breaking vis-à-vis network television and politically significant for
the purposes of my reading here is its subtle, sophisticated, and deft
approach to the subject matter of identity and sexuality. I will argue
that in its first season, *Six Feet Under* both promises and begins to
provide its viewers with something never before seen on television:
an illustration and illumination of the process of forming both gay
and straight sexual identities in the face of societal heteronormativity
– a demonstration that entails shining a light on the inner workings
of the closet.

The Television and the Closet

Of course, to anyone who follows portrayals of lesbians and gays on television, my thesis that *Six Feet Under* is the first television series to show viewers the closet and its politics may sound like bad history. It would appear to many that the closet door has already been thrown wide open by recent television offerings, a door that was previously cracked by shows such as *Soap* (ABC, 1977–81) and *Dynasty* (ABC, 1981–9). These programmes broke ground in television for gay themes and characters, ground that was then developed, though unevenly, during the 1990s (Atkinson 2004). NBC's long-term hit *Will and Grace* (1998–2006) not only won over audiences but also won Emmy awards – all with a gay lead character. Eric McCormack plays Will, a gay but also successful, reasonable, and mature Manhattan lawyer – officially described as 'likeable, handsome and charming' ('Will and Grace', NBC 2001). He is paired with Jack, his 'outrageous' (read flaming) comic sidekick.[1] Or, if mildly gay-themed situation comedy seems too tame, or just not political enough, then there is *Queer as Folk*. This groundbreaking show aired for two seasons in the UK (1999–2000), before the US cable channel Showtime decided to make their own version of the show and purposively repackage it as controversial. The rebranding was a success and the show ran for five seasons (2000–05). With *Queer as Folk* literally everyone is gay, every episode's theme is a 'gay theme' and no viewer of any episode can doubt the veracity of the 'graphic sexual content' warning before each episode.[2]

I have no need or intention to offer critiques of these shows. Instead, I suggest that perhaps they say less about what Eve Kosofsky Sedgwick has called the 'epistemology of the closet' than we might first think. Sedgwick's point of departure lies in the simple fact that for almost all gay people the closet constitutes the most salient feature of their social lives. This is the case whether someone is 'in' or 'out' of the closet, since all gay people, no matter how openly out they are, will eventually find themselves in the closet with someone who is close to them either personally, professionally, or economically (Sedgwick 1990: 68). But we are not, Sedgwick warns us, to conclude from these facts that the closet proves significant merely for gay people. On the contrary, Sedgwick provocatively suggests 'that the epistemology of the closet has ... been ... inexhaustibly productive of modern Western culture and history at large' (Sedgwick 1990: 68).

This is a bold claim. Sedgwick backs it up not with more sweeping rhetoric, but by way of example. She tells the story of the teacher in Montgomery County, Maryland, who was removed from his teaching position in 1973 when the Board of Education discovered he was gay; when he gave statements to the media, the Board fired him. He sued, and the federal district court sided for the Board, arguing that the teacher brought 'undue attention' upon himself when he spoke to the media. He appealed, and the Circuit Court of appeals disagreed with the lower court, saying that statements to the media were protected First Amendment speech. But they sided with the Board nonetheless, saying he had no standing to sue anyway, since he had failed to note on his employment application that he was an officer of a homophile organisation in college (Sedgwick 1990: 69). (School officials admitted that if the teacher had noted this on his application, he would never have been hired.)

Some readers might dismiss this story as an outdated example of homophobia from 35 years ago. But the story's significance lies in what it tells us about the precariousness of gay sexual identity. The epistemology of the closet produces the very fragility of this identity, something that may not have changed that much. In each ruling the court says that the teacher's sexual identity 'itself' offered no legitimate ground to fire him. Here we see the issue of knowing and its dynamic connections to power:

> Each of the courts relied in its decision on the supposedly protected and bracketable fact of [the teacher's] homosexuality proper, on the one hand, and on the other hand his highly vulnerable management of information about it. So very vulnerable does this latter exercise prove to be, however, and vulnerable to such a contradictory array of interdictions, that the space for simply existing as a gay person ... is in fact bayoneted through and through, from both sides, by the vectors of a disclosure at once compulsory and forbidden. (Sedgwick 1990: 70)

The defining feature of gay identity in a heteronormative society can thereby be articulated as follows: if you are gay you *must* disclose your sexual identity and you *must not* disclose that identity. But if gay sexual identity proves so precarious, what happens to heterosexuality – a term, it is important to keep in mind, that only arose in language *after* and *in relation to* homosexuality (Katz 1993: 147–50; Halperin 1990: 45; cf. Edelman 1994: 5–7)? It is in response to this somewhat rhetorical question that Sedgwick argues for the fundamental structural importance of the epistemology of the closet. Heteronormativity produces the closet, for without the presumption of heterosexuality there would be no closet. And heteronormativity constitutes the closet as a liminal realm – one, as I will discuss later on, that is impossible to fully inhabit or fully vacate.

I use the term heteronormativity quite consciously, in an effort to designate both the political power and the social structuring effects that heterosexuality has when it operates *as a norm*. Heteronormativity is at least two steps away from the term most commonly used to get at issues of 'discrimination' against lesbians and gay men: homophobia. The concept of homophobia often encourages two sorts of reductivisms that I wish to avoid at all costs. First, homophobia suggests a reduction to the individual, since it connotes an expressly intentional act of discrimination against gays or lesbians on the part of a single person. In this sense, homophobia is much like the racism of the bigot, a premeditated act of prejudice. Second, the concept of homophobia can also lead to a psychologising reduction. This further narrows the level of analysis down from the individual into the very mind of that individual. In other words, homophobia becomes a problem that exists only in people's heads – and can be explained, according to the terms of psychoanalytic theory, for all sorts of different reasons.

I wish to steer clear of both these reductions. If homophobia were the only term available to me, then I would insist that the problem of homophobia cannot be reduced to psychological issues, or even to the actions of a few overt homophobes. Instead, as a social and political theorist I wish to locate the problem of homophobia *out there* in political and cultural institutions and practices – which is not to say that homophobes do not exist, but rather to insist that the problems of homophobia can never be reduced to the actions of individuals who are homophobic. But to further facilitate that shift in analysis, I will consistently refer not to homophobia nor even to heterosexism (another term that emphasises structures and not just individuals, but still has individualistic connotations given its resonance with sexism), but to heteronormativity. Heteronormativity means, quite simply, that heterosexuality *is* the norm, in culture, in society, in politics. Heteronormativity points out the *expectation* of heterosexuality as it is written into our world. It does not, of course, mean that everyone is straight. More significantly, heteronormativity is not part of a conspiracy theory that would suggest that everyone must become straight or be made so. The importance of the concept is that it centres on the operation of the norm. Heteronormativity emphasises the extent to which everyone, straight or queer, will be judged, measured, probed, and evaluated from the perspective of the heterosexual norm. It means that *everyone and everything is judged from the perspective of straight.*

On the majority of television shows heteronormativity operates in the exact same way it does in society: invisibly. That is, we assume everyone is straight, and, pretty much, everyone is straight. But rarely do we see any discussion of sexuality, except perhaps for a certain comic distancing from homosexuality, something that looks a lot like homophobia. What is interesting about those shows that 'throw open the closet door', then, is that they do precisely that and a bit more: they open the closet door and remove it from its hinges entirely, since no one ever has to deal with being closeted. This removal or erasure of the closet has at least two significant effects. First, it erases sexuality as a possible problematic; that is, the sexuality of all characters is never in question or in doubt on those shows, so sexuality can never be problematised either for individual characters or for the broader culture. This means, second, that the elimination of the closet also eradicates the problem of 'knowing', the epistemological problem of who knows what about other people's sexuality. The epistemology of the closet seeks to capture precisely this problem of knowing, a problem that lesbians and gays face every day through the power of presumptive heterosexuality.

However, shows in which the gay characters are simply always already *known* to be gay falsely eliminate the problem of presumptive heterosexuality (i.e. the problem of heteronormativity) because they provide the viewer with a certain epistemological privilege: the viewer knows exactly who is straight *and* who is gay.[3] On *Will and Grace* we *know* that Will and Jack are gay and, more importantly, all of the main characters that surround them, and most of the tertiary characters that occasionally appear, know as well. The closet has been removed from Will and Grace's apartment (see Herman 2005 for an updating and overview of the 'coming out' literature). On *Queer as Folk* the viewer can be safe in assuming that just about everyone is gay. As Brian Kinney, the centre of gay sexual identity on the show, says when propositioned by a big-money client at work, 'Gee, isn't *anyone* straight anymore?' (episode 1.5).[4] With *Queer as Folk*, then, it is not so much that there is no closet as that the show itself takes place *within* the closet. The viewer knows that everyone at Babylon, the gay nightclub where much of the show is set, is gay, but the question of whether or not they are 'out' simply never has to come up because the show and its characters remain sheltered (in the closet) from the heteronormativity of the larger world. Ironically, and dangerously, then, the structure of knowing on these shows mimics the epistemology that defines heteronormativity, since in either case the majority of straight people are allowed to assume they know *everyone's* sexual orientation.

It goes almost without saying (but not quite) that the sort of identity reversal achieved by airing a show with primary gay characters has important effects, since seeing the world from a non-heteronormative perspective may perhaps make it possible to *mark* heteronormativity the rest of the time. But such a reversal does not offer viewers any sense or understanding of the complicated and ambiguous space that is the closet – that space and that process which Sedgwick tells us 'is productive of modern culture and history' – precisely because no one is really closeted on these shows.[5] *Six Feet Under*, on the other hand, introduces the reader to the closet – a theme familiar to fans of Alan Ball's award-winning screenplay *American Beauty* (Sam Mendes, 1999)[6] – in the very first episode. And it does so, I wish to argue, in a very significant manner. In the opening scenes the viewer meets David Fisher, the 'good son' who has done his duty and stayed at home to help his father manage and operate 'Fisher & Sons Funeral Home'. In this scene the camera triangulates on David's position at both the centre of domesticity (sitting in the kitchen with his mother) and in the workplace (since the Fisher's own home is also the funeral home), as David prepares for the viewing he must oversee that afternoon. At first glance from the camera David exudes straight-laced, uptight anality. With his pale skin and set jaw, his white, overly starched dress shirt, and his terse and taciturn responses to his mother, David seems boring and normal (i.e. he seems straight).

Shortly after exiting, David returns to the same kitchen in order to attend to his mother, Ruth, who has just had a complete breakdown/screaming fit occasioned by the news of her husband's sudden and tragicomic death (hit by an L.A. city bus while lighting a cigarette in his newly purchased hearse). David, however, does not break down nor even lose his sense of rationality, calm, and dignity. He takes over this difficult situation and begins to make the necessary phone calls: first to his high-school-aged sister Claire (located at a party where she has just smoked crystal-meth), and then to his brother Nate – who was supposed to have been met by his father at the airport, but instead was having sex in a janitorial closet with a woman he met on the plane. Again, amidst the backdrop of this surreal dysfunctionality, David provides the picture of normalcy, and after making his calls he returns to his duty and finishes his tasks at the viewing.

Much as he did in *American Beauty*, here Ball paints a mostly typical picture of middle America for his viewers and then he radically rearranges it. David is outed to the viewer, in a way that makes it clear he remains closeted to everyone else, when he receives a phone call in the embalming basement. David is overseeing Rico (the expert 'reconstruction artist' who has worked for Fisher & Sons for years) in the preparations for his father's funeral, when David's cell phone rings. As he answers, and then excuses himself into the hallway, the camera cuts from the bright antiseptic light (symbolising a transparency of knowledge?) of the Fisher's basement to a radically different setting. The shot opens on a scene of shadows marked by dark greys and blues, and then the camera pans across a large holstered pistol to the figure of Keith, a hulking, sexy African-American man (whom the viewer will soon learn is an LAPD cop). Compared with the viewer's introduction to David, the initial image of Keith is a study in contrast. We find Keith in the cramped but well-decorated quarters of his downtown apartment as car lights flash by out the window, signifying the movement, chaos, and excitement of urban life. With a shaved head and a muscle shirt that discloses his daily workouts at the gym, Keith exudes a sexuality absent from every other character to whom the viewer has been introduced – and that includes Brenda and Nate, whose sex in the janitorial closet comes across as anything but erotic.

Keith remains comfortable with his own sexuality and tries, genuinely, to console David. We see Keith at ease in his own setting in a way that only seems to exacerbate the tensions that David feels in his world; David returns from the hallway only to interrupt Nate and Rico in a picture-perfect moment of hetero-bonding. Rico has just told Nate that his wife is pregnant with their second child and Nate says, amidst a great deal of elbow-bumping, 'Ah, you stud!' This moment exemplifies both the operation and some of the effects of heteronormativity, and it depends upon the contrast with the conversation between Keith and David. Not only has David just been outed to us, the viewers, but when he returns to the embalming room, we feel (and fear) *with him* that perhaps the closet door has been left ajar. In another setting, the exchange between Rico and Nate might seem innocent or even touching; Rico is excited about having another child with his wife, and Nate wishes to congratulate him. But Ball constructs for us here the workings of the closet, and thereby shows us the darker underpinning of the presumption of heterosexuality. David has just hung up with his lover, who wishes to comfort him in his time of grief – Keith insists to David that 'he doesn't have to go through this alone' – and who, as we will see in later episodes, would like David to grow as comfortable with his own sexuality as Keith is with his. David exits that conversation to re-enter a world in which heterosexuality serves as the structuring norm, a world in which being in the closet offers a great deal more safety and apparent comfort than being out. The seemingly normal and perhaps even innocuous bonding between Rico and Nate serves to reinforce the boundary of the closet door. David can only respond, lamely, by chastising them for 'not respecting the dead' with their horseplay. David cannot leave the closet without causing serious disruptions on the other side, both for himself and for those around him.

Sedgwick asserts, somewhat obtusely, that '"Closetedness" itself is a performance initiated as such by the speech acts of silence – not a particular silence, but a silence that accrues particularity by fits and starts, in relation to the discourse that surrounds and differentially constitutes it' (Sedgwick 1990: 3). I take Sedgwick to suggest that being *in* the closet can never be reduced to or secured by one simple act or even one definite choice. Closetedness is constituted *only* in relation to the hegemonic discourse of heterosexuality, by what I have been calling heteronormativity. It is only in relation to heteronormativity that David's silences and vacillations keep him in the closet. And Ball and the other episodes' writers string out a long series of examples of this silence; each seems tiny and unimportant on its own, but in the aggregate they begin to 'accrue particularity by fits and starts'. Indeed, the first episode shows us that David is 'in the closet', but we really only understand what 'closetedness' means when we piece together the series of episodes in which David must constantly maintain his heteronormative balance – sometimes keeping silent, sometimes speaking, but always allowing the presumption of heterosexuality to go unchallenged. In this way, *Six Feet Under* makes a very simple yet utterly vital important point about heteronormativity and the closet: the fact that everyone assumes a straight world makes being in the closet both terribly difficult and terribly easy. The difficult directive: do not assert your own identity; the easy one: just don't contradict or correct people's assumptions.

However, as we will see in later episodes, *remaining* in the closet is no easy task because it requires constant vigilance. David will have great difficulty trying to come out of the closet, but he also cannot simply stay in the closet since his efforts to do so will create constant tension between himself and Keith. The series reveals quite clearly how complicated and often painful it can be to maintain a relationship across the boundaries of the closet – one partner in and one partner out is never a recipe for success. The closet expresses the contradictions of living a queer identity (see Warner 1993: xvi–xx), as we see in following this relationship through the first season.

Six Feet Under demonstrates for its viewers a point that has proved central to queer theory, and is perhaps best expressed by David Halperin. Following the lead of Sedgwick, Halperin's analysis of the closet tries to highlight these constitutive tensions and oppositions at the heart of any queer identity structured by closet space – that is, all queer identities. Halperin suggests that 'the closet is an impossibly contradictory place: you can't be in it, and you can't be out of it' (Halperin 1995: 34). For Halperin, you cannot be *in* the closet because by *trying* to stay in the closet you never know whether people are treating you as straight because you have tricked them or because 'they are playing along with you and enjoying the epistemological privilege that your ignorance of their knowledge affords them' (Halperin 1995: 34). And Halperin argues that being *out* of the closet is no less difficult since many people will refuse to give up that very epistemological privilege and continue to treat you as if they know a secret about you.

We witness a further dimension of this problematic when Claire gains epistemological privilege (i.e. comes to know that David is or might be gay), even though David is not even aware that she knows. Claire witnesses a minor but significant exchange between David and Keith – who has dropped in unexpectedly on the memorial service – as Keith tries to comfort David. As Halperin argues, there is rarely a symmetrical exchange of knowledge or knowing when it comes to the closet. Claire gains her knowledge in the first episode, but David does not know she knows. And even later, when Claire awkwardly tells Keith she knows, the circle of knowledge still remains doubly incomplete. First, because the viewer is given no sign that Keith has told David that Claire knows. Second, because Claire never tells Keith that although she knows, David does not know she knows. Tragedy and comedy meet. This incomplete circular movement of knowledge exemplifies the problem of coming out that Halperin describes. Closer analysis thereby reveals the closet as both a non-place, in that you can never occupy it fully, and an every-place – in that you can never escape it completely.

The difficulties of *being* out run much deeper than this formulation suggests. They do so because of the very performative character of both coming out and staying in – a significant issue that David's various attempts at coming out clearly demonstrate. The complex and intricate negotiations of both the space and time of the closet will saturate the actions and experiences not only of David, but also, as Sedgwick would be sure to remind us, of all the characters around him. And throwing both place and time off the tracks, as it were, will become somewhat of the norm for *Six Feet Under*, since each character in the show, but particularly David, will be haunted by ghosts.

GHOSTS AND THE CLOSET

I have already argued that the closet proves to be a properly liminal realm because it can never become a fully sutured space. Thus, one can never simply occupy the closet or leave it. In this way, ghosts are signifiers of closeted existence: ghosts are entities that can never fully regain a material existence, nor can they (at least not yet) enter a completely spiritual realm that leaves the material world behind. Ghosts are doomed to a liminal existence (see Turner 1967) that remains ill-defined with respect to the 'real' world and all those human beings they encounter within that world. The constant appearance of ghosts on *Six Feet Under* thereby marks a queer space in the most general sense: the realm of the spectre is a place in which characters renegotiate boundaries, a place where they can try to articulate to their ghosts (that is, to themselves) the very terms of their relational identity.

David's first haunting comes from his father, Nathaniel, who appears over David's shoulder to criticise the reconstructive work David is doing to prepare his body for viewing. Nathaniel points out to David that, 'You never really had much aptitude for this stuff'. The irony is not lost on David, who replies 'And that's why I sacrificed my life so that I could go to school to learn *this stuff*' ('Pilot', 1.1). It is hard not to sympathise with David over the course of the first few episodes. His brother Nate, who ran away from both his family and from the Fisher & Sons business as quickly as he possibly could, returns home to inherit half of the business, for which David devoted (or sacrificed) his twenties to help his father build. To add insult to this direct injury, Nate easily convinces their mother (who has no legal power in this decision, but holds quite a bit of pull nonetheless) that they should sell the business to Kroehner Service Corporation, a 'funeral services' conglomerate that has made them an appealing buyout offer ('The Foot', 1.3). David tries to reconcile himself to giving up this life and starting over, only to have Nate change his mind – after a visitation from his own version of the ghost of Nathaniel. Nate has an epiphany and winds up arguing to David and Ruth that being an undertaker might be what he was meant to do all along. Nate's changing his mind serves only to enrage Matthew Gilardi, the Kroehner representative who vows to put Fisher & Sons out of business in the shortest time possible ('Familia', 1.4).

In the midst of these traumas, David's relationship with Keith heads south; despite Keith's plea to David in their initial phone conversation 'not to go through this alone', that seems to be exactly what David tries to do. David skips the meeting of gay firemen and policemen that Keith invites him to – lying to Keith along the way – and gets drunk with his ex-fiancée, who has returned to town to offer condolences to the Fishers, particularly David. In this drunken state David makes a rather pathetic and uncharacteristic pass at his ex-fiancée, who turns him down in a way that suggests she knows David is gay (and that is what broke them up?). So David's larger problems dealing with his family and his career pivot around his problems with his own sexuality. After the pretence at heterosexuality falls flat, David shows up on Keith's doorstep and offers to satisfy his desires. But Keith turns David down as well, since, not surprisingly, David proves to be an awful liar ('The Will', 1.2).

Thus, as episode 4 begins, David has retreated further into the recesses of the closet and the safety it provides, and an early scene in this episode illustrates David's desire to stay there. This scene opens with Keith and David in the grocery store parking lot, loading grocery bags into Keith's car. A surly, anonymous character drives up in a truck, anxious to take Keith's spot. He asks if they are pulling out, and Keith mutters 'in a minute' while seemingly slowing down in his packing. The guy in the truck loses his patience and drives off, but not before he has had time to very clearly utter the words 'Fucking fags'.

Keith proceeds to demonstrate his aptitude for explosive anger: he chases the man down, rips open the door of his truck, and shouts, 'Say it again!' David tries to pull Keith away from the man, to which Keith responds by literally elbowing David out of the way. Then Keith escalates the confrontation by taking out his badge and shoving it into the man's forehead: 'Now you've got my badge number; file a complaint; I dare you.' As they turn to walk back to Keith's car, Keith appears satisfied with the outcome of incident, but David has a thoroughly stricken look on his face. David seems both horrified at the event and a bit appalled at Keith's behaviour: 'I don't think he meant anything by it.' Keith's response is to the point: 'Do you hate yourself that much?' ('Familia', 1.4).

We see here the utterly incommensurable worldviews of David and Keith when it comes to both the closet and heteronormativity. For David, the world just is the way it is, and his own sexuality should remain a private matter apart from that world. To allow his private desires and emotions to conflict with the public world – which, as David well knows, takes heterosexuality as the norm – is to 'be political', as he says in an earlier episode. Being political proves both unwanted and, David assumes, mostly unnecessary. It should be clear that the maintenance of this perspective depends upon and requires the sheltering space of the closet. Only the protection that the closet affords can allow David to: first, admit to himself that he is gay, second, recognise the heteronormativity of society, and, third, not see the tensions and contradictions between these two points. This centrality of the closet to David's worldview allows him to reflect honestly – 'I don't think he meant anything by it.' The closet may turn out to be a thoroughly uninhabitable realm, but its liminality is precisely what allows David to ignore the tensions between the heteronormativity of society and his own sexuality.

Keith, on the other hand, has rejected the closet and insists on being out in all aspects of his life. Therefore for Keith, heteronormativity, whenever it manifests itself, always serves as a threat and challenge to Keith's very identity as a gay man – a challenge that he experiences daily, as he will later tell David, in his career as an LAPD officer. From the perspective of Keith's worldview the conflict between Keith's sexuality and heteronormativity is not a result of 'being political'. That contradiction results merely from his very being, the result of the existence of gays and lesbians within a heteronormative society.[7] (And perhaps it is exacerbated in Keith's case by the tension caused by being a black man in a predominantly and normatively white society.) Given Keith's own rejection of the closet, he can simply never understand David's desire and ability to ignore or ameliorate that tension. It can only be explained through self-loathing – 'Do you hate yourself that much?'[8]

In order for David even to begin to understand Keith's worldview – that is, before he can ever seriously consider stepping out of the closet – he must first gain a slightly different perspective on his own world. In other words, David must see his own position as a gay man in a heteronormative society somewhat differently; he must deprivatise that relation without jumping to the opposite side and 'being political'. But quarrels with his lover and charges of self-hatred will not accomplish that goal; they serve only to scare David and push him further into the closet. Perhaps unlike the rest of us, who have not spent our lives working in funeral homes, it turns out that ghosts do not scare David – certainly not as much as the real life flesh and blood of Keith. And, more importantly, the sort of work David needs to do in order to transform his relation to the closet (and to his own sexuality) can only go on in the liminal realm inhabited by ghosts, spectres, and other assorted 'others'. The liminal realm of ghosts gives David a different perspective on the liminal realm of the closet.

The ghost of Manuel Pedro 'Paco' Antonio Bolin will serve as David's guide on this journey, showing David things about his gender, sexual, and cultural identity that he might not let anyone else reveal, and in the process spurring David to take actions that surprise even himself. Paco, an about-to-be-21-year-old L.A. gang member, found himself stranded on the wrong side of town, and, while trying to call a friend from a pay phone, was shot multiple times in the chest by rival gang members. In the scene that immediately follows the incident in the car park, the viewer sees David stitching up Paco's horribly scarred chest, and repeat viewers of Six Feet Under are unsurprised when Paco opens his eyes, looks around, and says to David: 'This is some fucked up way to make a living, you know that?' ('Familia', 1.4).

David, too, appears unperturbed to find the deceased Paco speaking, as he goes on about his business. So Paco tries again to get David's attention, by asking 'You ever see sunlight, or you gotta avoid it?' – a comment that subtly marks the huge cultural/racial barriers that would separate Paco from David. They would, that is, were David not an undertaker and Paco not a ghost. The fact that Paco is dead, however, allows Paco and David a conversational ease that they would never find in the world of the living. We see that very disjuncture manifested in David's complete inability to communicate with Paco's family and fellow gang members. And it is exemplified by the awful cultural and ethnic stereotypes that David makes – assuming that because Rico is not white that his family must have some experience with gangs.

More significant than this liminal boundary-crossing, however, is the ease with which David and Paco discuss the deeply personal and sensitive matter of David's relationship with Keith, which we see has everything to do with David's understanding of his own identity. Again, Paco broaches the subject in a way that would probably be thoroughly unacceptable to David in any other context; he asks, 'Hey, how come you don't call your bone-daddy?' David says nothing, but waits for Paco to continue: 'Still pissed at him, right? Hey, I'm feeling you, man. I mean what gives him the right to get all up in your world? You know, and be so fucking...' David nods along with this empathetic line of reasoning, and then interrupts here to complete Paco's sentence: '...so fucking self-righteous?'[9] The viewer sees understanding in Paco's eyes as he turns to David: 'That's what I'm saying.' Now, seemingly, thoroughly on David's side, Paco rails against Keith as a possible 'rage-aholic' ('Familia', 1.4). At this point in the conversation, David finally grows comfortable in voicing his own interpretation of the incident. Yet just when David takes a position in agreement with Paco, we see Paco alter the perspective, revealing to David an aspect of the incident in the parking lot that he would otherwise hide from himself:

Paco: 'I mean that boy went off.'
David: 'I know. Just because some kid calls him a fag. It's so unnecessary.'

Paco: [pauses thoughtfully] 'Well, he called you a fag too.'

David: 'So?'

Paco: 'So what'd you do?'

David: 'Nothing.'

Paco: 'Mmm-hmm. [the camera cuts to David to show significant recognition in his eyes] And Simon Peter stood and warmed himself. They said therefore unto him: "Art not thou one of his disciples?" He denied it and said, "I am not."'

David: 'John 18:25'

Paco: 'No wonder he went off on you, man. You know?'

('Familia', 1.4)

Paco allows David to catch a glimpse of Keith's worldview, to reveal to David that the preservation of David's own closet cannot be hermetically separated from Keith's life. For David to deny his sexuality and his identity as a gay man by assuming that the remark 'didn't mean anything' serves to undermine Keith's very effort to remain out of the closet and affirm his identity in the face of societal heteronormativity. In the liminal space of a conversation with a ghost, David sees things he would never allow himself to admit elsewhere.[10] Paco brings David into this liminal realm, yet also speaks David's language while there, by citing a biblical passage David clearly knows well.

And David responds by trying to share some 'street language' – or better, 'street ghost language' – with Paco. As David does a final check of Paco's body, fully prepared for the viewing, the ghost of Paco leans over his shoulder to survey the environment. Paco asks for some sort of night light, claiming he does not like the dark. David retorts: 'Well, then you shouldn't have gone and gotten yourself shot' ('Familia', 1.4). The put-down, like the biblical quotation, marks a moment of connection between Paco and David, as Paco replies by giving David credit: 'Shit, that's cold, man.' Ruth interrupts David, apparently talking to himself, to ask him why he stopped going to church with her. David says he has been going with 'a friend'. Never one to let these matters lie, Ruth asks in a somewhat intrusive and annoyed tone: 'That cop, the black man.' Paco whispers to David,

'Don't be a pussy.' David pauses, then smiles to Paco and himself in responding, 'Yes, mom. That cop. The black man' ('Familia', 1.4). The three-way exchange here, with Paco giving advice to David and David replying to Ruth, may seem like a minor scene, but I read it as significant precisely because along with the ghost of Paco there is another unmarked presence here: the closet. Ruth offers David yet another opportunity to closet himself, but this time David refuses to give the performance. Usually David would respond to Ruth's invasive question in a manner that made his presumptive heterosexuality more easily presumable; he would push himself just another inch back into the closet by saying, for example, 'Sometimes we play racquetball on Sunday, so it's easier to go to the Church by the gym', or perhaps even by making a remark that implies Keith is straight. Paco gives David the confidence not, of course, to come out to his mother but at least to suspend the performance of the closet for just a bit.

The irony and complexity in this brief scene lies in the fact that Paco uses a very gendered (some might say sexist) language, 'Don't be a pussy', in order to push David closer to asserting his sexual identity. Indeed, throughout their conversations and confrontations Paco will continually use a language of machismo that appears both sexist and homophobic in order, and herein lies the irony, to spur David to confirm his own identity as a gay man (an identity that on most interpretations proves utterly at odds with machismo). Paco says to David, 'Be a man.' We would typically oppose this being a man to being a woman, but both Paco and David know that for David 'being a man' means precisely being who he is – it means being a *gay* man. Paco develops a language that ties together machismo with gay identity. Thus, he tells David directly at the funeral: 'You've got to apologise to your boy Keith. Otherwise you're just a born bitch.' And David takes Paco's advice, catching Keith after church and apologising.

This is a small but important step in David's relationship with Keith, but the truly transformative work that Paco achieves with David comes when David prepares to meet with Gilardi, the Kroehner representative, for a hastily called meeting. David asks Paco what he would do in the same situation. Paco points out that he would never have gotten into the funeral home business, but then he takes the question seriously, quite seriously. Paco suddenly lunges for David's throat, pinning David's head on the back of the couch with a fierce grip from his right hand. A look of utter terror and panic takes over David's face, and he gasps for air while vainly trying to pull Paco's hand away. As David struggles in fear, Paco says with deathly seriousness: 'I'd say pick this motherfucker. Five o'clock, you near me, my corner, and my shit. I'll cut your fuckin' stomach and watch your guts spill out. And then I'll let you live, till you slowly bleed to death, in front of your fuckin' kids' ('Familia', 1.4). Finally, Paco releases the death-grip on David's throat; David falls the rest of the way to the floor, gasps for air, and looks up at Paco in astonishment and fear. Paco pats his heart:

Paco:	'You feel your heart racing?'
David:	[nods and gasps]
Paco:	'Cuz when the other guy feels like that. You won. C'mon David, you gotta stand up, man. You gotta step up.'
David:	'Yeah, you stepped up. Look what happened to you.'
Paco:	'That's right. For 20 years I lived my life like a man. When are you gonna start?'

('Familia', 1.4)

At this point the viewer cannot even be sure whether David is unharmed, and the direction leaves both that question and the overall import of the scene hanging in the air as the camera cuts directly to the diner, with Gilardi, Nate and David. Here the viewer's questions will be answered as we discover that perhaps David is better than ever. Nate looks through some papers, and then notes that Kroehner has lowered their offer. Nate says thanks but no thanks, and Gilardi proceeds to state matter-of-factly: 'I'll make it simple. You either accept our offer by the end of the day, or I'll make it my personal mission to bury you by the end of the month' ('Familia', 1.4). Gilardi then turns to David who has a look in his eyes so steely and cold that it shocks Gilardi, the viewer, and even Nate. David shoves his plate across the table, before delivering the following not-so-thinly-veiled threat:

You have the entire Kroehner organisation behind you. And what do we have? ... [looks Gilardi directly in his eyes] You. Because one day when your mind isn't on Fisher & Sons I will find you or someone you love. [Gilardi laughs nervously] I'm not saying anyone's going to die. There are tragedies far worse than death. Things you couldn't even dream of, you spineless candy-ass corporate fuck. Just give me a reason. ('Familia', 1.4)

Needless to say, at this point Gilardi has stopped laughing, as David reports that lunch is over. In this very brief scene we witness David's first coming out. No, David has not revealed his sexual identity to anyone, but we can safely call the act a sort of coming out precisely because David performs a completely new and utterly unexpected identity. So radical is the performance, in fact, that it shocks both Nate, who asks immediately 'What the fuck was that?', and David himself, who responds 'I think I'm going to throw up' ('Familia', 1.4). This performance will set the stage for David's first real step out of the closet in episode 5, as I will discuss in detail below.

However, first David has to say goodbye to Paco. 'Powerful', Paco's gang leader, approaches Rico to ask if the Fishers are around, and Rico assumes he wants to lodge a complaint. But Powerful merely wishes to include the Fishers in a final group prayer before Paco's burial. So the viewer witnesses, once more, a connection drawn across cultural and racial boundaries within the liminal realm of death. It doesn't matter, as Nate puts it, that the Fishers are 'sooo white', for they, too, have lost a member of their family. The ghost of Paco enters the room to join the circle. And as the prayer ends and the pallbearers take up the casket, Paco and David are still holding hands. Paco, with tears in his eyes, says, 'Hey, let go of me you fucking fag. I gots to go.' David replies, this time looking at the casket and not at the ghost, 'Jesus, you're just a kid.' But Paco points out, 'So are you.' As the casket is carried from the viewing room, the ghost of Paco follows it out. But he pauses before leaving, to say with a small smile, 'Hey David, don't be a bitch' ('Familia', 1.4).

Paco leaves David with this complicated, problematic, and very important charge, before literally going to his grave. We see here again, and in striking terms, the language of machismo directed to

David in the form of advice. In a way, 'Don't be a bitch' as Paco's last words to David, sums up their entire relationship and encapsulates the transformations that this episode carries out. 'Don't be a bitch' might be read literally as one of the most clear expressions of homophobic hatred. That is, we can interpret it as meaning simply 'don't be a fag' since 'bitch' is often used as a term of derision not only for women but also for men who seem effeminate. In a certain context, then, 'don't be a bitch' might imply the very avoidance of one's gay identity. However, in the context of the encounter between Paco and David this apparently sexist and homophobic phrase belongs to a completely different discursive context and thereby takes on an utterly different set of meanings. Paco has taught David to 'be a man', and even though Paco's own language often borrows from an apparently homophobic discourse, Paco knows very well that for David to not be a bitch is precisely for him to come to terms with the fact that he *is* a gay man. And in a completely different discursive universe, this means precisely to own up to being a 'bitch' (i.e. a gay man). 'Don't be a bitch' directs David to see and be who he really is and thereby to refuse the performance of the closet.

COMING OUT, STAYING IN: DON'T TELL, DON'T ASK, AND THE NEGOTIATION OF CLOSET SPACE

The life lessons David learns through his conversations with the ghost of Paco prepare him for his first real move out of the closet in episode 5, the first episode since the pilot that was written by Alan Ball himself and which Ball quite appropriately and certainly intentionally titles 'An Open Book'. In interviews discussing *Six Feet Under* Ball himself maintains a rather straightforward position on the subject of openness, honesty, and truth: 'the truth is always better than maintaining a facade or a lie or trying to live up to some expectation' (Ball 2001a). His position on coming out can easily be deduced from these observations. Indeed, while obviously somewhat sympathetic to the character he created, Ball takes an almost adversarial position against David. Ball makes it quite clear that David *should come out* and that David's problems are mostly his own fault:

here is somebody whose main obstacle in life is himself, and that's something that's very interesting to me. I get bored by television or entertainment that sort of presents gay characters as victims of such an oppressive society. I mean, yes, there are oppressive elements of society. But *you make a choice* to be a victim ... (Ball 2001b)

Perhaps despite Ball's own idealist assumptions about the freeing ability of truth and openness (see also Ball 2001a), there is absolutely nothing straightforward, simple, or even necessarily liberating about David's first tentative step outside the closet. As I have suggested from the beginning, such a complex and subtle approach to the epistemology and politics of the closet is precisely what makes the show so interesting and important. This complexity belies Ball's own statement, and I will show how it refutes the very voluntarist position that Ball takes here on coming out.

In episode 5 the intricacy and political significance of negotiating closet space is foregrounded by a seemingly separate storyline involving David. The viewer has learned a number of important points from previous episodes: first, David met Keith at a church they go to together, second, Ruth met the man she had an affair with at the family church, which David now no longer attends, and third, now that Ruth has broken off her affair and since the death of her husband, she asks David to come to church with her on occasion. This episode opens with a scene from the church service: David sits next to his mother as the choir sings, all the while cruising a certain young choir singer. After church, the young (and perhaps not-so-straight-looking?) priest greets David warmly, noting his delight that David has returned to church. Their noteworthy exchange is as follows:

David: 'Oh, I've been going to church, I was just ... going to a different church.'

Priest: 'Really. Which one?'

David: 'Saint Stephen's?'

Priest: 'In the Palisades?'

David: 'Um. No ... Saint Stephen's in West Hollywood.'

Priest: [Pause ... small smile] 'Well I hope you always feel as welcome here as you did there.'

('An Open Book', 1.5)

The effect of this dialogue, particularly the last line and its delivery, suggests strongly to the viewer that the priest knows that 'Saint Stephen's in West Hollywood' is a lesbian/gay friendly church – as the viewer has already discovered in a brief scene from episode 4. So by telling the truth, David has quite subtly outed himself to the priest. Or has he? If David *has* outed himself, he has done so in a rather safe mode, since the priest will only 'know' David is gay if he also 'knows about' David's other church – and the chances of the latter increase in proportion with the chances that the priest himself is gay or 'gay friendly'. And David certainly has not 'come out of the closet' with this exchange, since he has outed himself to the priest only while simultaneously making it clear that David himself is not 'out'. The entire exchange occurs in the presence of David's mom, who seems to take no notice at all – and whose silence preserves the structure of the closet.

However, she excitedly enters the conversation when the priest somewhat abruptly changes the topic and asks David if he would be interested in being considered for a deaconship at the church. This is a transformation of identity that Ruth can certainly get behind. And while somewhat surprised by the offer, David, too, seems to have had his interest piqued. As he tells Keith later that night, 'It will certainly be good for business' ('An Open Book', 1.5). For his part, Keith plays the supportive role, while lamenting that they will no longer be able to go to their own church together. In an exchange of sorts, he asks David to accompany him to a Saturday night event hosted by the gay firemen and police association. In an effort to make up for his previous mistakes on this front, David happily agrees. In doing so, the scene suggests that perhaps David *is* moving closer toward an exit from the closet after all, and the scene foreshadows his overt act of coming out later in the episode.

With the closet, however, matters are never so simple. Ball brilliantly illustrates (perhaps despite his own intentions) the constitutively contradictory space of the closet through a powerful and poignant scene in which David interviews for the deacon's position with a bishop. In this short scene we witness a very brief and seemingly 'to the point' interview. However, 'the point' will only be talked around obliquely, through allusion and vague referents. After quickly establishing that David wants to serve God and not merely increase his potential client base, the bishop declares that this is 'an old church, a conservative church, a church that doesn't need to have its boat rocked'. The over eager priest answers this non-question on David's behalf, assuring the bishop that David meets precisely those qualifications. Yet the bishop continues to press the point (but again obliquely): 'Are you married?' he asks. David answers, 'Uh, no sir', but then goes on to add: 'I was engaged … briefly.' That move in the conversation seems to satisfy the bishop, who pauses before saying, 'Is there anything else you'd like to tell me about yourself?' David mirrors him, 'No sir. Is there anything specific about me that you'd like to ask?' Bishop: 'No' ('An Open Book', 1.5).

In this exchange we see the politics of the US military's so-called 'don't ask, don't tell' policy played out in inverted fashion. We also witness the mutual complicity that structures closet space and reinforces its boundaries. David and the bishop literally cite 'don't ask, don't tell' in reverse. The bishop makes it clear to David that he does not want 'the boat to be rocked' as it were, one of the many possible euphemisms for saying that homosexuality is non-traditional. And David gives the bishop exactly what he wants to hear with the unnecessary (at least literally) and perhaps even dishonest reference to his previous engagement. Yes, it turns out, David was once engaged, but that constative fact has little to do with the performative force of David's statement, which disingenuously suggests, 'I don't have a "family" now, but perhaps I will one day.' Indeed, the subtext here proves much longer and richer than the text itself and reveals the mutual performativity that forms and preserves the closet.

Sedgwick emphasises that coming out rests upon the performativity of a speech act that 'may have nothing to do with the acquisition of new information' (Sedgwick 1990: 3). For this reason, coming out may only rarely be performed through 'I am gay', one of the few speech acts in which locutionary meaning and illocutionary force coincide.[11] As she notes, often one comes out only by referring in conversation to a previous act of coming out; in other words, John would come out to Jane precisely by mentioning in conversation that he had previously come out to Jeff (Sedgwick 1990: 4; cf. Halperin 1995: 34–5). But if coming out is *more often* a performative rather than a constative speech act, then – as I suggested in the first section above – closeting oneself must *always* be performative. After all, the statement 'I am not gay' can just as easily function performatively to demonstrate the opposite – that one is, in fact, gay. In the case of the interview with the bishop, David performs his closetedness *in cooperation with* the bishop. Since there could be no adequate answer to the question, 'Are you gay?' – either a yes or a no could equal a yes – the bishop asks about family. This rather oblique question actually produces a context in which David's response can be *clearer*, because he can offer a statement with the strong illocutionary force of 'I'm not gay.' This context allows the bishop to say, in effect: you stay in the closet and you can have the privileges and benefits that accrue to those with presumptive heterosexual identity. David responds by as-suring the bishop – 'I was engaged' – that if he can get those benefits, then he will make sure not to undermine or question that very set of assumptions. Heteronormativity is preserved precisely because it supports heterosexual privilege.

The scene illustrates another crucial dimension of the closet, one that has been suggested by my analysis up to now, but not yet fully specified. The closet exemplifies the mutual interdependence of structure and agency – and thereby undermines either a voluntarist or determinist approach to agency[12] – since neither society nor indi-vidual gays or lesbians can ever be held *culpable* for closetedness. The exchange with the bishop serves to closet David all the more, but the cause of that closeting cannot be found, *simpliciter*, in the bishop, Da-vid, or society in general. It is hard to lay blame on the bishop, since he never even mentions 'sexual orientation', and says nothing overt that could be construed as homophobic or anti-gay. Many viewers, perhaps even Ball among them, might have been hoping for David to respond to the bishop's last question by saying 'Yes, I'm gay and while my sexuality is a crucial part of who I am, it makes me no less spiri-tual a person – no less faithful to God.' Even so, we have no reason to *expect* David to respond in this way, that is, we have no grounds from which to demand that he take those risks and expose himself to those dangers. As David himself might say, in the context of an in-terview for such an important position, why should he 'be political'?

– which in this instance roughly translates as, 'Why make an issue out of sexuality when it is not an issue?' Ball wishes to fault David for 'choosing to be a victim', but we see here that this voluntarist approach to the question of sexual identity is *far* too narrowly framed. Being in the closet is not *simply* a choice one makes, since heteronormativity continually pushes lesbians and gay men toward the closet. The choice remains significantly constrained by context. I will return to the general question of choice in relation to norms of sexuality in Chapter 5, where I insist that the critique of heteronormativity fails if it merely falls back on a voluntarist notion of agency.

In this context, the key argument about agency vis-à-vis heteronormativity and the closet can be further developed by looking at the one scene in which David (clearly?) comes out. David decides, rather spontaneously, to come out to his brother Nate, but the context itself is certainly not something of his choosing. It just so happens that Nate and Brenda have decided to have breakfast at the same trendy L.A. spot as Keith and David. The camera switches back and forth between Brenda and Nate's dialogue inside the restaurant and David and Keith's outside (in the physical space of the scene, David is already out). Brenda gives Nate a key to her apartment, a significant move in their turbulent relationship, which marks a decision to open up to Nate in a way that suggests a coming out of its own. Brenda spots David as she and Nate are leaving the restaurant, so the two of them head over to the table for the following awkward-yet-rich conversation:

Nate:	'Dave...'
David:	'Uh ... hi'. [Nate looks at Keith] 'Keith, you remember my brother Nate.'
Keith:	'Yeah, how's it going?'
Nate:	'Hey.' [They shake hands] 'This is Brenda ... my uh ... my girlfriend!'
Brenda:	'I prefer the term fuck-puppet.'
	[David laughs, awkwardly of course.]
Nate:	'So, what are you guys doing here? You, uh, just play racquetball?'
David:	'Uh, no, no we just worked out.'

Nate: 'Oh, so you guys work out together?'

David: [Looks at Keith, takes his hand, and turns back to Nate]
          'Yeah, yeah we do.'

Nate: 'Oh, well, that's great. ... Uh ... ok, great, uh ... ok, you
          guys have a great day.'

David: 'You too.'

                                              ('An Open Book', 1.5).

Again, David makes the bold choice at this moment finally to come out to Nate, but, of course, he does so in a strange setting that has been bizarrely thrust upon him, with Nate and Brenda 'catching' David and Keith together in a difficult-to-explain situation. The scene above explores the power dynamic of the epistemology of the closet. Heteronormativity secures a certain epistemological privilege for straights as their sexuality is always assumed (correctly) as is most gays' (incorrectly) except for those who are very actively out.[13] But coming out can often provide a reversal of power, by exploding the myth of presumptive heterosexuality right in front of someone. So we see in this scene both the power and liberation offered by coming out – David is overcome with emotion when Nate and Brenda leave, and Keith could not be more proud of him – and the difficult position it can create for unsuspecting straight friends or family members.

Indeed, the act of coming out can place the person to whom one comes out in a similarly contradictory space to that of the closet itself, and coming out creates one of the few instances in which a straight person experiences the tensions of the closet. So the viewer feels compelled to empathise at least a little bit with poor Nate: his 31-year-old brother comes out to him by taking the hand of his lover in public at the restaurant. And he does so, no less, just as Nate himself is trying to 'come out' a bit by defining his relationship to Brenda by consciously (if awkwardly) choosing to use the term 'girlfriend'. Again, in its own way, this is a courageous step for Nate, but it is thwarted not only by David's coming out, but also by Brenda's bizarre comment (this is not the first time Brenda has come across as a bit unstable). And when David does come out, he places the burden of silence that he has experienced in the closet all these years squarely back on the shoulders of Nate. What *can* Nate say, aside from the awkward mumblings he does offer? Just as the gay person is often robbed of a chance to come out in the way he or she might like, the straight friend is robbed of any sort of carefully considered response. Perhaps David comes out in the most authentic way possible: not just by telling Nate that he is gay but by showing Nate the effects of epistemological privilege precisely by reversing them. Here we see the multiple, problematic levels of the epistemology of the closet as they affect both gays and straights.

This scene proves one of the central arguments of queer theory that I worked through in detail above: the closet itself can never be fully inhabited nor fully vacated. This subtle but important point comes across forcefully in David's coming out scene, where we see the closet emerge, almost literally, as that thoroughly contradictory space that one can never occupy and never totally leave behind. Yes, David has just come out of the closet. But that does not mean he simply *is* out of the closet. Indeed, David finds himself right back in the closet a mere five minutes later. Keith and David happily leave the restaurant, enjoying, in fact, the awkwardness experienced by Nate. Says Keith: 'I know I shouldn't be laughing, but he just seemed so stupefied' ('An Open Book', 1.5). But then David reports to Keith that he cannot make it to the Saturday party in Laguna, because he really should be at church on Sunday morning while they consider him for the deaconship. Keith recovers quickly: 'Fine, we'll come back Saturday night.' And David interjects, 'That'll work', before Keith finishes: 'I can go to church with you on Sunday.' This proves to be one step too far out of the closet, and at that moment David retreats to its safety, saying 'I don't think that would be such a good idea.' Keith simply explodes, accusing David of taking a small step forward and 'a giant leap backwards right into the arms of the enemy'. Keith calls David a 'fucking coward' – perhaps Ball's own sentiments expressed through Keith's rage – before an abrupt exit ('An Open Book', 1.5).

So where do we locate David: in the closet or out? This question proves difficult to answer, and I would suggest that is just the point. One's existence in relation to the closet can never be fixed; with respect to the closet one's identity is always in a state of becoming, but never of being. That is to say, one can *come out* of the closet or one can *closet* oneself, but one can never *be* in the closet or *be* out. In the space of ten minutes, David does both. First, David outs himself to Nate with a gesture – and not, significantly, with a speech act[14] – but then, David closets himself precisely by *prohibiting* a similar gesture on Keith's part. As David is well aware, Keith's very presence at David's church would undoubtedly enact another series of coming out performances by David – or, it would require another series of more difficult performances of closetedness. In the end, we see that the state of *being out* of the closet actually relates to the performativity of *constantly coming out*. The state of *being in* the closet refers to the performativity of constantly closeting oneself.

No doubt, heterosexual identity works the same way, in that the being of heterosexuality is also always a retroactive interpretation of a series of performative acts (see Butler 1999 [1990]). Heterosexuality, too, is a state of becoming (see Halley 1993). But the contrast with homosexuality still proves profound: since heterosexuality *is* the norm, one has to work quite hard to deviate from it, therefore most actions, words, and gestures can easily be interpreted within the frame of heteronormativity. It is easy to perform a straight identity: just do not do anything queer. The hegemonic power of heteronormativity preserves the *being* of heterosexuality, unless one's heterosexuality is called into question, that is. And this is precisely why the performative character of heterosexuality is most clearly apparent in those spaces and places where it is most precarious or where homosexuality poses the greatest perceived threat – such as football locker rooms or any other space of charged masculinity that from the perspective of the hetero norm would be most compromised by the appearance or existence of homosexuality.

That very power and privilege of the heterosexual norm always makes it tempting to recoil from the dangers outside the closet. David attempts precisely this move, not only in the scene that ends his relationship with Keith but then again at church on Sunday. We discover that David's interview has been a success, as he is announced in church as a new deacon. Nate congratulates David afterwards –

apparently the first time they have seen one another since the restaurant – and then asks, innocently enough, 'Where's Keith?' David
replies hotly, 'He's just a friend, Nate', and walks away ('An Open
Book', 1.5). As if David could return to the closet where Nate is concerned. But perhaps he can, if Nate is willing to let him go. That is,
the capacity for David to *return* to the closet vis-à-vis Nate depends
on the depth of Nate's presumption of heterosexuality. The viewer
feels quite confident that David simply is not straight, but perhaps
the view for Nate, knowing much less than we do, proves a bit less
clear. And the power of heteronormativity makes it easy to assume a
person is straight, particularly if the one making such an assumption
is straight. Examples from popular culture indicate this differential
impact of heteronormativity. A famous movie like Hitchcock's *Rope*
(1948), or a well-known advert like the Volkswagen commercial from
the late 1990s – where two twenty-something guys find a free chair
on the side of the road and fit it in their VW, only to discover that it
reeks – are illustrative: most gay viewers feel *certain* that the characters are gay, while very few straight viewers ever *consider* that the
characters are anything but straight.

The force of heteronormativity thereby assures that the perme-
ability of closet space will always remain quite high; this proves to be
the case for David, even after he has come out. Indeed, in many ways,
this episode in which David comes out actually marks a transition
in which he grows more closeted. His relationship with Keith – the
one person in his life with whom he did not hide his sexuality – has
ended, and he has taken on a public position at the church predicated
upon his presumptive heterosexuality, something only the closet can
preserve. Further, the viewer discovers in episode 6 that with Keith
gone, David will seek to express and satisfy his sexual desires by pick-
ing up strangers at gay clubs. While David will have to be honest with
his sexual partners about being gay, we discover that he can lie to
them about almost everything else. He tells the first such partner
that he is a lawyer from Boston named Jim. And his brief relationship with Kurt revolves around David trying to perform the identity
of a member of the young gay club scene, an identity that even David
must admit is just not him.

David's perhaps failed attempt at coming out (but could there be such a thing as success?) illustrates the two crucial elements of producing and maintaining both gay and straight sexual identities in the face of societal heteronormativity that go missing not only on most television offerings but also on ostensibly 'gay-themed' shows. First, David's performative effort to come out offers by far the best illustration of the problematic epistemology and politics of the closet; it provides a prime example of the complex negotiations of closet space. Second, it shows that the very process can never be brought to a close. And this is the case because the negotiation of closet space never ends – unless, of course, you are straight. No matter 'how out' or 'how closeted' the character of David becomes throughout the life of the show, he, like every other gay member of a heteronormative society, will continue to have to deal with the asymmetrical power and knowledge relations that constitute closet space. *Six Feet Under* shows its viewers the complicated and difficult nature of those negotiations; it thereby breaks new trails in television portrayals of lesbian and gay sexual identity while illustrating some of the most important insights of queer theory.

NOTES

1   The character of Will offers viewers an extremely positive gay role model, as Will defines the normal in contrast to the pathological; he is the least deviant character, gay or straight, that any writer could think up. In contrast, Jack's character provides comic relief while admitting that some gay people are different from straights, but emphasising that they are, indeed, very markedly different.

2   For those readers unfamiliar with the show, I should make it clear at the outset that *Six Feet Under* is by no means a 'gay show'; only one of the main characters is gay, and in focusing on the plot lines that centre on that character I pick but a small percentage of the overall number of plot lines in, and issues raised by, the show.

3   One might take *Frasier* (NBC, 1993–2004) as an example of the reverse phenomena in that many of the characters seem somewhat obviously gay, but they are all written to be straight.

4   In relation to the above discussion of heteronormativity, we can see that these shows construct a false front of 'homonormativity'. It is false

to just the extent that it denies the hegemony of heteronormativity. Norms are not things that one can just go around making up, since they are sustained by larger cultural, social, and political forces. The norm of heterosexuality remains dominant in society precisely because broader discursive and cultural practices, along with an enormous legal edifice, support that norm. Heteronormativity can only be challenged by fighting the hegemony of heterosexuality, not merely by constructing tiny islands of homonormativity.

5   To be more precise and perhaps more fair, on *Queer as Folk* some characters are not out at work, but the show rarely makes that angle relevant since the viewer only sees these characters from within the lesbian and gay community.

6   The climax of *American Beauty*'s plot hinges on the murder of Lester Hayes (Kevin Spacey) by Colonel Frank Fitts (Chris Cooper), the certainly homophobic but also apparently closeted nextdoor neighbour of the Burnhams.

7   To repeat myself in order to remain clear: this is not to say that heteronormativity seeks the extinction of homosexuality, since in order for heterosexuality to operate as a norm, there must be a marginalised other (homosexuality) to which to compare and oppose itself.

8   Here I confine my reading of David and Keith's relationship to their initially contrasting understandings of sexuality and publicity within season one, in order not only to illuminate the epistemology of the closet but also to make an argument about the power of heteronormativity. It should be noted, however, that the entire series story arc for David and Keith has worrisome resonances with heteronormativity: in the end, David and Keith adopt kids, commit to monogamy, and reject many aspects of non-normative sexual practices. I do not develop this line of critique here, but I recognise its tenability.

9   Here David breaks the very rule that he incessantly invokes against Nate and Rico, not to disrespect the dead by cursing in the embalming room. In doing so, David's actions reinforce for the viewer the liminal nature of the space; they make palpable the *ghostly* presence of Paco.

10   This liminal realm also proves productive for David's (and the viewer's) reappraisal of the closet and his sexuality due to the fact that Paco is so comfortable with his gender and sexual identity. As a member of a gang, Paco, unlike David, knows where he belongs, and understands precisely who makes up his community. David, as we will continually see in later episodes, is torn between the lesbian and gay community that will accept his sexuality and those political and religious conservative groups that share his broader ideology.

11   Speech act theory is grounded in the insight that any particular state-
     ment, phrase, or sentence can be analysed and understood on three sep-
     arate levels. First, through the locution, the textual content/meaning
     of the sentence. Second, through the illocutionary force, the speaker's
     intention in saying what he or she has said. Third, through the perlo-
     cutionary effects – the impact or effects that the statement has upon
     the addressee or audience (Austin 1962; Searle 1969). For example, if I
     say, 'We're supposed to have record temperatures today', the meaning
     should be clear enough (locution), my intention in saying it may be to
     suggest we go to the lake to cool down (illocutionary force), and the
     impact it may have is that you decide to stay inside, in air-condition-
     ing, all day (perlocutionary effect). Some writers working with speech
     act theory would argue that both locutionary meaning and illocution-
     ary force can be adequately and accurately interpreted through enough
     work; others would suggest that misunderstanding is always a possibil-
     ity (Derrida 1982). Perlocutionary effects can never be fully controlled.

12   In other words, the experience of the closet indicates that human choice
     can never be acceptably theorised as totally free (as voluntarism might
     suggest) nor ever validly conceptualised as completely constrained (as
     determinism might conclude). Human agency exists, but always re-
     mains dependent upon context. This certainly does not constitute a
     unique contribution to the structure/agency debate, but merely dem-
     onstrates one more plank of support for a contextualist position.

13   Here I would note that gay celebrities are the exception that prove the
     rules of power which structure the closet. For only celebrities can be
     sure that they are always out, since everyone knows who they are. Of
     course, this means as well that gay celebrities can never retreat to the
     very real physical and emotional security offered by the closet. This
     makes their decision to come out both much easier and much harder.

14   David will not utter the words 'I am gay' until episode 11. Even then, he
     says these words to a female stripper who finds herself 'unsuccessful' in
     giving David a lap dance; David, always the nice guy, does not want her
     to feel bad ('The Trip', 1.11).

2

The Alterity of the Present

The character of Will Truman from NBC's *Will and Grace* offers a pithy summary of most people's understanding of the closet: 'Coming out of the closet is something you only do once. It's like being born' ('William, Tell', 1998). This claim turns sexuality into a rigid, binary framework of 'sexual orientation', and it suggests that people who find themselves in the closet must be figuratively reborn as gay through the act of coming out. This singular birth will thereby produce a gay sexual identity for them, which will then persist throughout their lives. Of course it goes without Will saying it here, but his claim presupposes the fact that only gay people come out. Straight people never need to declare their sexuality at all; all they must do, quite literally, is be born.

The character of Russell from HBO's *Six Feet Under* seriously troubles this view of both the closet and of sexuality, when he unexpectedly says to his close friend and confidante, Claire: 'I'm not gay you know' ('Nobody Sleeps', 3.4). How do we interpret this claim? What does it reveal about the structures of power and knowledge produced by the closet? What does it tell us about *Six Feet Under*'s configuration of sexuality? And above all, in light of a claim such as this, how are we to *read* sexuality?

These are the questions to which this chapter seeks to provoke responses. It builds on my argument in Chapter 1 that *Six Feet Under* is the first show on television to explore thoroughly the internal workings and political dimensions of the closet. While previous television shows may have contained gay characters, they did not raise the problems with *presuming* (hetero)sexuality, nor did they explore the difficulties of *interpreting* sexuality.[1] This chapter will argue that in its third season *Six Feet Under* revisits the closet from a radically different yet still politically salient angle, through the character of Russell. From the pilot episode on, David always remains certain about his sexuality (even if he questioned the morality of it), and he never wavers in his knowledge that he is 'gay'. Thus, while the viewer experiences others' questioning of David's homosexuality – or incorrect presumptions of his heterosexuality – the viewers themselves, like David, still 'knew' he was gay. The viewer is thereby given a certain epistemological privilege in the case of David, and the question of sexuality is always already decided, at least from the viewer's perspective.

With Russell, it does not work that way: he never claims to be gay or straight. And the viewer sees Russell's sexuality through the eyes of Claire, who never attains the certainty about his sexuality that she so desperately (and perhaps phobically) longs for. We can only understand or discuss Russell's sexuality through our (and Claire's) interpretation of a series of phenomena: his outward signs, his actions, and his own denials about his putative homosexuality. Russell's sexuality is *never* fixed because it is never clearly *legible*. I will argue here that precisely this illegibility of Russell's character – understood through the storyline that covers the triangular relationship between he, Claire, and Olivier – shakes our confidence in the solidity of sexuality, and it troubles the assumptions that a heteronormative society insists on making.

Therefore, despite his refusal to declare a gay sexuality – or better, *because* of that refusal – Russell proves to be a much more queer character than David. Through Russell's character, the third season of *Six Feet Under* continues the show's pioneering and unparalleled tradition of exposing and thereby challenging heteronormativity.[2] Russell produces, for both the characters around him and for the viewers of the show, a significant disruption of the terms of modern sexuality; he rejects the offer to claim the modern category of 'the homosexual', while he refuses to play the normative role of 'the heterosexual'. This chapter elucidates that very disruption in the form of a reading of sexuality in the third season of the show. Its goal is to reveal the very alterity of those present categories of sexuality and to contest the heteronormativity that preserves, fixes, and reifies them.

HETERONORMATIVITY

Central to the argument that I wish to advance in this chapter is the concept of heteronormativity as I have introduced and developed it in Chapter 1. Here I will lay out my working theory of heteronormativity that I use throughout the book. I add another layer to the development of the theory of heteronormativity as it can both be brought to light by readings of television and put to work to elucidate various television series and episodes. Part II of the book centres on concrete investigations into the operation of heteronormativity – exploring unexpected spaces for both the reification of heteronormativity and its subversion. In this chapter I want first to elaborate a general understanding of heteronormativity, and to show again, and from a different angle, how it moves beyond the conceptual framework offered by homophobia, or even by the epistemology of the closet.

Heteronormativity was coined by Michael Warner (who does much important work *with* the term, but very little conceptual or theoretical work *on* the term), but its roots extend back at least to Adrienne Rich's famous argument concerning 'compulsory heterosexuality' (Warner 1993; Rich 1980). Some define heteronormativity as a '*practice* of organizing patterns of thought, basic awareness, and raw beliefs around the presumption of universal heterosexual desire, behavior, and identity' (Dennis 2003), while other definitions emphasise either 'the *rules* that force us to conform to hegemonic heterosexual standards' ('Guide to literary and critical theory' 2004) or 'the *system* of binary gender' ('Heteronormativity' 2004). Heteronormativity certainly involves rules, systems, and practices, but to my mind none of these definitions does enough to emphasise the importance of *norms* that proves so central to the concept. This is why, in Chapter 1, I put so much effort into distinguishing heteronormativity from both heterosexism and homophobia, as the latter terms emphasise individual acts or practices of discrimination in such a way as to neglect the importance of normalising forces.

Heteronormativity carries a certain disciplinary power with it: a power of judgement, a power of the gaze, and a power that impacts on all persons, straight or gay. Thus, we can see that heteronormativity, as a social and political force exercised through norms, structures and sustains the social, political, and cultural worlds not just through its impact on ideas and beliefs, but also materially, in the way that it operates through institutions, laws, and daily practices. For examples of such practices, we can think of marriage, of course. But we can also think of adoption, immigration, and taxes. We can think of autoclub memberships and car insurance. We can ponder blind dates, bathrooms, and St Valentine's day. And none of this is to mention weddings. Any list of laws, customs, and practices like this points to the fact that heteronormativity accrues privilege to those behaviours, practices, and relationships that more closely approximate the norm, while stigmatising, marginalising, or perhaps rendering invisible those behaviours, relationships, and practices that deviate from the norm.[3]

I will develop my argument as follows. In the next section I explore the problem (both theoretical and practical) that Claire and Russell face so concretely: how does one know one's own, or someone else's, sexuality? 'The problem of knowing' lies at the heart of the operation of heteronormativity, and the Russell–Olivier–Claire relationship reveals new and significant dimensions of that problem. This problem leads me to enter a crucial debate in queer theory, one that centres on how we understand sexuality both historically and in the present. I focus on what it means to grasp or experience the 'alterity' of sexuality and I pose the question of how to 'read' someone's sexuality. This framing leads me to argue, as a contribution to this debate, that Russell forces both the characters around him and the viewers to experience modern categories of sexuality as somehow alienating or inadequate. Russell throws into disarray both epistemological and hermeneutic practices in regard to sexuality; that is, he makes it impossible to *know* sexuality, and he makes it terribly difficult to *interpret* sexuality. I make good on these claims by way of an interpretation of the *illegibility* of Russell's sexuality; in other words, I offer a *failed* reading of Russell's sexuality, a reading designed to show that when it comes to sexuality our efforts to *know* will always

be thwarted by a structural impossibility that results in the very illegibility of sexuality. It is precisely this illegibility that makes the
character of Russell so very queer. Finally, I will conclude with some
brief remarks about the political significance of revisiting the closet
through a reading of sexuality in Six Feet Under, suggesting along the
way that the show makes a crucial contribution to emerging cultural
politics. And it is precisely this cultural politics of heteronormativity
that I will take up in greater detail in Chapters 3 and 4.

Knowing Sexuality

How do we know if someone is gay (see Miller 1991)? When she meets
Russell on her first day of art school, why does Claire immediately assume that Russell is gay? How can she know? She never tells us how
she knows, but her assumption can only be based upon her reading
of outward signs: the way Russell dresses, the way he wears his hair,
the way he talks, or even the mere fact that he is a man in the art
world. For a long stretch of modern, Western history, the question I
ask here had no answer because it had no space in which to be asked.
The presumption of heterosexuality – what I have already defined
and will continue to elaborate upon as heteronormativity – meant
that one simply could not *be* gay. The question could not be asked.
The gay liberation movement of the 1970s and 80s gave a direct and
concrete response to the issue of 'how to know if a person is gay'
through the strategy of coming out. The answer: we know because he
or she tells us. But, of course, Russell certainly never *tells* Claire he is
gay, so all she has to go on are the signs she reads.

Seen from a certain angle, coming out breaks through the homophobic barriers of heteronormativity by calling into question the
very presumption of heterosexuality. Put more simply, saying 'I am
gay' undermines the heteronormative assumption that everyone is
heterosexual. More significantly, the more people who say 'I am gay'
and the more often they say it, the more likely that the assumption
of heterosexuality needs to be made explicit. In other words, coming
out may throw heteronormativity into starker relief *as a norm*, thereby limiting some of its powers – since the power of norms only grows
when their status as norms need not be revealed. 'Coming out', then,

both gives an answer to the question 'How do we know if someone is gay?' and also increases the relevance of asking the question in the first place.

Neither the gay liberation movements nor mainstream hetero-normative society have come up with many *other* responses to the question with which I open this section. Perhaps this is for the best, especially when one considers the phobic nature of the question. That is, why not ask, 'How do we know if someone is straight?' The first answer here proves to be the same as above: we need not ask, since everyone is always already presumed to *be* straight. But un-like the first question, we can find no second response to this query. One does not 'come out' as straight, except to the extent that one merely exists in a heteronormative society. Indeed, the presumption of heterosexuality must remain just that, a presumption, since to declare one's heterosexuality is precisely to call it into question. As Halperin puts it: 'as all the world knows, there's no quicker or surer way to compromise your own heterosexuality than by proclaiming it. After all, if you really were straight, why would you have to say so?' (1995: 48).

In one sense, then, we can answer the question 'How does Claire know Russell is gay?' with the response '*Because he tells her he's not gay*'. Russell tries to do precisely what Halperin says one cannot do: declare a heterosexual identity. But heterosexuality is the iden-tity that need not, indeed should not, be declared. Thus Halperin reverses the famous claim about 'the love that dare not speak its name', by applying it to heterosexuality rather than homosexuality (1995: 48). What happens to our understanding of sexuality – of Russell's in particular but of all of those around him as well – when he abruptly says to Claire one night while the two are studying: 'I'm not gay you know' ('Making Love Work', 3.6)? How do we read this claim?

The problematic of reading this declaration returns us to the po-litical and theoretical importance of both the questions, 'How do we know someone is gay?' and 'How do we know someone is straight?'. Folded together these questions reduce (or add up) to the following: How do 'we' 'know' the sexuality of another person or persons? The

multiple sets of quotation marks here serve to mark off the problematic of *knowing*: how can sexuality even be something to *know*, and
who is placed in the position of knower and known (see Sedgwick
1990: 70; cf. Chapter 1)? If sexuality cannot be presumed (and out
from underneath the weight of heteronormativity, it cannot) and if
it is not always clearly declared, then how do we come to terms with
it? Without a guiding framework that makes sexuality a given, and
without a clear declaration, then sexuality must be interpreted. It
must be *read*. Claire and the viewers are pushed into the position of
reading Russell's sexuality, both before and after he declares he is
not gay. This logic suggests that the epistemological question (how
do we know) must be rewritten as an interpretive question: how do
we read sexuality?

Doing the History of the Present

Perhaps the place to start in assessing answers to this final question
would be with the work of historians in the 1980s who produced
what can best be called 'gay history', a project that creates what I will
name a *universalising hermeneutic* in its interpretation of sexuality.
Gay history emerges out of and furthers the rise of lesbian and gay
studies in the 1980s, itself dependent on the political movements
of the 1970s. This body of work is diverse and often involves internal debates, but it can nevertheless be characterised in the broadest
terms as follows: a project designed to go back in time and discover
a history of gay practices and gay ideas, and thereby to demonstrate
the very universality of homosexuality (see Boswell 1982–3[4]). This
'reading' of sexuality invokes an incredibly wide-angled hermeneutic,
in which all male–male sexual activity can be read *through* the modern category of homosexuality. That hermeneutic, in turn, rests on
the grounding assumption (defended or not) that homosexuality as
we know it today can be thought of in generic terms as an extremely
broad category of identity, associated with and encompassing a very
broad range of acts. Through this hermeneutic, Russell will be (or at
least become) gay at the moment that he 'fools around' with his art
school professor, the provocative, manipulative, and always sexually
charged Olivier.

Gay history, as I suggested above, sustained the creation of lesbian and gay studies, just as it supported the very important politics of gay pride. Nevertheless, its *reading* of sexuality was quickly
called into question, most pointedly and powerfully by the work of
Halperin. Drawing on the insights of Foucault, Halperin's *One Hundred Years of Homosexuality* (1990) argues for its title, suggesting that
the ancient Greek system of sexuality simply cannot be appropriated
to or reconciled with our modern understanding of sexuality as identity fixed through desire. Halperin treats the historical creation of
the category of 'the homosexual', in the late nineteenth century, as a
serious topic for historical inquiry – thereby making a powerful defence of constructionism (over essentialism) as the most appropriate
(if not necessarily 'true') approach to the history of sexuality. Thus,
Halperin offers a *constructionist hermeneutic*. The goal of this reading
of historical sexualities was, as he describes it a decade later, 'to snip
the thread that connected ancient Greek paederasty with modern homosexuality' so as 'to restore Greek erotic practices to *their alterity*'
(Halperin 2002: 4, emphasis added), and thereby to describe modern
categories of sexuality in their very *specificity*.[5] Russell's sexuality remains unclear through this interpretive lens, but this hermeneutic
does foreclose a reading of his sexuality as reflecting a universal essence of homosexual desire.

Eve Sedgwick's *Epistemology of the Closet* (1990) offers an important critique of Halperin, along the way producing what I will call a *de-
constructive hermeneutic*. Sedgwick praises the work of Halperin (and
Foucault) for helping us to move beyond gay history, but she presents
two worries in light of Halperin's work. First, Halperin's thoroughgoing constructionism leads him to implicitly pose a 'supervenience'
model of sexual change. This means that in the historical shifts from
Greek paederasty, to 'inversion', and on to modern homosexuality,
each successive model replaces (and erases) the previous one entirely. Thus, on this view, Greek paederasty can be said to have nothing
to do with modern homosexuality; hence the thesis of *One Hundred
Years*. Sedgwick quite properly insists that vestiges of the old model
always live on in the new one, and in his eagerness to win the constructionist debate, Halperin effaces this crucial fact. Second, in his

effort to locate the alterity of the Greeks, Halperin reconsolidates the normalcy of our current categories. 'In counterposing against the alterity of the past a relatively unified homosexuality that "we" *do* "know today"' the constructionist hermeneutic 'has tended inadvertently to *re*familiarize, *re*naturalize, [and] damagingly reify an entity that it could be doing much more to subject to analysis' (Sedgwick 1990: 45). Sedgwick insists we read sexuality by always insisting on a deconstruction of the homosexual/heterosexual binary, which in her case means showing that the two terms cannot be taken as mere opposites since they are mutually constitutive (1990: 10). Russell's sexuality makes perhaps the most sense through this reading, since Russell's refusal to declare either a straight or a gay identity works to undo the homosexual/heterosexual binary.

In *How to Do the History of Homosexuality* (2002), Halperin takes up Sedgwick's critique, and he takes it quite seriously. Halperin accepts the terms of the supervenience critique, and responds by proposing what I will call a *historicist hermeneutic* to read the history of sexuality. Halperin defends a refined and sophisticated historicism, one that he defines as follows: 'an approach to the history of sexuality that foregrounds historical differences, that attempts to acknowledge the alterity of the past as well as the irreducible cultural and historical specificity of the present' (Halperin 2002: 17). Rather than resting on a dogmatic constructionism, historicism responds to Sedgwick by reading sexuality genealogically (Halperin 2002: 13). This approach still maintains the key principles of constructionism, but it asserts, with Sedgwick, that more recent categories and systems of sexuality are products of shifting discursive practices – and today's discourses always retain elements, remainders, and blind spots from yesterday's discourses (Halperin 2002: 12).

Halperin thereby offers a corrective to his own approach to the history of sexuality that takes into account Sedgwick's first critique. Unfortunately, as I will argue here (and as I will put into practice in order to 'read Russell'), Halperin does not take Sedgwick's second critique seriously enough. Sedgwick chastises constructionism for naturalising our modern categories. While historicism's commitment to genealogy could potentially be taken as an effort to show the contingent nature of our modern categories, Halperin himself focuses on historicism's ability to reveal the 'alterity of the past' and to show us the 'specificity of the present'. Halperin suggests that the problem with his earlier work was not, as so many critics claimed, that it was under the sway of Foucault, but quite the contrary, 'that it wasn't Foucauldian enough' (Halperin 2002: 13). Yet, four pages later Halperin defines historicism in a way that, I would suggest, isn't Foucauldian enough. What Foucault called a 'history of the present' must do more than reveal the present's specificity; it must expose within the present the very alterity that constitutes it. I wish to propose a hermeneutic of alterity as my own corrective to the limited Foucauldianism of Halperin's historicism.

Halperin's work on the erotic life of the ancient Greeks follows his methodological presumption of historicism in order to assert, rather adamantly, the irreducibility of their sexuality to our modern categories. But how can we be so sure that our own sexualities fit within those very modern categories? With this rhetorical question I am trying to get at the extent to which we read our own sexualities through the very modern categories of homosexual and heterosexual identity, and to grasp the mechanism by which we use those readings to reconsolidate the self-same categories. In other words, our modern categories lead us, not only, as Halperin's early work shows, to misread the Greeks but also to misread ourselves. This practice of reading serves only to shore up heteronormativity, since it consolidates homosexuality to the margins, preserving the power of the norm through precisely the deviations from it. My instinct, however, is to insist in my own way on reading sexuality against the grain of heteronormativity; this reading requires a commitment not to the specificity of the present but to its alterity.

A hermeneutic of alterity demands that we read sexuality in order to denaturalise 'what we know' about homosexuality (and heterosexuality), just as much as we read ancient texts in such a way as to render their conception of sexuality distant, or other. Halperin's recent work quite clearly proposes a better way to 'do the history' of sexuality, or, for my purposes, to 'read' sexuality. The historicist hermeneutic when applied to historical texts serves a valuable purpose.[6]

But what do we do with contemporary texts? How do we read sexuality today? Here I think we still need to 'do the present' of homosexuality, not just its history. I would even go so far as to suggest, in dialogue with Halperin, that to 'do the (history of) the present' in this way may turn out to be a more Foucauldian activity. Put simply, Foucault was not a historian, and his history of the present was more than merely a connection between history and the way it makes our present feel contingent. Foucault's work offers an 'othering' not only of historical characters, but also of ourselves. Foucault's genealogy, like Nietzsche's, can never be reduced to a way to 'do history'. It must also always be taken as a way of rendering problematic our relationship to ourselves. Perhaps it proves worth quoting once more the famous lines that open Nietzsche's *Genealogy of Morals*:

> We are unknown to ourselves, we men of knowledge – and with good reason. We have never sought ourselves – how could it happen that we should ever *find* ourselves? ...So we are necessarily strangers to ourselves, we do not comprehend ourselves, we *have* to misunderstand ourselves. (1967 [1887]: 15)

READING RUSSELL THROUGH THE HERMENEUTIC OF ALTERITY

Like just about any other first-year 18-year-old art student, Russell is unknown to himself. This distanciation of self from self is mediated by Russell's own sexuality, about which the only thing that can be said clearly is that Russell himself is trying to come to terms with it. I use the phrase 'come to terms with' to distance myself explicitly from notions of acceptance and recognition. Russell finds his own sexuality illegible to himself, but this is not because he is 'denying the truth' of that sexuality. It is the inadequacy of the modern binary homosexual/heterosexual framework that makes his sexuality illegible, not the fact that he 'really is gay' but cannot accept it. Just as we are, Russell is attempting to *interpret* his sexuality, not *define* it. Russell therefore engages in a practice of reading his own sexuality, but so far as we can tell it makes no sense to him. Russell's sexuality remains thoroughly, stubbornly unclear when read through the modern categories of homosexuality and heterosexuality. In other words, Russell seems to experience those categories themselves as *other* than what he takes his own sexuality to be; or, perhaps better, he takes his own sexuality to be 'other' than the categories available to him. In distinct ways, Russell refuses both available categories of modern sexual identity.

We grasp Russell's resistance to heteronormativity and we bring to light the queer positionality of his sexuality when we read his actions and words neither through Claire's eyes nor through our given modern categories, but rather through the hermeneutic of alterity. This hermeneutic allows us to take Russell at his word when he refuses the modern categories of sexuality. Russell thereby shows us the need for a hermeneutic of sexuality that can resist modern categories, just as applying that hermeneutic to Russell makes more sense out of his own choices and decisions.

First, Russell insists (more obstinately before, and less adamantly after, his encounter with Olivier) that he is not gay; he engages in repeated acts of *not* coming out. As Sedgwick has argued, and as *Six Feet Under* has demonstrated through the character of David, to maintain an open gay identity in a heteronormative society requires and depends upon continued acts of coming out. The presumption of heterosexuality repeatedly reasserts itself, and consistently and tacitly forces even the most 'out' individuals back into the closet. Coming out is *never* a singular act. The character Will from *Will and Grace* thus makes a truly *awful* (in its full etymological sense) statement when he claims: 'Coming out of the closet is something you only do once. It's like being born.' Here Will somehow manages to assimilate coming out, an act of potential resistance to heteronormativity, into the terms of heteronormativity. To be born in a heteronormative society is precisely *to be born straight*. And being born also proves to be the only singular act that determines one's sexuality; in other words, it is all you have to do to be straight. Norms cannot be overturned, replaced, or erased by singular acts. Coming out reveals the functioning of heteronormativity and it may offer a real challenge to that norm. But it cannot undo it. And an individual who comes out in one context will almost immediately find him or herself under the presumption of heterosexuality in another. I am not sure how else to say it: coming out is something you must, by definition, do a great deal more than once; it is absolutely nothing like being born. It is easy to be straight, then, unless of course one *appears* queer.

Perhaps because he rejects the essence of desire that freezes in place a 'homosexual' identity, Russell finds himself in the rare position of feeling the need to declare a non-gay sexuality, to come out as straight. I have already mentioned that Russell makes such a declaration to Claire, but I have also quoted Halperin to the effect that such a claim actually *undermines* the authority of the speaker and calls into question the statement that he or she makes. But perhaps I am wrong to say that Russell 'comes out as straight', since Russell never asserts any sort of heterosexual identity either. He does not pick one essence (heterosexual) over another (homosexual); he only rejects the notion that he is gay. The fine distinction in terms proves significant, since it means that Russell never actively *identifies* with heterosexuality, even as he makes his *disidentification* with being gay quite clear. Indeed, the power of heteronormativity and the narrowness of modern categories of sexuality intervene at precisely the point that Russell says 'I'm not gay you know'; they intervene in such a way as to *determine for others* that Russell must be straight. To deny being gay will always be taken, under the power of heteronormativity, an implicit declaration of being straight. Heteronormativity tries to determine readings of sexuality *for us*.

Russell may reject those readings, but as viewers of the show we also take up the practice of reading Russell's sexuality. We tend to do so, however, in a way that remains disconnected from, outside, Russell's own hermeneutic. We view Russell's sexuality mostly through the eyes of Claire; yet we are aided as we do by the writers and directors who engage us in that process, leaving all sorts of hermeneutic clues, signs for us to try to decipher. Claire interprets those signs in line with the binary choices offered by modern categories of sexuality, and in a way that remains constrained by the influence of heteronormativity. That is, her interpretation of Russell never follows the rules of the hermeneutic of alterity. Instead, her reading of Russell's sexuality traces the following path:

1) She presumes he is gay, because of his outward performances of gender and desire.

2) She assumes he is straight, not because he says he is, but because he denies being gay.

3) She comes to question that very declaration, when she feels a variety of jealousies toward Olivier.

4) She reverts to the previous assumption that he is gay, again, not because he says so, but because his having sex with Olivier forces him (in her understanding) into the category of homosexuality.

At the beginning of their friendship, Claire tells herself and others that Russell is gay. Taking Russell as her gay male friend may provide Claire with a sense of security and safety: she feels she can build a strong friendship with Russell, and that he can be her sounding board for her boyfriend troubles. Declaring to those around her that Russell is gay may also help her to *secure* those very notions, by reflecting them onto others. However, often the 'knowledge' about someone's sexuality circulates in disjunctive ways. As I discussed in Chapter 1, Claire knows early on in season one that her brother David is gay, and she reveals her knowledge to David's partner Keith, but David himself does not know that Claire knows until much later. Now, in season three, Claire not only assumes that Russell is gay, but also declares this as fact to David. This act comes back to haunt Claire: in a later conversation with David (after Claire starts to doubt her certainty about Russell's sexuality), David says to her that he thought Russell was gay. And for Claire, David's assertion that Russell is gay takes on the 'authenticity' of another member of the 'club'. But the tautology is revealed when David explains to Claire that he bases his claim not on some innate 'gaydar' (a notion he makes fun of) but solely on Claire's earlier 'knowledge'. With the Claire–Russell relationship, the incompleteness of knowing someone's sexuality is therefore further complicated. Claire's agitated reaction here betrays the extent to which she may *still* be reading him as something other than straight ('Making Love Work', 3.6).

That agitation is only exacerbated when Claire speaks with Billy, Brenda's brother. Billy and Claire have already had their own share of sexual tension, so when Billy tells Claire that he and Olivier once had a sexual relationship it multiplies her frustration and paranoia with respect to Russell. Certainly Claire had already sensed that Olivier's intense interest in the life and work of both her and Russell also extended to sex, but the confirmation that Olivier's sexual encounters with his students also extends to guys puts her more on edge. Billy, in a sense, tries to reassure her, saying: 'It was a sex thing, not a gay thing' ('The Opening', 3.9). Yet, under the terms of heteronormativity, there is no non-normative sexuality that is not in some sense 'gay'. Or, to put it in other terms, the sexual tension between Russell and Olivier may not represent a future 'gay relationship', but it further erodes Claire's confidence in the notion – derived from his refusal of a gay identity – that he is straight. (Along the same lines, one sees no reason to conclude that Olivier is gay, but he is certainly not simply straight.)

Claire is discomfited by the fact that Russell's sexuality stubbornly remains so hard to read. She insists with some urgency that Russell declare precisely whether he is gay or not, ignoring along the way the plain fact that Russell himself does not seem to know. After the revelation of his encounter with Olivier, his claim to be uncertain about his own sexuality only angers Claire all the more ('Everyone Leaves', 3.10). And she will not allow such confusion to stand in tandem with Russell's positive and forceful declaration of his love for her. For Claire, still reading Russell through modern heteronormative categories, Russell cannot love her and be confused at the same time. Claire's insistence not just to read but *to define* Russell's sexuality, probably has much to do with the way she understands her own sexuality. She can only reconcile her current feelings for Russell and his past feelings for her when she 'knows' the 'truth' about his sexuality. If he is gay, then their relationship was a front. If he is straight, then his feelings for her may have been real, and their sexual encounter would be validated. But his queerness queers their seemingly heterosexual relationship (Williford 2004). That is, if Claire were to read Russell through the hermeneutic of alterity, to

accept the undefinability of his sexuality, then she would, by implication, render her own sexuality less fixed. She would be forced to
look at her own sexuality differently. Thus, Russell's queerness would
potentially queer Claire.

If we use the crib of heteronormativity, then it seems easy
(though still confusing) to read Russell's sexuality: he is either gay or
straight, and he just cannot figure it out for himself. Once he does,
it will be incumbent upon him either to (a) come out, or (b) begin to
live a consistently and thoroughly heterosexual life. If, instead, Russell merely denies a gay identity once again, or if he tries to claim a
straight one, he will find himself back in the third modern category:
'confused'. To reconcile oneself to modern categories requires a recognition that one cannot come out as straight: one can either be/act/
perform straight or come out as gay. One could complete this line of
logic as follows. Russell refuses to commit to a heterosexual identity,
while remaining committed to a relationship with Claire. His refusal
of identity, however, causes Claire to reject him. His very queerness halts their 'heterosexual' relationship because of the fact that
his sexuality cannot be defined clearly by his actions or feelings. For
Claire, Russell's sexual ambiguity precludes the possibility of a relationship with him. Although it proves significant to note that Claire
goes on in the next season to 'experiment' in a lesbian relationship,
quite possibly because of the queering effect that Russell has on her
own sense of 'fixed' sexual identity ('The Dare', 4.7). For Russell, being with Claire does not affirm a sexual identity; their 'heterosexual'
relationship does not really consolidate heterosexuality for Russell.
For this very reason it constitutes an extreme threat to heteronormativity. In other words their relationship proves to be more queer
than a homosexual relationship because of its challenge to those categories themselves.

If we read Russell against the grain of heteronormativity, then we
come to a completely different conclusion than the 'gay or straight'
options found within the terms of heteronormativity. *We cannot
read Russell's sexuality.* Read through the framework of modern categories, his sexuality remains illegible. Russell experiences his own
sexuality as 'other' than the modern categories, and his presence on

the show can serve to denaturalise those categories for us (something much easier for us than for Claire, because we are not in love with Russell, and she may well be). Russell's refusal to come out or to perform heterosexuality effectively leads to a rejection of the terms of heteronormativity; he refuses the only things that heteronormativity would allow him to be – gay or straight. His sexuality, then, remains in a state of becoming. The resistance to static identity and the embrace of becoming lies at the centre of the meaning of queer, as Halperin defines it:

> Unlike gay identity, which, though deliberately proclaimed in an act of affirmation, is nonetheless rooted in the positive fact of homosexual object-choice, queer identity need not be grounded in any positive truth or in any stable reality. As the very word implies, 'queer' does not name some natural kind or refer to some determinate object; it acquires its meaning from its oppositional relation to the norm. Queer is by definition *whatever* is at odds with the normal, the legitimate, the dominant. *There is nothing in particular to which it necessarily refers*. It is an identity without an essence. 'Queer', then, demarcates not a positivity but a positionality vis-à-vis the normative – a positionality that is not restricted to lesbians and gay men but is in fact available to anyone who is or feels marginalized because of his or her sexual practices. (1995: 62, emphasis in original)

Russell's queer identity emerges precisely through his refusal to claim an identity with an essence. The illegibility of his sexuality produces a queer positionality, and it is precisely his rejection of his only heteronormative options that constitutes his resistance to heteronormativity.

THE CULTURAL POLITICS OF *SIX FEET UNDER*

Six Feet Under first reveals the operation of heteronormativity by showing its viewers the workings of the closet. In watching the character of David negotiate the parameters of heteronormativity, viewers experience the power of presumptive heterosexuality. Yet it seems crucial to note that the system of heteronormativity continues to marginalise even 'out' individuals – now not despite, but because, they are out. The discourse of 'tolerance' operates by way of the same epistemological privilege as 'discrimination' (Brown 2006a; see also Carver and Chambers 2007). In other words, that discourse says, we as a society will tolerate you, but we insist on *knowing* whether you are gay or not. It remains unacceptable, however, for your sexuality to remain an undecided. And this means that transgender identities are erased whenever possible, while bisexuality either means a transit point on the way to being truly gay, or a lifestyle option of sexy younger women. These effects of heteronormativity will be explored in much more detail in the next chapter.

The power of heteronormativity to co-opt even the discourse of gay rights points to the continued significance of *Six Feet Under* as a show that participates in cultural politics (Atkinson 2004). With the character of Russell we witness a more radical form of resistance to heteronormativity (even though Russell could never serve as a poster child for the mainstream gay movement). As if we needed another way of putting it, Russell reveals the ludicrous nature of the claim that 'coming out ... is like being born'. The reading of Russell's sexuality shows us exactly how alienated we can be from our very own categories of sexuality. It shows us that our sexual practices and identities are both specific and 'othering'. We can arrive at this important conclusion only by putting the hermeneutic of alterity to use in our practices of reading sexuality. Only through this lens can we see that it is not Russell who is weird in his sexuality, but the very presumptive categories of sexuality that are bizarre in their heteronormative expectations.

Those expectations and their attendant coercive capacities are heightened and strengthened through a variety of cultural and political practices that seek either to prop up the heterosexual norm explicitly or merely to presuppose that norm and thereby support it implicitly. These practices, as I explained in the introduction to this book, help to constitute the context in which the queer politics of television takes shape. Political struggle within this context must certainly go on in the electoral arena, and must undoubtedly be routed through the circuits of public policy. However, as I maintain consistently throughout this book, such struggles must also be carried out through cultural politics. And in its continued ability to undermine the power of heteronormativity, *Six Feet Under* remains a valuable asset in the battle that is cultural politics.

The readings of *Six Feet Under* offered in Part I of the book thereby set the stage for the arguments to come in Parts II and III. In Part III I will return specifically to the question of cultural politics and queer theory through a detailed exploration of the contemporary politics of the family. First, however, in Part II, I wish to deepen and refine the theory of heteronormativity, and to bring its power into sharper focus by way of perhaps unexpected readings of two very different shows. The Showtime series *The L Word* appears to be an obvious case of 'queer television', as it centres on a cast of characters almost all of whom are lesbians, while *Desperate Housewives* from ABC looks like a typical romantic soap opera. Appearances notwithstanding, I will argue that the former show tends to re-entrench heteronormativity, while the latter may well subvert it.

NOTES

1   On the rare occasions when such issues do arise, they tend to be played only for their comic effect (see Battles and Hilton-Morrow 2002).

2   This is not to say that there are not precedents for Russell's character. The character of Ferdy from *This Life* (BBC, 1996–7) provides some of the same resistances to the modern categories of gay and straight identity, although in this case the challenge to heteronormativity is blunted by the reification of a third category, 'bisexuality', which would sometimes appear to leave the other two categories largely undisturbed.

3   Precisely because heteronormativity works best by operating invisibly the theory of heteronormativity (and the critique that it implies) is easily mistaken for something else. Most prominently, when the challenge to the dominance of heterosexual norms is made explicit, some see this as a radical challenge to life as we know it. More precisely, many see it as a critique of heterosexuality, as a challenge to straightness. They thus align this critique with a narrow understanding of other radical politics – such as black power, or radical feminism, for example. But the critique of heteronormativity can in no way be reduced to an opposition between straights and gays. Resistance to heteronormativity may prove more obviously necessary for gay men and lesbians, but there are reasons for everyone to resist the entrenched dominance of heterosexual norms.

4   For a detailed and thorough reading of some of this literature, and for a long list of citations, see Halperin (1990).

5   Halperin himself remained committed to a historical reading of sexuality 'written from the perspective of contemporary gay interests' (1990: 28). Thus, he did not seek some kind of scientific objectivism or cultural relativism in his challenge to the idea of 'gay history' – his was still a 'gay hermeneutic' – but he did permanently call into question the notion that ancient identities and practices could be subsumed under modern categories. Moreover, none of this is to say that Halperin somehow 'saved' gay history from reading identity into the past, as he himself would be the first to emphasise that certain writers doing gay history, especially those influenced by Foucault, had already made this move.

6   Halperin himself, especially when addressing some of the contradictions present in contemporary discourses of sexuality, moves much closer to an embrace of this hermeneutic of alterity (see Halperin 2002: 130–7).

PART II
The Politics of Heteronormativity

3

From Representation to Norms:
Reifying Heteronormativity

Television should be watched – and written about – as television.

(Lawson 2005: xxi)

Theory can only be judged by what it enables, by what it opens up and closes off.

(Grossberg 1992: 13)

he L Word's significance lies in its very existence. On one level this claim proves irrefutable: who could deny the political and cultural impact of airing a show centred on the lives of lesbians, and portraying the main characters (their relationships, their experiences, their struggles) in a positive, healthy light? Even a cursory glance at the recent political history of gay and lesbian television, and the portrayal of queer issues on television – from the cancellation of *thirtysomething* (ABC, 1987–91), to the protests that stopped a gay kiss on *Melrose Place* (Fox Network, 1992–9), to the firestorm over Ellen DeGeneres' coming out (and that of her character Ellen in *Ellen* (ABC, 1994–8)) – demonstrates the political import of *The L Word*, a commercially successful show running for six full seasons, all with relatively little backlash or scandal.

If one takes for granted *The L Word's* significance in simply portraying the lives of lesbians, then the political question quickly and easily shifts to an analysis of that portrayal, that is, how *well* does the show *represent* the lives of lesbian women. Unsurprisingly, then, a rich debate has already arisen to address the question of representation on the show, one I feel certain will continue (productively) into the future. Despite my belief in the validity of this question, in this chapter I will not merely eschew the debate over representation but will directly reject it. And despite my belief in the importance of *The L Word* for even being aired, I will offer a polemical critique of the show. This chapter works in tandem with the one that follows. Here I formulate the critique of a narrow politics of representation and make the case for shifting to a politics of norms. This shift makes possible, in Chapter 4, my elaboration of an alternative politics of subversion.

In this chapter I contend that the identity politics that centres the debate over representation tends to constrain the political possibilities for both *The L Word* and writing about it. I therefore urge a move away from the question of representation and toward a queer politics that considers the problem of norms. This shift facilitates my critique (a sympathetically motivated critique, but a critique nonetheless) of the show. Focusing on the first full season, I argue that the narrative structure of *The L Word* – despite (and perhaps because of) its central cast of characters – often serves to perpetuate, preserve, and sustain the normativity of heterosexuality. In short, one might best describe the show as an aporia: *The L Word* is a heteronormative show about homosexuals.

BEYOND REPRESENTATION;
OR, EVERYONE IN LA IS BEAUTIFUL

Much has been written, posted, and probably even texted about the question of representation on *The L Word*. In this chapter, however, I wish to take a detour around the politics of identity and the question of representation. For the purposes of my argument, the problem with representation is (at least) two-fold. First, the representation game, as we see in discussions of *The L Word*, can never be brought to a close. The game usually runs as follows. In the first round, *The L Word* wins an enormous number of points by having so many lesbian characters. In the middle rounds that follow, points are consistently lost for the show, since that group of lesbians is overwhelmingly white and overwhelmingly feminine in appearance, dress, and behaviour. Late rounds may include more losses (for subtle critiques, e.g. over class) or small gains based on tertiary characters. And sometimes moves will be made to stop the game after round one, by claiming that the gains here are so important that nothing else matters (Warn 2004a).

In the end, we come out with no clear winners or losers in the representation game – both sides admit that in the case of *The L Word* we have a cast of 'Beautiful People' (Lo 2004b; Warn 2004a) – since we never find a perfect solution to the puzzle. The predicament can be articulated as follows. If *The L Word* cast of lesbian and bisexual women had included a balanced (proportionate to some statistical average) number of butch and femme characters, and then gone on to pick a handful of racial minorities – perhaps one African American, one Latina, and one Asian American – to round out its representation of lesbians, then it would have run headlong into another waiting 'representation' critique. To put it simply, a multicultural pastiche would prove utterly unrealistic, both for the setting (West Hollywood) and for the group of friends. How many of us are a part of, or know of, a group of friends that are as close as the group of female friends on *The L Word* and in which the group is evenly populated across lines of sexuality, gender-identification and performance, race and class? We know the world does not work that way. Thus, *The L Word* will be (rightly) criticised for being too white and too femme, but if it had not been, it would (rightly) be challenged for its departure from any semblance of reality.

Second, and more significantly, the question of representation only gets at one small dimension of the politics of gender and sexuality. Representation can have an important political impact – here we might think of the common 'thought experiments' concerning how the world would be different if, for example, women comprised 50 per cent of a given country's legislative body – but it has no necessarily determinant effect on the *norms* that both structure the political world and saturate society. 'Representation' in the sense I have been discussing it here (i.e. not political representation in an electoral democracy, but in terms of TV characters representing reality) can provide absolutely no political guarantees. Norms of gender and sexuality may be changed by a show about lesbians, or they may not. In Chapter 4 I argue that one way to change norms is through the process of subversion, but here I maintain that to get at this political level of the show requires both a different approach (no longer fixated on representation) and a clearer conception of norms.

I turn explicitly to the theory and politics of norms so as to expand my work on heteronormativity (in distinction from homophobia) and in order to capture something crucial about the queer politics of television. As I explained in the introduction, the notion of a 'queer politics' does not rest on gay identity; rather, it depends on a relational understanding. Such an approach is necessarily bound up with particular conceptions of norms. Thus, to elucidate the nature, power, and importance of norms, I follow Judith Butler's work in *Undoing Gender*. In a key passage for my argument in this chapter, Butler describes norms as follows:

> A norm is not the same as a rule, and it is not the same as a law. A norm operates within social practices as the implicit standard of *normalization*. Although a norm may be analytically separable from the practices in which it is embedded, it may also prove to be recalcitrant to any effort to decontextualize its operation. Norms may or may not be explicit, and when they operate as the normalizing principle in social practice, they usually remain implicit, difficult to read, discernible most clearly and dramatically in the effects that they produce. (2004: 41)

Norms, I argue, must not be conflated either with any sort of specific, politically enforced edict (a rule or a law) or with a statistical average; they are related to but always distinct from both of these. A norm is not a piece of legislation (though it may be sustained by legislation), and it is not merely 'what people do' (though it is usually, also, 'what people do'). A norm implicitly, and sometimes explicitly, demands, presumes, expects, and calls for the *normal* (see Warner 1999). This means that norms construct and continually reinforce (even if only in the background) our idea of 'the normal' – a process or power often referred to as *normalisation*. This is the power that repeatedly judges and marks us in relation to an idea of normality. It evokes the statistical bell curve, with a median point at the top of the bell that contains 'normal' identity/behaviour, and with marginal tails that hold the abject, deviant cases. Normalisation affects those at the margins in often obvious ways, by marking their existence as other. But it also impacts those near the centre of curve, since they must *remain* 'normal'. (If this point seems counterintuitive, just ask the 'cool kids' in school if they find it easy being the cool kids.)

As a constitutive element of culture, television participates in both the fashioning and refashioning of norms. To make this connection clear it must be stressed that a norm is not a structured, static position; rather, norms are always produced socially and they remain variable, *contingent*. Norms have no independent or transcendent standing: 'the norm only persists as a norm to the extent that it is acted out in social practice' (Butler 2004: 46, 48). Their status as norms depends upon their daily reproduction and implementation, even while they somehow always exceed those particular instantiations. One can clearly extend this logic to the politics of television, since one of the daily practices through which norms are continually reproduced must also be discursive practices that include cultural objects – media and television. Television must be thought of not merely as a 'representation of reality' – a reality ostensibly 'out there' beyond the screen – but as a cultural practice that produces and reproduces the norms of gender and sexuality that *are* our lived reality (both political and social).

To reduce the politics of television to the politics of representation would be precisely to mistake TV for nothing more than a mimicry of a reality that supposedly exists in a separate realm. But television, like any other cultural artefact, participates in the constitution of our reality (Hall 1973; Lavery 2005; Lawson 2005). We cannot therefore analyse television solely by checking its adequacy against an idealised standard, one that somehow stands apart from the show in question (since norms do not work that way). Thinking of politics in these terms more clearly illuminates *the politics of television*. Television, to put it starkly, proves political because of the way it participates in the reproduction of norms (and therefore culture, and therefore reality). This explains why, quite often, important critical work on gender and sexuality gets done on shows that are not 'gay shows' at all: *Six Feet Under*, as shown in Chapters I and II, exposes the workings of the closet through the character of David, while it questions the very straight/gay duality through the character of Russell; *Star Trek* explores the taboo against same-sex desire through the metaphor of alien species (Capsuto 2000; Ferguson 2008); and *Desperate Housewives*, as I will argue in Chapter 4, subverts traditional gender roles while working from precisely within their terms. And the converse may be true as well: there is nothing *inherently* radical or subversive about a show that centres on gay characters.[1]

In the case of *The L Word* we find narrative structures that actually mimic and help to reify the structures of heteronormativity. If we insist on moving away from a politics of representation and toward a politics of norms, then it becomes clear that one cannot make political judgements about a television show based solely on its 'identity-ingredients' (e.g. how many straights, how many gays, how many blacks, how many whites?). Only when trapped within the narrow frame of identity politics would we wind up with the crude reduction – lesbians are good, straight guys are bad – that marks the 'final rounds' of the representation game.

A queer politics of norms proves much 'wider' because it can assess a show on different terrain. Thus, exploring lesbian relationships (from friendship to sex to business to politics), challenging societal presumptions about gender and sexuality through the portrayal of lesbian characters and their interactions (both with one another and with society as a whole) and articulating a normative vision of gender and sexuality that surpasses heteronormativity can all be described as 'good things' (socially progressive, politically democratic) to the extent that they do the important and productive work of cultural politics. On the other hand, practices that reify the structures of heteronormativity – by either mimicking the heterosexual norm or upholding patriarchal visions or assumptions – may, and should, be criticised for their conservative and freedom-limiting effects. The key for my analysis is this: one can, and indeed one must, analyse *The L Word* in terms of this politics of norms, regardless of how we assess it with respect to the politics of representation. This demonstrates precisely why shows that are not at all 'gay shows' can often prove quite successful in subverting the heterosexual norm, while, at times, so-called 'gay shows' can wind up (perhaps unwittingly) maintaining heteronormativity (Havrilesky 2004; Lawson 2005: xx).

Both criticisms and praise of *The L Word* miss their mark to the extent that they remain trapped within a politics of representation[2] and fail to take into consideration the question of heteronormativity. The profound importance of Sarah Warn's work on *The L Word* cannot be denied; it provides the starting point for any serious consideration of the show (Warn 2002, 2003, 2004a, 2004b, 2005c). And this is not to mention Warn's broader work on gay and lesbian entertainment. I focus on Warn's arguments precisely because of their prominence and significance. And, on my reading, Warn's approach to the show proves problematically narrow, not because she fails to see the weaknesses in the show – Warn does a wonderful job of remaining balanced in her treatment of *The L Word*, despite the obvious fact that she is a fan – but because she fails to assess the show in terms of norms. In the debate she stages with Malindo Lo over 'butch representation' Warn's opening tactic is to take the position of moderation: 'to ask *The L Word* to reflect the full diversity of the lesbian community when it already has so many hurdles to jump just to survive is too much otherness to put on one show' (Warn 2004a). One could certainly debate this point – Lo does – either on its own merits, or in terms of the extent to which it mimics conservative political responses to gains in civil rights for lesbians and gays; 'don't go too far, too fast' has been a constant conservative refrain in the face of civil rights advances, whether it be challenges to segregation in the US south or claims for gay marriage in recent years.

The political pitfalls of taking the representation tack emerge clearly if we follow its logic to the concluding point:

> *The L Word*'s biggest achievement is simply in improving the visibility of lesbian and bisexual women on television by leaps and bounds, which will make it that much easier to challenge traditional concepts of gender and appearance in the future. (Warn 2004a)

But, put simply, this logic will not hold. It *might* be the case that having a show about lesbians will help to challenge gender norms, but it *might also* be the case that having a show about lesbians will make it *harder* to challenge gender norms in the future. There is no way we can tell what happens to norms of gender, or to norms of sexuality, simply by checking the sexual orientation of the main characters. If a show about lesbians reinforces heteronormativity, if it preserves traditional conceptions of femininity, if it maintains binary gender, if it rejects queer sexuality, then it cannot blithely be assumed that it will prove progressive in terms of the politics of gender and sexuality. The argument that lesbian visibility is progressive by definition can be challenged if we shift (read: broaden) the frame of analysis to a politics of norms. This frame reveals that there is nothing automatically positive about having lesbian characters maintaining given norms of gender, not to mention potentially mimicking heteronormative structures. The claims for lesbian visibility do little, if anything, to assess whether the show challenges heteronormativity or upholds its structures.

For her part, while often debating Warn within the terms of the politics of representation – by calling attention to what is missing in the representational spectrum – Lo regularly gestures toward the politics of gender norms. She does so by emphasising that the debates over representation have a great deal to do with the show's refusal to question gender:

> What these discussions boil down to is not whether *The L Word* represents all lesbians – it simply cannot do that, being a 13-episode Showtime television drama – but whether *The L Word* is willing to engage with issues of gender. [As one of her friends put it:] 'They're willing to talk about sexual orientation but not about gender. They clearly did not want to blur any gender lines.' (Lo 2004a)

Making the crucial distinction between sexual orientation and gender could mark the first move toward interrogating the heteronormative nature of the show – exploring the norms of gender and sexuality as they are instantiated in particular episodes, finding out whether the show subverts heteronormativity by calling the so-called naturalism of heterosexuality into question, or reifies heteronormativity by imitating its terms (see Halberstam 1998).

Yet Lo fails to carry out this analysis, and thus her critique falls short exactly because it stays within the terms of identity politics. She writes: 'Like many viewers who posted their thoughts online, my friends and I felt that the inclusion of men in numerous sex scenes ... pandered to a straight male audience and was outright offensive to lesbian viewers' (Lo 2004a). I am fully sympathetic to Lo and her friends' general reaction; I share it. But I do not think that Lo's heading title, 'Too many straight men', quite captures what is sometimes so very wrong with the show (see also Lo 2004b). The problem that Lo puts her finger on cannot be boiled down to a problem created by the appearance of men. The presence of men no more sustains heteronormativity than the presence of lesbians undermines it. We must get to the question of norms, which far surpasses games of counting heads, to ask after much deeper questions concerning constructions of gender and sexuality. The weakness of the show does not arise from 'having men around', since, in the world, men (especially straight men) are 'around' quite a bit. Neither inclusion nor exclusion can decide matters here. To put it crudely: have the guys around, just don't have the threesomes.

REIFYING HETERONORMATIVITY;
OR, LESBIANS ARE HOT

The structure, focus, dialogue, and stories in the show, not the mere presence of men (or representation of lesbian identity), lead to heteronormativity. I will take as my frame the first full season of the show, focusing particularly on the opening episodes. In doing so, I seek to analyse the initial presentation of *The L Word* to its audience, in order to capture the impact of the show on norms of gender and sexuality.[3] I will argue specifically for four distinct, but certainly intertwined, manifestations of heteronormativity: the bizarre fixation on straight sex, the (re)production of heterosexual desire, the consistent construction of narratives of straight romance and the presumption of a straight audience (in the form of a 'student'). In all of these areas,

The L Word produces the paradox I mentioned in my introduction: it takes a cast of mostly lesbian characters yet still manages to mimic, support, and even reify the norm of heterosexuality.[4]

Straight sex

I am not the first to comment on the (straight) sex in *The L Word*, but it cannot be ignored, and its importance should not be downplayed. Well before the pilot episode initially aired, when it still had the bizarre working title of *Earthlings*, the show drew constant comparisons to *Queer as Folk*. The latter show proved groundbreaking not only for centring on the lives of a cast of gay characters, but also for its direct, honest, and some might say graphic portrayal of gay sex. For the first time on television, viewers had the chance to see not just gay characters, but male–male desire, eroticism, and a rather broad spectrum of sex acts. And *Queer as Folk*'s pilot episode was filled with lots of sex; sex that delighted most of its gay fans, surprised many of its gay and straight viewers, and shocked a portion of its straight audience. When *The L Word*'s own pilot finally aired, many viewers keenly anticipated a chance to see, finally, lesbian sex ('Pilot', 1.1 and 1.2).

Those viewers had to wait. The pilot has plenty of sex, just not very much between two women. The first sex occurs between the only straight characters on the show, Jenny and Tim, and while lesbians have a 'presence' it occurs only through Jenny's fantasy. In terms of supporting heteronormativity, this last fact proves much more significant than the fact of the straight sex itself, since lesbian sexuality has long *had a role* in the structure of heterosexual fantasy and the circuits of desire. So-called 'lesbians' have been an object (phantasmic or not) of heterosexual desire in popular culture and pornography for quite some time; after all, if the cinematic gaze is both straight and male, then lesbianism can easily be reduced to a mere object of desire and fantasy (see Mulvey 1989 [1973]). Thus, two straight people having sex doesn't tell us much about the normativity of heterosexuality (although, from a psychoanalytic perspective it might tell us a great deal about the psychic structure and animating fantasies of heterosexuality). However, by including lesbians in that circuit of desire as objects of fantasy to supplement straight desire, this first sex scene fully supports the heterosexual norm – not merely by ignoring lesbianism but by giving lesbians a specific, secondary place *within* the heterosexual norm (see Butler 2004).

Perhaps readers might see this as an 'over-reading' of a simple sex scene? To dispel this sense one only needs to continue watching the pilot. The second sex scene repeats the first in structure, only adding the variation of beginning with oral sex. Now the first sex in general, and the first oral sex in particular, belong to the straight couple. The point, it would seem, has been made. But just in case it has not, the pilot episode takes one more step into the fantasy life of the straight male. When viewers of *The L Word* finally get their first full sex scene with two women in it (the earlier make-out session in the pool served only as a turn-on for Jenny), they have to abide the inclusion of a man. Almost everything about this scene proves hard to believe: that the show would even include this ultimate straight male fantasy, that Tina and Bette (the two central characters who form the primary couple at the start of the first season) would choose this route to conceive their baby, that as intelligent citizens of LA, they would have unprotected sex with an utter stranger (that the guy really drives a motorcycle). The scene could serve at least two plausible purposes, both of which reify heteronormativity.

First, it sells the show to a straight male audience (see Lo 2004a), and this marks a *crucial* difference between *The L Word* and its constant companion in comparison, *Queer as Folk*. *Queer as Folk*'s primary audience is gay men, with a secondary audience of straight women, and this latter group need not find the main characters attractive as objects of desire. *The L Word*'s perceived secondary audience is straight men, a group that within the structures of heteronormativity *has* taken lesbians as objects of a certain kind of desire. To include scenes that make lesbians attractive to straight men cannot be explained away in marketing terms (even if that explanation proves valid), since this move undercuts significantly any plausible chance the show might have of challenging heteronormativity. The threesome scene proves this point, for another reason: it serves to *mask* the one example of lesbian sex in the pilot. By cutting from the sex scene between Marina and Jenny, to the threesome with Bette and Tina, the pilot sneaks in lesbian sex, covering it up with the classic example of heteronormative fantasy.

Eventually, of course, *The L Word* offers numerous and repeated portrayals of lesbian sex, even lesbian sex that excludes both straight participants and straight voyeurs. Yet reminders of the implicit message that lesbians are sexy, attractive objects of desire, even for straight men, crop up repeatedly, whether in the form of the straight man observing lesbian sex ('Lawfully', 1.6) or in the representation of lesbians in or as the pornographic model (e.g. the 'lingerie sex' between Marina and Jenny that Tim walks in on in 'Losing It', 1.7). These reminders reinforce the message of the pilot – that lesbians are attractive, desirable, feminine beauties (cf. 'Let's Do It', 1.3) – and they help to blunt any challenge that the presentation of lesbian sex might pose to the preservation and exaltation of heteronormativity.

Straight desire

This message is subtly reinforced by the show's construction and production of desire. Desire proves essential to the politics of heterosexual norms, since heteronormativity operates by way of excluding the possibility of same-sex desire; it manifests itself in the world through the constant presumption of opposite-sex desire and heterosexual identity (Butler 1999 [1990]). It follows, then, that shows centring on gay characters – much like the individual and social practice of 'coming out' – hold the potential to undermine heteronormativity by questioning this assumption. Thus, 'gay TV' can undo the heteronormative supposition and belief that remains dominant in the world, much as it can be reversed within the context of a lesbian and gay community; within these situations the presumption *might* be that everyone is gay. In a sense this happens on *The L Word*: anyone who patronises The Planet (Marina's coffee shop) or attends a party hosted by Bette and Tina is more likely to be gay than straight, and this is the view taken up by most of the gay characters.

This makes it all the more surprising and consternating that the show can so consistently both presume and produce straight desire. Viewers see this most clearly through the triangular relationship among Tim, Jenny, and Marina. The appropriately titled episode

'Longing' (1.4) foregrounds this issue nicely. As Jenny has begun her affair with Marina, we see Tim as utterly clueless about his own betrayal. Tim positively and repeatedly encourages Jenny to spend time with and to befriend the very person with whom she is cheating. It simply does not enter Tim's head that Jenny might betray him by sleeping with a woman. Even when Jenny changes her appearance rather drastically, dressing up to go out with Marina, Tim simply finds it attractive. Jenny makes herself up to be the object of a woman's desire, yet the effort only serves to reinforce straight male desire. Tim operates in the world of binary sexuality produced by heteronormativity, that is, if Jenny has sex with him, she cannot be a lesbian, and thus she cannot desire Marina. Like Claire in *Six Feet Under*, Tim allows heteronormativity to make 'straight' and 'gay' the only options. But at least Claire was *paranoid* about the possibility of her lover cheating on her with someone of the same sex, whereas for Tim this seems inconceivable. Ironically, Tim seems absolutely confident in Jenny's heterosexuality. The irony, of course, stems from the fact that Jenny's desire for Marina positively oozes from the screen, and Marina's passionate focus on Jenny proves obvious to anyone *not* utterly blinded by the heteronormative logic of exclusion – the logic that unilaterally and universally prevents straight women from having sex with other women. Tim's making Jenny into an object of straight male desire reinforces the message that lesbians do not, and will not, endanger the heteronormative order.

It would be possible, of course, through a more self-reflective portrayal, for the show to be making fun of Tim and thereby questioning his heteronormative assumptions. Unfortunately, *The L Word* rarely, if ever, achieves such self-reflection; it thereby misses the mark of critical parody and serves conservative ends. Thus, within the very same episode, we sink to deeper heteronormative depths (and, in inverted fashion, we reach greater heights of irony). While Tim harbours no jealousy toward Marina, Jenny *does*. Despite the fact that Jenny has no reason to think Marina is bisexual, she immediately grows jealous of Marina's interactions with Tim. The heteronormative presumption of straight desire proves so strong that even though Jenny herself is sleeping with Marina, even though she knows Marina is gay, she worries that Tim wants Marina as well. Heterosexual desire moves in a circle here, both presumed by the characters on the show and reinforced by their actions. This is the circle in which actions both follow the edicts of a norm *and* instantiate that norm.

One might try to explain away these examples as the product not of heteronormativity, but of a relation in crisis (e.g. Jenny's jealousy masks her guilt, Tim's naivety hides an underlying knowledge of Jenny's betrayal). Yet the show presumes straight desire in other ways and it continues to construct straight desire well after Jenny and Tim's break-up. Despite the fact that Jenny cheated on him with a woman, Tim finds a way to be comfortable with Jenny's living on the premises and bringing over dates. Somehow lesbian desire fails to appear as a threat to Tim, even though it clearly is one (it ends his relationship with Jenny). Tim shows no jealousy toward the women Jenny brings home to have sex with, but he immediately reacts with anger and frustration when she merely *receives a phone call* from an old boyfriend ('Lies, Lies, Lies', 1.5), and he becomes temporarily insane when she brings home a guy ('Limb from Limb', 1.14). Thus, the narrative consistently communicates the notion that lesbians pose no threat to heterosexual male possessiveness. Therefore Tim does not really 'lose' Jenny to Marina; he rejects her for her betrayal. And Tim's actions say that, if Jenny is a lesbian, it does not matter that he loses her anyway; he competes for her only with men.

Here *The L Word* conveys a vision of the world much like the one in which we live; in it, usually only gay people ever consider the possibility that someone else might be gay. This structure preserves heteronormativity, since the world will continue in the foreseeable future to be populated by a large majority of straights, and smaller minorities of gays, lesbians, transgender people, and others who are queer with respect to the norm. By reproducing heterosexual sex and reifying heterosexual desire, *The L Word* obviously fails to challenge heteronormativity.

Narratives of straight romance

Worse, it fails in other, more subtle, perhaps more insidious, ways. When the show is not explicitly working with and through a heteronormative frame of sex and desire – that is, even when it deals explicitly with sex and relationships between women – it often goes well out of its way to replicate a narrative structure of heterosexual romance. The first scene of the pilot offers the most obvious example. The scene opens at the epicentre of domesticity, in the bathroom off the couple's master bedroom; there Bette and Tina learn that Tina is ovulating. The scene perfectly imitates, in generic fashion, the hundreds of scenes from movies and television in which the wife happily discovers that she is pregnant, or the recently married couple heroically decide to do the most romantic thing of all, 'make a baby'. The pilot's opening scene only falls short of the straight romantic script when, rather than having sex (can't have that) Bette says instead, 'You get dressed; I'll drive you [to the clinic] on my way to work' ('Pilot', 1.1).

Perhaps this interruption at the end could be read for its disruptive potential, making the scene a politically powerful parody of the straight script, rather than a mere repetition. Episode 1.3 ('Let's Do It') rejects this reading outright, by *repeating* the same scene, only this time Bette and Tina *do* have sex at the end (as they have decided to do the insemination at home, rather than at the clinic). Thus *The L Word* opens both of its first two episodes with a narrative so familiar to its viewers as to be beyond cliché; it tells those (straight) viewers that lesbians are just like 'us', they desire nothing more highly than reproductive sex in the family bed. Unlike *Queer as Folk*, which opened with daring portrayals of gay *desire* and eroticism, *The L Word* tames the lesbian sex, even before it portrays it. After all, Bette and Tina's attempt to make a baby at the beginning of episode 1.3 marks the first uninterrupted sex between two women on the show. Where the pilot and other episodes throughout the first season tell the straight male viewer 'Lesbians are hot', this episode says, again to a straight audience, 'Worry not, there is nothing scary or even all that different about lesbian sex' ('Let's Do It', 1.3).

To fortify this case, the first season consistently returns to clichéd heteronormative narratives that will strike the straight viewer as comforting and familiar (see Havrilesky 2004). Thus, we have some of the obvious cases: the ultrasound scene with Bette and Tina ('Lies, Lies, Lies', 1.5) and the marriage announcement from Dana and Tonya ('Limb from Limb', 1.14). The former proves to be so tired as to be uninteresting, in any context. The latter not only mimics heterosexual marriage, but also runs the risk of trivialising gay marriage, since Dana announces her 'engagement' to a woman that she hardly knows and that both her friends and the viewers can hardly stand.[5]

None of this is to say that lesbian desire can be portrayed as a single, monolithic entity, nor is it to deny the possibility that same-sex desire may participate in power relations related to those of opposite-sex desire (see Bersani 1995). As has been shown, however, *The L Word* often mimics heterosexual symbolic structures on the *primary* level, thereby closing off any portrayal of same-sex desire or lesbian eroticism. This reflects the privileging of straight male desire, and the male gaze within the order of heteronormativity. The conveyance of (same-sex) female desire has the potential to disrupt this order; hence the disappointment that a show about lesbians so rarely depicts lesbian desire.

Teaching to straights

This failure can be directly and easily linked to missed opportunities in exploring lesbian sexuality. Dana's relationship with Lara offers the most lucid example. Like Justin in *Queer as Folk,* Dana is the sexually inexperienced character in the group, one through whom the audience could potentially explore lesbian sexuality. *Queer as Folk* used the relationship between Brian (a much older, *much* more experienced gay man) and Justin (an inexperienced, but not necessarily innocent 17-year-old[6]) to, for lack of a better word, 'teach' the audience about gay sex. Like Justin, Dana is learning about her own sexuality in the context of a same-sex relationship. But instead of exploring the sex between Dana and Lara – with all the nuances, complications, discoveries, and embarrassments it might entail – *The L Word* chooses to provide yet another mimicry of straight narratives. The viewer does not witness the first sex between Dana and Lara; instead, the scene opens with the two of them in bed just afterward. There we witness the rehearsal of another worn-out dialogue, as Dana expresses her embarrassment and disbelief at something that has 'never happened to her before'. The references to straight male impotence scenes can be missed by absolutely no one, even though those references make no sense (how could Dana possibly be impotent?). We learn later, in the safe space of discussion in the coffee shop, that Dana had experienced female ejaculation, but the intimate sexual encounter has now been reduced to comedic relief and the moment to investigate both the logistics and the meaning of sex between women has been lost.

The L Word does offer its share of 'teaching' about lesbians; however, it confines that teaching to a narrow, often desexualised teaching to straights. Thus, in the pilot we have the scene in which Jenny meets Tina, and Tina explains that she has quit her job to stay at home and have a baby. Jenny reacts with awkward surprise, as if she cannot process how this could possibly be. Tina explains. That is, she points out to Jenny that women (even lesbian women) can, indeed, have babies (even without men). But this explanation proves necessary only if one makes the rather ignorant and certainly heteronormative (if not homophobic) assumption that a baby can only and ever be brought into the world by 'a man and a woman'. That is, this embarrassing and cumbersome 'explanation' that Tina offers to Jenny might be helpful to those state and federal legislators across the USA who are most convinced that 'families' cannot be constructed with gay members, but it seems hard to see why Jenny or the audience would require it. Perhaps this scene could have a more critical edge if it served to expose precisely the ridiculousness of the heteronormative idea that women cannot have babies. To achieve that effect, however, would require Jenny to look a bit stupid – rather than funny and cute.

Presuming an unreasonable level of ignorance (appropriate only to rather dense straights) appears elsewhere. Take the example of Dana showing up to a cocktail party with her doubles tennis partner, named Harrison ('Pilot', 1.2). The viewer has almost no reason whatsoever to suspect that Harrison is straight. First, we know that Dana is gay, so if she attends a cocktail party with a man, there is a decent chance he is gay. Second, Harrison does not look much like a typical straight male: his outward appearance, dress, manner, and behaviour all read as more likely gay than straight. But if that were not enough, Harrison hits on Tim. Tim may be clueless about it (see above), but it proves obvious to the viewer. Still, in the face of all this (just in case), Dana later makes certain to say explicitly that Harrison is gay.

The act confirms the heteronormative operational principle that one can only be gay through an unambiguous, affirmative declaration. This situation clearly resonates with the problems of 'reading' Russell's sexuality in the preceding chapter, where heteronormativity always intervenes in our reading practices to render individuals straight unless they actively resist this coding by 'coming out'. What we see here, in the case of *The L Word*, is that this aspect of heteronormativity serves to closet, in many aspects of their lives, even those lesbians and gays who have no desire or intention to keep their sexuality a secret. It demands of gays what would never be expected of straights: to declare outwardly their sexuality, or be prepared to have everyone assume wrongly about it. And, of course, in the face of being forced by heteronormativity to announce their sexuality much more often than anyone would want to, lesbians and gays will then be accused of making too much of it, of 'shoving it in our faces'. If the world were not so thoroughly and consistently heteronormative, if it did not shove heterosexuality in *everyone*'s face, *all the time*, then there would be no need for gay people to continually make it known that they are gay – a point already made clear in Chapter 2 (Sedgwick 1990; Halperin 1995). By refusing even the slightest degree of subtlety about sexual identity – and one should not forget that Dana finally comes out in a full-page magazine spread, the loudest declaration possible – the show reinforces heteronormativity in yet another way.

TELEVISION AND THE SUBVERSION OF HETERONORMATIVITY

In demonstrating the show's maintenance, preservation, and furtherance of heterosexual norms, I have attempted to make my critique of *The L Word* as lucid, stark, and forceful as possible. Nevertheless, this critique would prove misdirected if it implied, and misread if it were taken for, a dismissal of the show. Norms are not the sort of thing that one can avoid, transcend, or otherwise get outside of. This crucial fact about norms has two entailments. First, the subversion of heteronormativity must come from within its terms. Second, to ignore heteronormativity entirely would be, in its own way, to sustain it by letting it go unchallenged, and this is something, as shown in Chapter 1, that other so-called 'gay shows' often do. By refusing to construct a 'homosexual utopia' *The L Word* holds the potential to offer genuine challenges to heteronormativity, and occasionally does just this, especially around the character of Bette and her family and work conflicts.

The ongoing battle against heteronormativity – whether it comes in the form of legislative politics or the cultural politics of television – requires a two-pronged approach. Challenges to heteronormativity must be foregrounded and acclaimed (even if they appear where least expected) in order to increase their chance of becoming successful subversions. I pursue this strategy in the next chapter as I deepen both my theory and critique of heteronormativity through a reading of *Desperate Housewives* – a reading that mines the show for its unexpected subversive potential. Subversions of heteronormativity can occur when the norm itself is brought to light, and this may happen in unanticipated places and ways. In these cases, the task becomes how to bring these subversions to the surface and how to further their effects.

At the same time, however, failures to confront heteronormativity must also be called out in order to be questioned, discussed, and debated (even if *they* occur where least hoped or planned for). My effort here clearly operates within the second prong of this battle: *The L Word*'s problematic reification of heteronormativity cannot persist uninterrogated. The show deserves criticism on this account – that is, within the politics of norms – even if it makes a contribution in the politics of representation. I insist on reading this critique as part of a larger struggle against the power of heteronormativity. Queer politics can challenge heteronormativity in two distinct but complementary ways: first, by calling attention to the reification of heteronormativity, as I do here; and second, by identifying and sustaining subversions of heteronormativity, as I do in the next chapter.

NOTES

1   I stress the word 'inherently' here, since shows that centre on gay characters (just like those that do not) certainly have the *potential* for contributing to radical critique. Moreover, and to echo my opening sentiment about the importance of *The L Word*'s very existence, even if a show based on gay characters serves to reify heterosexual norms it at least does so in a way that acknowledges their existence.

2   Here I reject a narrow approach that would confine a reading of the show to the politics of interest group pluralism – to the limited question of whether the distribution of characters 'matches up' to some predetermined distribution. I do not, for that reason, wish to abandon the broader philosophical question of representation – the question of what it means in the first place for one thing to stand for another. For an incisive overview of and contribution to contemporary debates in political theory over representation see Rehfeld (2006), cf. Disch (2008).

3   Some would suggest that the show does not find its lesbian audience until the end of the first season, and that the second and future seasons prove much 'queerer' for this reason. But in the terms I am working with here, a show that speaks only to a gay audience loses much of its potential to challenge heteronormativity and therefore cannot be all that queer. Heteronormativity cannot be subverted merely by being evaded or ignored. The first season therefore remains crucial in the sense of how it engages with the dominant norms of sexuality and gender.

4   If one sought to advance a very generous reading of *The L Word* on this point, one might suggest that even in its apparent mimicry of heteronormativity – in playing out straight male sexual fantasies about lesbians and multiple sexual partners – the show still manages to interrupt the hegemony of reproductive and heterosexual norms. I do not reject the theoretical possibility of such a reading, but I doubt very much that the text of the show could be made to support this interpretation.

5   Here I simply defer any engagement with the broad and complicated debate over whether gay marriage in general can be thought to *queer* marriage in a radical fashion, or to ape heterosexual marriage in a conservative one (see for example Sullivan 1996; Warner 1999). Rather than rehearse the arguments within this debate, I make a particular and oblique entry into, and engagement with, this set of arguments in Chapter 6.

6   The character of Justin was 15 years old in the original UK version of *Queer as Folk*, but Showtime found that too controversial.

4

Desperately Straight:
Subverting Heteronormativity

D*esperate Housewives*. That truly is the title of the show, as I had to reassure myself (repeatedly) when I saw the first advertisements for it before the series premiere. 'Really?', I asked out loud to the television set. (And I was not the only one asking – see KATC3 2004; Peterson 2004) Then I backed up the TiVo to check again. Yes. Really. The first commercials in the USA ran back-to-back with announcements for *Wife Swap* (ABC, 2004–). 'Are they serious?', I queried, turning my exchange with the TV into a full-fledged conversation. It turns out, they were, indeed, quite serious. This chapter poses the question of just how serious, and answers: perhaps much more than we might at first imagine. *Desperate Housewives* centres, as the title would clearly indicate, on the lives of five suburban women – three married housewives, one divorced housewife, and one, well, 'slut' (Zeman 2005) – and their struggles with being ... housewives. There are no central gay characters. The entire show is set (and shot) in manicured, whitewashed, sun-splashed (un-named, but clearly Californian) suburbia. Everyone is what Americans call 'middle class', which means quite rich. The exception to the all-white cast comes in the form of Carlos and Gabrielle Solis, the most materialistic, high-class members of the group. In other words, the show appears to be about as straight as one can humanly conceive.

Not despite all of this, but rather because of it, I seek to argue here that *Desperate Housewives* mobilises a crucial *subversion* of mainstream sexual politics and heterosexual norms. While we often conceive of subversion as the overturning of a system from outside it, the concept can also be thought of as the challenge to, or even erosion of, a set of norms *from within*; in this chapter I will articulate and argue for this latter concept of subversion. I will both *reveal* the concept through a reading of the first season of *Desperate Housewives* precisely as I *employ* that concept in order to expose a certain (unexpectedly radical) politics in the show. Thus, I argue that, in what appears to be their very effort to maintain normalcy – within their straight, white, suburban world – the actions and choices of the characters on the show ultimately call mainstream American 'family values' into question. In the effort to shore up the heterosexual norm, *Desperate Housewives* reveals its operation, and despite any and all intentions, this amounts to a subversion of heteronormativity.

THE POLITICS OF SUBVERSION

To claim *Desperate Housewives* as a subversive show for its sexual politics sounds rather nonsensical on the surface. After all, to reverse the slogan: this is not HBO, it's TV. And *Desperate Housewives*, a show airing on the *least-watched* (at the time) major network, ABC, certainly bears little resemblance to the latest path-breaking, cutting-edge, never-before-aired (or pick your own favourite television marketing cliché) product from Home Box Office. Even worse than the show's failure to create its own new genre is the status of the already-existing genre into which TV critics typically place it. As if being on network television were not bad enough, *Desperate Housewives* is a night-time soap opera. Thus, it simply cannot be the next *St. Elsewhere* (NBC, 1982–8), *thirtysomething*, *Hill Street Blues* (NBC, 1981–7), or *My So-Called Life* (ABC, 1994–5). Rather, for genre comparisons, readers/viewers of *Desperate Housewives* find themselves stuck with *Dallas* (CBS, 1978–91), *Dynasty*, or *Melrose Place*. Perhaps more awkwardly, multiple members of the *Housewives* cast are veterans of multiple night-time soaps (Doug Savant and Marcia Cross both from *Melrose Place* and *Knots Landing* (CBS, 1979–93), and Nicollette Sheridan from *Knots Landing*).

Thus, if I am to make good on my claim for the show's subversiveness, evidence will have to come from somewhere other than the novelty, genius, or heavy-handed seriousness of the show; on all these counts, *Housewives* will be unlikely to measure up. The first step lies in a careful consideration of the concept of subversion. According to the *Oxford English Dictionary* the verb 'to subvert' has three main definitions: (1) to demolish, raze, or overturn, (2) to undermine, corrupt, or pervert, and (3) to disturb, overthrow, or destroy (*Shorter OED* 2002: 3094). When it comes to radical politics, I suspect that the first and third sets of meanings tend to predominate in our minds: subversion sounds like a revolutionary act, an attempt to destroy or demolish a set of institutions or practices. But let's face it: television seems like an unlikely place for this sort of radical overthrow.

For precisely this reason, I wish to focus on the second meaning of subvert, and by following a particular reading of the works of Judith Butler, to conceptualise subversion as a practice of *undermining from within*. Particularly when it comes to the idea of challenging norms, subversion is best thought of as a practice that works from *inside* the terms of the norms. This means that subversion must operate from *below*. Norms of gender and sexuality cannot easily be overthrown from the outside, but they can be overturned from the inside. Here we have a theory of subversion that remains fully inside the terms of culture (norms are cultural artefacts), working with those terms so as to rework them. The subversion of law (and of behaviours, norms, traditions, and practices) operates inside the law (see Butler 1999 [1990]: 119). This conceptualisation of subversion calls up the Latin etymology of the word, *subvertere* – to turn from below.

On this account, we can never get outside the system that we wish to subvert; to claim that we could would be instead to undermine the possibility of subversion (Butler 1999 [1990]: 185, cf. Butler 1993, 1995, 1997). For this reason, the agency involved in a subversive act or a subversive reading appears from inside the system that it attempts to overturn. Indeed, because it must remain internal in this way – yet still serve to overwhelm or transform the system to which it is internal – subversion undermines the very distinction between inner and outer (Butler 1999 [1990]: 174, cf. Butler 2000).[1]

This particular theoretical articulation of subversion raises pointed questions for our reading of *Desperate Housewives*. Can a show working within (fully or partially – a debate I will leave for others) the soap opera genre serve to challenge certain norms of gender and sexuality? Can a show centred on the lives of (mostly white) suburban family housewives somehow wind up thwarting or eroding heteronormativity? Can a prime-time network soap prove subversive?

WISTERIA LANE I:
A VERY STRAIGHT ROAD

The task of situating *Desperate Housewives* inside mainstream norms of gender and sexuality proves undaunting, to say the least. In the first season's introduction of the characters, to which I confine my formal analysis, all circuits of the show run through the five central female characters. Bree Van De Kamp, Gabrielle Solis, and Lynette Scavo fill the role announced by the title of the show. Each of these characters takes up a different version of the traditional role of a 'wife' who does not work outside the home. No television critic can stop from describing Bree as a 'Martha Stewart-like' character; Bree is a mother (to two teenagers), a wife, and, above all, a *homemaker*. While Bree lives the subject position of wife to its maximum, however, Lynette struggles with the constraints the role places upon her: as a former high-powered business executive, she now wages war (to great comic effect) with her home and children as a mother of three young boys. Gabrielle deviates from the norm slightly; she is the only wife who is not also a mother. But Gabrielle remains firmly within the role, serving as her husband's trophy and doing all she can to spend his money.

Neither Susan Mayer nor Edie Britt are married, but they round out the 'housewife' subject position by appearing just outside its contours. On one side we find Susan, a divorcée with a teenage daughter and a fragile heart of gold. Susan upholds the role of wife because her exclusion from it comes at the hands of a cheating husband. The viewer has little doubt that Susan wants nothing more than to marry again some day; she is the wife who was and the wife who would be. And finally, on the other extreme we can locate Edie, the exception that proves the rule. Edie has been divorced multiple times, for reasons – unlike the case of Susan – never made clear to the viewers. But one has every reason to suspect that Edie often *chose* to leave her husband, just as she regularly chooses whom to sleep with. Edie is the 'slut', the abject other that clarifies and shores up the role of 'wife' played (or potentially played) by all the other women. Edie, as 'slut', forms the constitutive outside to the housewives: she is that which they reject and exclude in order to constitute the subject position of wife. And frequently the show literalises this symbolic function; Susan, Bree, Gabrielle, and Lynette form a close circle of friends, with Edie actively ostracised. And yet, as will become clear in the sections below, like all constitutive outsides, Edie often proves to be that which the housewives cannot make do without. They need her, not only outside their circle, but sometimes also within it.

This formal analysis of the central characters can easily be complemented with a few other facts about the relative 'straightness' – by which I mean the extent to which the show upholds norms of binary gender, standards of femininity, and presumptions of heterosexuality – of *Desperate Housewives*. The list of rather banal examples proves long. First, one may note that all three husbands work in professional, high-status, suit-wearing environments, while none of the wives work at all. Susan (again, the wife to be) works at home, allowing her daily life to mimic that of her housewife friends. Edie, of course, works as a professional (again, the exception that proves the rule). However, as a real estate agent, Edie holds a job that is today gendered very much female, one that has her relying heavily on her looks, and one that places Edie working in the neighbourhood (we never see her in the office). Mike, the central male character who is not a husband, pretends (as his cover) to be a plumber. In reality, we witness Mike's involvement with guns and money and then with covert and illegal actions. Finally we discover Mike's past: conviction for murder and time in spent in prison. How could anyone possibly be any more masculine than Mike?

Cataloguing the straight attributes of Wisteria Lane certainly requires mentioning that none of the main characters on the show is gay.[2] This fact is perhaps not all that shocking in the context of network TV generally. However, one might expect that in 2004 a nighttime soap opera would include at least one gay character; after all, most daytime soap operas now do. More significantly, the universe that *Desperate Housewives* creates proves significantly unqueer, since the vast majority of the show is shot *on* Wisteria Lane. That is, the show operates almost exclusively within suburban space, the one place in America today where one is, supposedly, least likely to find gay and lesbian citizens (Lynch 1992; Dunlap 1996; Peyser and Jefferson 2004).

Finally, the mainstream press has done an excellent job making certain that the show stays within traditional norms of femininity. No case better makes this point than the infamous flap over the perfectly timed *Vanity Fair* cover story on *Desperate Housewives'* amazing popularity (Zeman 2005). The article profiles the success of the five main actresses on the show, contains a detailed interview with creator Marc Cherry, and chronicles the surprise success of the show. Yet none of this material made it into the endless rehashings of the piece on entertainment news shows and other media outlets. These frequent retellings turned the story into only one event, and reduced even that to one worn-out metaphor: the photo shoot that turned into a cat fight.

The caption to the *Vanity Fair* cover image reads: 'You wouldn't believe what it took just to get this photo.' This caption, rather than the specific claims and the general mood of the article itself, provided the hermeneutic key to the dozens of press reports written *on* the *Vanity Fair* article. Almost all of these 'reports' – really nothing more than Cliff's Notes glosses on the longer article – mislead terribly. They all give the impression that the actresses on the show are whiny, fighting, crying, hair-pulling little girls. No doubt, conflict moves a narrative, and in order to make it plausible to *report* as a newsworthy event a photo shoot for a magazine article, journalists

that 'covered' the 'events' from the photo shoot just had to emphasise that conflict. Such emphasis, however, quickly turned to outright distortion.

A careful reading of the entire *Vanity Fair* article leads one to believe that the writer and/or the magazine's editors were engaging in
a meta-political debate with, in general, publicists in their attempt
to control access to 'talent' and, in particular, the ABC rep on this
photo shoot who sought to micromanage all details. In contrast, the
press reports written about the article detail the prissy nature of the
actresses, their conflicts with one another, and their emotional fragility. In sum these reports play on, and play up, the idea that, given
their essential feminine nature, a group of five women cannot possibly work together as professionals.

If this account sounds at all overstated, I simply ask the reader
to imagine the articles on the conflict if they were written about a
group of five male actors. As Felicity Huffman herself states, 'the
prurient interest is gender-specific' (Traister 2005). As I have demonstrated in Chapter 3, 'gay-themed' shows such as *The L Word* are
easily co-opted as sites of heterosexual fantasy; coverage of *Desperate
Housewives* operates along the same lines of logic, serving to reinforce both heterosexual and feminine norms. A group of five strong
women cannot possibly get along, and so the masses scream for a cat
fight. I conclude here that the mainstream press wants to read the
show as just as straight as we might think it is. *Desperate Housewives*:
a show about housewives in traditional roles, a show about suburbia,
a show populated by thoroughly 'feminine' actresses. We will have to
dig quite a bit deeper to find subversion here.

WISTERIA LANE II:
NOT AS STRAIGHT AS YOU THINK

Lucky for us, then, that the text of the show, the vision of creator
Marc Cherry, and even (if we get past the accounts of the cat fight
to the actual text of the interviews) the statements of the actors,
all point us toward unexpected, hidden, and perhaps even politically productive aspects of the show. Despite surface appearances,

hidden queer moments and unknown queer spaces can be found up and down Wisteria Lane.

The most obvious case may appear in the unexpected form of Andrew Van De Kamp, Bree's son. Finding himself in the strictest, most uptight (read 'straightest') family on Wisteria Lane, Andrew is either the most likely or unlikely (depending on your perspective) character for the viewer to find making out with his male friend, Justin, in the swimming pool. That is precisely where we locate Andrew in episode 15. Andrew and Justin's on-screen kiss, some viewers and readers may be surprised to hear, turns out to be just the sixth male–male kiss in US network television history – and the first one hardly even counts (Warn 2005a).[3] Much like Russell from Chapter 2, Andrew himself turns out to be a very queer character to the extent that he actively refuses any particular sexual identity – first denying his homosexuality, then coming out to his parents as gay, and finally telling his pastor that the coming out was itself a lie ('Impossible', 1.15; 'Children Will Listen', 1.18; 'Live Alone and Like It', 1.19).

As if this were not enough queerness to thoroughly trouble the heteronormativity of the nuclear Van De Kamp family, we later discover that Rex Van De Kamp, Bree's husband, has significantly non-normative sexual proclivities: he thoroughly enjoys S/M role-playing and has been paying a prostitute to fulfil his desires. Even worse, the prostitute in question is another housewife just down the street on Wisteria Lane. When Bree discovers these 'unspeakable' (in her mind) transgressions, she is, needless to say, not amused. Bree denigrates Rex, stigmatises him for his actions, and upholds her normative vision of narrowly constrained sexual practices. And yet her very devotion to a vision of the nuclear family eventually leads her to agree to role-play with her husband. Thus, we find queerness at the very deepest element of the heterosexual norm.

Perhaps most interesting in Bree's case is the fact that well before finding out about Rex's sexual tastes, and long before he asks her to experiment with him, Bree's very chastising and stigmatisation of Rex follows the aesthetic of S/M. While she may be unable to see herself this way, Bree has always played the dominatrix in the family, even if she never took up that role in the bedroom. Thus, viewers cannot really be all that surprised that Rex – *the man who chose to marry Bree*

– likes to play the submissive. In many senses the formal logic of their relationship, in its paralleling of S/M roles, proves more subversive than the fact that they also try out non-normative sexual practices.[4]

Finally, we have perhaps the hardest case to make or to even make out – perhaps also the place in which we find the *queerest* moment on the show, and a moment absolutely central to the story. From the very beginning of season one, viewers know plainly that something is not right with Zach Young. His mother committed suicide under suspicious circumstances, and his father appears to be one of the least trustworthy individuals one can ever imagine meeting. If unsavoury situations were not enough to make us question Zach's character (or at least question the normality of his family), the show adds more fuel to the fire by, first, partially exposing the family secret – that there is something, quite likely a body, buried underneath the backyard family pool – and then by having Zach's dad commit murder on screen. The entire story arc of the first season of *Desperate Housewives* revolves around one question – *what is the secret?* – posed by Susan at the end of the pilot episode and by Paul in the flashback contained in the season finale: what has Mary Alice done?

While many viewers will know the tale well, I should quickly reveal the secret here before offering my particular reading of the story that eventually, gradually exposes it. In brief, 15 years previously, Mary Alice, unable to conceive herself, bought a child named Dana. Dana was the child of drug addict Deirdre, who at the time was happy to give up her offspring for the money to buy another fix. But a cleaned-up Deirdre returns a few years later to claim Dana. Mary Alice panics and murders Deirdre, while four-year-old Zach looks on from the top of the stairs. Mary Alice's husband, Paul, then dismembers and hides Deirdre's body. *Desperate Housewives* begins with Mary Alice's suicide and the first revelation of the backstory: that Mary Alice had received a note on the day of her death, a note that read simply 'I know what you've done' ('Pilot', 1.1).

However, the tale has different meanings as it unfolds in partial form over the course of the first season, and some of those meanings prove more radical than the complete account could ever be. I want to focus on one particular moment in the conveying of this secret tale. We can locate it in episode 18, during the conversation between Zach and Felicia: Zach concludes, without Felicia really telling him, that he *was* Dana ('Children Will Listen', 1.18). Prior to this point in the season, the viewer already knows about 'Dana' through the discovery of the baby blanket ('Anything You Can Do', 1.7). From this point onward the characters on the show all make the common assumption that 'Dana' names a girl, leading the viewers to do the same. And, indeed, it seems like a safe assumption: in recent history 'Dana' has been used as a 'boy's name' only very rarely and of the total occurrences of the name, only a tiny fraction are boys.[5] But it is not merely that we assume upon first hearing the name that Dana was a girl: the continued circulation of the name in the conversations of the characters, the frequent references to Zach's 'baby sister', and Zach's (misplaced) admission that he 'killed [his] baby sister' ('Suspicious Minds', 1.9) all *reify* the character of Dana as a girl.

Thus, at the moment that Zach and Felicia reveal for us the first (real) crucial part of the secret, that Zach and Dana are the same person, we are already fairly certain that Dana was a baby girl and we are beyond positive that something scandalous happened in the Young family's past. We also know, from the earlier exchange between Paul and Zach, that Zach's own earlier tale told to Julie – that he killed Dana – may not be true after all, but here the ambiguity proves high, since Paul seems an untrustworthy source ('Your Fault', 1.13). Finally, the text of the exchange between Zach and Felicia does nothing to give away the later revelation that Dana really was a boy:

Felicia:	I bet you miss your mother. I'm sure things were different when she was alive. Such a warm, loving woman.
Zach:	You knew my mother?
Felicia:	Yup. Years ago in Utah. We worked together.
Zach:	I didn't know that.
Felicia:	It's true. In fact, I'll tell you a secret. I once met you when you were a little baby.
Zach:	Really.
Felicia:	Mmm hmm. Your mother loved you so much, Zachary. Of all the things I remember, I remember that the most.
	[Zach begins to cry...]

Felicia:	You want to know what else I remember? How lovely your original name was.
Zach:	Dana.
	[Felicia nods]

('Children Will Listen', 1.18)

How are we to read this scene? Its ambiguity, along with the very suspense and mystery that the show has been building for the entire season, creates a moment of cognitive dissonance: how can Zach have been Dana in the past? That obscurity, along with almost all the rest, will be removed in the 'tell-all' season finale, where it will simply be asserted and assumed that Dana was a boy all along. Who would think otherwise? But rather than take the perspective of what we know at the end, I want to pause here, to read the question of Dana's/Zach's identity at this very moment. In doing so, I wish to locate this as the queerest moment of the season. Before we 'know' that Dana was a boy in the season finale, how do we understand the revelation that Zach was Dana at *this* point in time – a point at which we 'know' Dana was a girl?

Could the secret scandal from the Young family's history be that their 'daughter' Dana was born, like so many children throughout the world (Fausto-Sterling 2000), without clear male or female genitalia? Could it be that Dana *became* Zach after a surgical procedure altered 'her' ostensibly female genitalia into 'his' putatively male genitalia? Could Dana/Zach be one of the many intersexed children that today's heteronormative societies insist on 'correcting' so that they will fit into the normative grid of binary gender? Of course, the season finale will answer all of these not-so-rhetorical questions both clearly and definitively, with its own version of a resounding 'No!'. And yet, the very ambiguity of Zach's/Dana's past leaves open a space from which all these questions might appear. The fact remains that upon an initial viewing of season one of *Desperate Housewives* from beginning to end, it will be reasonable (maybe even prudent) to raise questions such as these at the moment this scene airs. This ambiguity, the possibility of such radical questioning, of broaching such important yet neglected political issues, produces in turn a potentially rather subversive moment.

OUT OF THE SUBURBS AND
INTO THE STUDIO:
'REAL-LIFE' POLITICAL SUBVERSION

Perhaps the very idea still sounds far-fetched. Perhaps readers remain unconvinced that a prime-time soap opera could possibly allow a space for such subversion. Many might raise the spectre of intentionality by asking the following: is it plausible to broach radical
questions of gender and sex subversion when the show itself has no
intention to consider such a radical sexual politics? My first answer,
unsurprisingly, will be that the choice to constrain the interpretive
field based upon the intentionality of the author proves increasingly
difficult even with singly authored texts; it sounds downright impossible in the medium of television, where the final product is the
result of creators, directors, writers, and editors, not to mention the
actors themselves. Nevertheless, why not play the 'intentions game',
briefly, by seeing what some of the 'authors' of *Desperate Housewives*
have to say. Their own comments open and maintain space for this
queer reading of the show.

One might start with the rather phobic 'scandal' surrounding
Marcia Cross. As reported in the *Vanity Fair* piece, in February 2005
media madness produced swirling rumours that Marcia Cross was
gay and that she planned to come out by way of a cover story in the
Advocate (Freydkin 2005; cf. Warn 2005b). The real shock comes from
the source for the story: an anonymous post by an unregistered user
on a gay gossip message board. Mainstream media outlets – including CNN and *USA Today* – ran with stories reporting on the 'rumour'
and 'speculation' without making any attempt to verify the information. The *Advocate* was planning to put Marcia Cross on their cover,
but she had no plans to come out in their pages, and yet the *Advocate*
was the first to contact Carl Pritzkat, the president of the company
that runs the message board, in an effort to verify the information.
In his turn, Pritzkat simply declared his 'shock' that the media would
point to the message boards as a source at all.

Nevertheless, by the time Marcia Cross co-hosted ABC's *The View*
on 8 February 2005, the question of her sexuality had already be-

come a full-blown 'news' story. Still, Cross herself saw no need to
address the issue, having had her publicist issue a statement the day
before calling the rumours 'completely untrue' (Slan 2005). *The View*
hosts saw things differently, raising the issue repeatedly. Barbara
Walters went directly to the topic, giving Cross something explicitly
to deny: 'There is a big rumour about you – that you are gay' (Giantis 2005). Cross instead took the opportunity to question the entire
problematic: 'Well it was very odd. I just assume this is what comes
of being 42 and single. I don't know if they just needed to find a reason why I wasn't married or – I mean, I'm not' (Giantis 2005). One
might wish to take this final 'I'm not' as an answer to the more-than-
implicit question 'Are you gay?', as focused by Walters following the
media frenzy. Indeed, a number of transcriptions of the interview
that one finds online choose to write the quotation this way: 'I'm not
[gay]', and this is not to mention the perverse manner in which a few
sites report on Cross's 'angry denials' of the rumour, despite the fact
that one can find (either cited in these articles or elsewhere) not one
shred of evidence to suggest that Cross was either angry about the
rumours or gravely intent on denying them ('*Desperate Housewives*
Marcia Cross denies lesbian slur' 2005; 'Movie/TV News' 2005). At
this moment in the conversation, a different host, Star Reynolds, offered to fix Cross up, confirming Cross's point that folks just are not
comfortable with the idea of a famous, beautiful, single 42-year-old.

Still, the 'I'm not' proved too ambiguous for the ladies of *The
View*; thus Joy Behar followed up with this rather subtle question:
'So you are not a lesbian?' To this, Cross repeated the 'I'm not' (this
time, given context, less ambiguously) before elaborating: 'I did think
it was really weird, though, that there was all this curiosity about
something like that, about sexuality. And I thought, what a world we
live in that that's so important' (Giantis 2005). Again, it is hard to
locate an angry denial here. What we find instead is not merely – as
would be expected from most heavily managed Hollywood personali-
ties – an incredibly careful and diplomatic response from Cross, to a
series of questions that she should never have to answer in the first
place. More than this, we also witness a rather significant elaboration and critique of the power of heteronormativity. Cross takes no
offence at the idea that someone might think she is gay, but she does

take the opportunity to question the notion that any of this should cause controversy and she challenges the idea that this question must even be definitively answered. In my opinion, Adam Vary puts it quite eloquently and accurately in the *Advocate* article – a piece that, in fully postmodern self-referentiality, wound up being *about* the controversy over the cover story itself. Vary claims that Cross 'handled herself [graciously] on *The View*, where she appeared more incredulous that anyone would care about her sexuality at all than that anyone would think she's gay' (Vary 2005). She directs her incredulity toward three key heteronormative assumptions (with the first two being homophobic assumptions as well): (1) being gay is bad or wrong, (2) being straight is important or essential, and (3) all women should be married.

In her own way, then, and from within the particular constraints of the Hollywood context, Cross hereby challenges the power of heteronormativity by refusing the terms of the question. Even her dry and succinct publicist's statement achieves this goal. It states: 'In response to recent rumours about Marcia Cross, they are completely untrue. She is, however, very supportive of the gay and lesbian community' (Slan 2005). Once again, the last line of support for the gay and lesbian community might be expected as good PR (although even at that, few would take the time to make the claim), but I would prefer to focus on what is *not* said in the first sentence. The statement calls the rumours 'untrue' but it refuses to say 'Marcia Cross is a straight woman' or that she is not gay.

None of this was enough to stop the news reports from proclaiming just that, sometimes even from their headlines. *USA Today* ran this headline: 'I'm single and straight, Cross says' despite the fact that she said no such thing, either on TV or in her official statement. *Entertainment Weekly* went with this headline, offering a similar, and similarly falsely attributed quote: 'Marcia Cross: I'm not gay!' Perhaps most amazing of all, *TV Guide* online ended their brief entry with this sentence: 'Just don't call her a lesbian!' ('And the plot thickens' 2005; Freydkin 2005; Susman 2005;). Here we see clearly the same force, though greatly magnified through the power of the media, as the one we witnessed in Chapter 2: Claire's insistence that Russell must be gay if he sleeps with a man is mirrored here in the media's demand to translate Cross's demurral into a full-fledged rejection of homosexuality. In other words, all of these media mis-reports serve as efforts to reconstitute the power of heteronormativity in the face of Cross's small confrontation to that very power. Such a challenge proves politically significant, that is, potentially subversive, even if it requires archaeological work to uncover.

Much less buried will be the political work of Felicity Huffman. The most critically acclaimed but perhaps least well-known actress on the show, Huffman is certainly one to participate in subversive on-screen work. While shooting the first season of *Housewives* Huffman also filmed the movie *Transamerica* (Duncan Tucker, 2005). In it, Huffman plays the lead role as a transgendered woman travelling cross-country with her son, a role for which she won the Best Actress award at the Tribeca Film Festival. In April 2005, before the film made its North American debut at Tribeca, *Salon* interviewed Huffman about the movie. Not surprisingly, this interview addresses complex and subtle questions about gender and sexuality, focusing specifically on the difficult, abjected lives of transgender and transsexual individuals. It also addresses in some detail the very practical and mundane, but also quite radical issues of living life as a transgender person: specifically, since Huffman's character in the movie is shown removing her penis from her trousers to urinate by the side of the road. None of this comes as too much of a shock (even if the scene would be shocking to many viewers), in that one expects a media outlet like *Salon* to take up these issues.

What is surprising, however, is how quickly, how easily, and how utterly seamlessly the interview transitions from a discussion of *Transamerica* to questions and answers about *Desperate Housewives*, and does so without really shifting the topic away from themes of gender and sexuality. Huffman and her interviewer both stress what is obviously path-breaking about the show: all the lead roles have gone to actresses in their thirties and forties. When asked why such a show would emerge now, when in the past there have been almost no good roles for women over 35, Huffman gives a rich and significant answer:

I think gay men appreciate women differently than straight guys do. It's funny; we're not the objects of their sexual desires, but they always consider us sexual objects. They appreciate women. And I think that's because it's OK now to be gay in Hollywood – and that's taken a while – that finally maybe there are opportunities now for Marc Cherrys to be the source for a series. I think gay men write women differently and appreciate them and maybe it took them getting in a creative position of power for us to be seen that way. (quoted in Traister 2005)

Huffman's response calls on the logic of a long-standing feminist argument: women should be in positions of power not merely for fundamental egalitarian reasons but also because many things will change in society (in ways we perhaps cannot foresee) when the powerful positions are no longer dominated by one, rather singular subject position (the straight, white male). Yet the argument has been completely reworked and amplified, since Huffman suggests that it is creator/producer Marc Cherry's position as a gay man that provides the show with a different take on gender roles.

Thus, to complete the logic in a way that ties together the previous two sections of this chapter: *Desperate Housewives* does indeed deal with characters confined within very narrowly drawn, 'traditional' gender roles, but the perspective it takes on those roles proves totally different than we would traditionally suppose (and this point holds no matter the reason for it – whether it be Cherry's sexuality or some utterly different explanation). Huffman's comments in the *Salon* interview find a faint, but otherwise hard to read, echo in her brief remark in the *Vanity Fair* article. Observing Cherry's skill at dealing with on-set problems, Huffman states: 'I think he has a vagina in his brain' (quoted in Vary 2005: 204). I call the remark 'hard to read' since in the *Vanity Fair* article it appears to have no context at all; the *Salon* interview provides such a context, filling in the notion that Cherry's talent and the spark of the show both partially emerge from Cherry's unique perspective – a gay man writing a show about suburban housewives.

For his own sake, Cherry provides a name for this perspective, calling it 'post-post-post-feminist' (quoted in Vary 2005: 265). I have no idea what Cherry means by that, and I am even less certain that he knows himself.[6] But if feminism takes an oppositional stance to traditional gender roles, in an effort to seek women's liberation, and if post-feminism wrongly assumes that no such change in gender roles, no such liberation is necessary since women are somehow already equal to men, then whatever lies beyond the second category would need to consider the case to be made for resistance to those categories of gender and sexuality – resistance that can only come from within, a radical political praxis through subversion.

NORMALISATION AND SUBVERSION, ON AND OFF WISTERIA LANE

To delineate this politics of subversion fully requires a clearer understanding of normalisation. In both its narrative and dialogic structure *Desperate Housewives* makes a concerted effort to maintain the surface appearance of both heterosexual normality and traditional gender roles. However, on the reading offered here this is precisely the point: the show *tries so hard* to uphold straightness, that it betrays itself. The reason that Wisteria Lane proves something less than straight lies in the very desperation to remain straight. Often the characters on the show work so hard to preserve normality that in the process they *reveal the workings* of gender and sex norms.[7] Certainly Bree comes to mind in this regard: she is so intent on preserving her vision of the perfectly mannered, brilliantly behaved, normal nuclear family that she will take her cheating husband back into their home and participate in S/M sexual scenarios with him. Clearly, her effort to uphold normality serves instead to undermine it.

In general, to reveal the norm may be to subvert it since norms work best when they are never exposed. In other words, the optimal operation of the norm is an invisible operation. Once norms reach the point that they require significant shoring up, then they have already been significantly weakened. This means that reinforcing a norm can never bring it back to full strength, since the very act of reinforcement serves to expose the norm as weaker than it could be. Examples abound. Within a society in which marriage law dictates women to be the property of men, and in which women do not work (one would say 'outside the home' but even that suggests a visibility to the norm that is necessarily lacking in the case I sketch here), then there simply is no need to 'show women their place'. Prior to Stonewall and the burgeoning practice of 'coming out', heterosexuality was never even considered a norm. It simply *was* – taken to be so fundamental, so natural as to never need description as natural. The movement of gay liberation challenges the norm of heterosexuality, not simply through offering alternatives to it, but (through this process) by bringing heterosexuality to light as something other than a given – making it visible *as a norm*. Put another way, and as I have already discussed in some detail in Chapter 2, the best way to call one's heterosexuality into question is to declare it, since if one is really straight one need never say so (Halperin 1995: 48). For viewers of the show, this argument will likely call up the scene in which Susan catches Andrew and Justin making out in the pool, and Andrew immediately and adamantly declares, 'I'm not gay' ('Impossible', 1.15).

By revealing the heterosexual norm and exposing its operation, *Desperate Housewives* proves successful (despite whatever its intentions might be) in undermining heteronormativity. The show subverts the norm from within, not by eroding it from the margins but by undermining it from the centre. To capture this particular meaning of subversion (and its political significance) requires maintaining a clear distinction between 'what the majority do/are', on the one hand, and *normalisation*, on the other. This distinction entails *not* taking heteronormativity as a mere description of the fact that a super-majority of people in the world act or identify as heterosexual. As a political concept heteronormativity offers not a bare description of fact (most people 'are heterosexual'). Rather, heteronormativity provides a political articulation of the *normativity* of heterosexuality (see Butler 2004).

In other words, 'heteronormativity' tells us that heterosexual desire and identity are not merely assumed, they are expected. They are demanded. Thus, heteronormativity must not be reduced to the idea of an assumption in the heads of individuals that says, 'My guess is that you're straight.' Heteronormativity is written into law, encoded in the very structures of institutions (think bathrooms, think locker rooms), and built into an enormous variety of common practices – particularly since so much of society remains structured around dating/romance. Put another way, most people (75 per cent) have attached earlobes, but that does not (necessarily) mean that attached earlobes are normative. It would mean *that*, only if those with detached earlobes were subject to different laws, if their sexuality was criminalised, if they were excluded from social or cultural practices, and if their behaviour was considered deviant or abject.

Thinking heteronormativity in this more expansive yet more precise manner serves to specify *Desperate Housewives'* particular form of subversion. The show does not subvert heteronormativity by emphasising the margins. Obviously, the women of Wisteria Lane are neither political radicals, nor gender or sexual deviants. If they were, they would not live on Wisteria Lane. Across their differences, Bree, Lynette, Susan, Gabrielle, and Edie all find themselves relatively close to the median point on the normal curve. Yet, here we see a crucial point about normalisation: it produces its effects even on those it marks as ostensibly 'normal'. The power of the norm is felt in different ways (sometimes more violently) by those at the margins of the curve, but it is still felt by those toward the centre. The norm wields a terrible force against the women of Wisteria Lane, and we witness their struggle with, through, and sometimes against that norm. Obviously resistance to norms can come from the margins, but resistance may arise at the centre as well. As the women of Wisteria Lane wage their struggle with normality, they often expose heteronormativity – and sometimes they even undermine it.

Indeed, challenging the norm from the centre has the potential to wield a much greater force than questioning the norm from its margins. This logic can be illuminated with the following rhetorical question. Whose gender deviations prove more disturbing to the power of the norm: those abject others whose very difference consolidates the power of the norm, or the 'normal' ones themselves? If gays, sexual radicals, and even (occasionally) single people challenge norms of sex and gender, this behaviour is to be expected (even if it is not 'normal'). But to challenge sex and gender norms from inside the upper-class, white, nuclear family is, potentially, to do serious damage to heteronormativity. No wonder the American Family Association (AFA) was so upset about *Desperate Housewives* (Potts 2004).

The paradox and power of *Desperate Housewives* arises from its ability to do two things at once. First, it constructs a *severely constrained* context. As I detailed in the second section, the role of housewife does, indeed, confine these women. One sees no vision of liberation from the show: the political goal will not be a place beyond sex and gender, it will not be complete equality, it will not be equal work (for equal wages), and it will not be shared child-rearing responsibilities. Nonetheless, and second, while the show never concerns itself with women's 'oppression', it also refuses to take their condition for granted. Any viewer of the show (especially viewers who watch past the first two episodes, which marks the limited viewing given by most progressive or quasi-feminist critiques of the show, see for example Peterson 2004) will recognise that the characters we watch from week to week prove, consistently, to be strong, sometimes brilliant, often fierce, and always *agentic* women. This agency comes from within the context of their roles as women, and here we see a politics of subversion emerge.[8]

If a politics of subversion sounds weak or somehow hollow, if it reads like a feeble attempt to praise a show that, in the end, one might wish to condemn as nothing more than a soap opera, then perhaps it will be worth reminding readers of what *Desperate Housewives* manages to carry off. Unlike a whole host of ostensibly more 'radical' shows on television, *Desperate Housewives* successfully (and perhaps surprisingly, with little controversy) raises a number of contentious, complicated, and important questions concerning the politics of gender and sexuality. As noted briefly above, *Desperate Housewives* aired one of the very few kisses between two males, but it seems worth adding that the *Housewives* kiss had an important context – the characters were both teenagers, and they were alone at night, ostensibly naked, and in the swimming pool. Beyond this, as is also well known, the show plots an affair between an older married woman and another teenage boy.[9] And then we have Rex Van De Kamp's infamous sexual proclivities; unlike 'gay kisses' I am unsure if anyone has bothered to document serious characters with a taste for S/M, but I will run the risk of conjecture: if Rex is not the first, he finds himself on a very short list indeed.

All of this could be trivialised, and certainly the show's dark humour plays many of these examples as much for their comic effect as for any other more serious purposes. Nonetheless, one should not downplay the significance of the fact that *Desperate Housewives* has been able to raise issues such as these, ones that would never appear on shows such as *Will and Grace*. And while they may certainly crop up in other quarters, such as *Queer as Folk*, they are just as likely to be dismissed there. In other words, audience is always important, and *Housewives* speaks to a very different, much larger one. These factors all come together to produce the counterintuitive but nonetheless powerful conclusion that *Desperate Housewives* motivates a significant cultural politics, one that is subversive of heteronormativity.

My interpretations of both *Desperate Housewives* and *The L Word* in Part II of the book serve to elaborate and deepen the theory of heteronormativity. This entails not only a further exploration of how heteronormativity functions but also a more detailed engagement with the potential tactics and strategies for challenging or resisting heteronormativity. My critique in Chapter 3 of *The L Word*, and my call to shift from a narrow interest-group politics of representation to a broader politics of norms, serves to support my argument in this chapter in favour of a politics of subversion. In the Part III I will narrow the focus of the argument in this book further, by engaging directly with the contemporary politics of the family – a central and crucial site for both queer theory and the cultural politics of television.

Notes

1   For further elaboration of the concept of subversion and the politics thereof, particularly as read through the writings of Butler, see Chambers 2007, Carver and Chambers 2007, and Chambers and Carver 2008.

2   In terms of secondary characters, Andrew Van De Kamp is another story, parts of which I tell later in this chapter.

3   I say the first one does not count because the kiss between Will and Jack
     on *Will and Grace* was itself a completely artificial performance, even
     within the terms of the show. As Christie Keith points out, viewers had
     to wait five full years after the 'joke' kiss with Jack, before lead character
     Will would actually kiss a man with whom he was romantically involved
     (Keith 2006).

4   Thanks to Jairus Grove for thoughts on this argument.

5   See Baby Name Wizard at *http://www.babynamewizard.com*.

6   Anecdotally, Cherry's own politics fall to the right of the spectrum, and
     he freely declares his support of the US Republican party. Certainly
     some of Cherry's own idealisation of 1950s suburban America inflects
     Desperate Housewives. Yet, as I make clear throughout this book, read-
     ings of television shows can by no means be confined to intentionality,
     even when dealing with the intentions of the creator and executive pro-
     ducer.

7   One could take a similar line of argument in reading Todd Haynes' 2002
     film, *Far From Heaven*.

8   One could conceptualise this phenomenon through the lens of what
     we might call the 'practical feminism' of *Desperate Housewives*. By this I
     mean that while *Desperate Housewives* certainly does not portray a femi-
     nist utopia of liberated women, we must pause before merely condemn-
     ing it for this portrayal. What if feminism must sometimes be narrowed
     to the question of acting in and through the subject positions that we
     are given? What if it cannot be a matter of constructing new ones out
     of whole cloth? In that case, then, feminist action must be thought of
     in the same way I have considered subversion here – as actions taken or
     choices made *within the terms* of gender norms. From this perspective
     we can call to light the strong agency of these women. The show has to
     be about subversion or about agency within the given categories, be-
     cause for these characters there is nothing else.

9   On this point one might fruitfully compare the relationship between
     Justin and Brian on *Queer as Folk* to that of Gabrielle and John on *Des-
     perate Housewives*. The latter relationship demonstrates the heteronor-
     mative assumption that straight sexual practices are so normal as to not
     need learning. During their affair, John almost always acts like a mature,
     adult, movie star lover. Justin, in contrast, has to have Bryan teach him
     what to do – has to be inculcated into sexual practices. This explains why
     the original actor who played John, Kyle Searles, was dismissed because
     he 'lacked chemistry' with Eva Longoria. Searles, age 18, was replaced
     by Jesse Metcalfe, age 25 (Keck 2004). Perhaps Searles proved to be too
     (authentically) vulnerable; he needed coaching. Gabrielle and John have

an utterly unrealistic relationship not because older women never sleep with teenagers, but because when it comes to sex, she seems to teach him nothing. Marc Cherry's comments about the network's reaction to teenage sex also speaks to the power of heteronormativity: 'We have her [Gabrielle] in bed with a young teenage boy [John], and the network's note was, "Must she smoke?" ... We had to cut the footage so you don't see the cigarette as much, and then it was just peachy keen' (Walker 2004). The message seems clear: teenage sex, as long as it is straight sex, is less deviant than smoking.

Part III
Family Politics

5

The Meaning of 'Family'

It's an eensy more complicated than that. Family always is, isn't it?
The Hell-God 'Glory' ('Blood Ties', 5.13)

B*uffy the Vampire Slayer* is not just a television show. It is a canonised and sometimes deified intellectual object, the source of hundreds if not thousands of interpretations, analyses, critiques, and excursus. Around this object forms a field of academic study. But beyond the academy *Buffy the Vampire Slayer* (frequently abbreviated as *BtVS*) centres and animates a worldwide community and in many respects forms a movement. To analyse, interpret, or make an argument about the show means to encounter these broad and powerful phenomena, but my goal here will not be an attempt to interpret or sum up either the show, the field of study, or the community. Consistent with my treatment of other – always far less famous – television shows in this book, I want to read *Buffy* as a text, to mine it for the ways in which it participates in a certain cultural politics and to explore the extent to which it speaks to and reads as queer theory.

In doing so, I take an intentionally, and I would argue very much necessarily, narrow approach to *Buffy*. I focus on the meaning of family articulated by the show, particularly *in relation* to dominant, mainstream, and certainly heteronormative understandings of family. That is, I offer an interpretation of *Buffy*, focusing particularly on the episode from season five titled 'Family', to develop and to articulate *a radical conceptualisation of family*. In my emphasis here I am trying to distinguish between a 'radical understanding of family' and a 'radical reading of *Buffy*'; that is, I am making the former claim and not the latter. In other words, my goal is to develop an understanding of family that I think makes a radical break from *both* mainstream and conservative understandings of family, on the one hand, *and* liberal criticisms of those conceptions, on the other. In order to accomplish this goal, I offer a reading of *Buffy* that is very much distinct from other interpretations that deal with family.[1]

Put very simply, I argue that the show *resignifies* family. Numerous authors (I cite them below) have argued that *Buffy* offers us powerful representations of 'non-traditional' families, or that *Buffy* generates a conception of family as *choice*. While I accept the veracity of the first thesis, I eschew repeating this line of argument: it has already been successfully established and – following my arguments about representational politics in the previous chapters – it proves relatively less important for my purposes. *Buffy* may well offer us representations of non-traditional family arrangements, but I hope to show that it does far more than that. I reject the second thesis outright; one does not *choose* one's family. The *resignification* of family means that the show does not simply offer 'alternatives' to the standard, nuclear family, nor does it merely broaden our understanding of how a family comes to be (e.g. through choice). Instead, it *reworks and refigures the very meaning* of 'family'. Ultimately, in line with my arguments about the queer politics of television throughout this book, I suggest that this is radical political work.

To make my case I start not with *Buffy* but with my own theoretical work on the idea of 'family'. That is, in order to argue that *Buffy* provides a radical model of family, I first need to lay out what I take to be the normatively dominant model of family operative in the contexts to which *Buffy* speaks – I will call this the *sanguinuptial* model of family. From here I address the *BtVS* literature on ideas of family, showing how this literature, while certainly making strong claims about family, still remains trapped within the dominant understandings. I can then give a reading of the episode 'Family' designed to show how *Buffy* provides a powerful critique of common models of family – a critique more far-reaching than previous *BtVS* literature on family has entertained. I then go on to show how we can, and why we should, grasp this distinct understanding of family as a *queer* one (and here I draw some distinctions with other putatively 'queer readings' of *Buffy*). I conclude with some thoughts about the cultural politics involved in resignifying 'family' in the manner suggested by this interpretation.

WHAT IS 'FAMILY'?

Both here and in the title of this chapter, 'family' appears in inverted commas. This is not because I doubt its existence; rather, this presentation signals a significant methodological choice on my part. In the first instance I focus very little, if at all, on the historical practices of family. I offer no anthropological cataloguing of family forms, no genealogical explanation of family's transformations. Instead of trying to sort out all the contradictions inherent in the history of family (from the various rules for marital and sexual relations, to the deviations from those rules in actual practices), I want to analyse the way in which 'family' functions both in and as a discourse (and does so regardless of the contradictions). In other words, I am most interested in the way that 'family' is mobilised in political discourse, particularly in the USA but also in the UK and Europe. 'Family' can have a very powerful set of political effects because of the meanings that it takes within specific discourses, and it can do this not merely despite, but indeed *because of the fact* that the actual rules, actual practices, and actual history of family prove to be variously *contradictory* to these mobilised political meanings. No matter how family gets practised, both inside and outside Western liberal democracies, 'family' functions in politically salient ways.

For these reasons, while I wish to explore the meaning of family in this chapter, I insist on understanding that meaning in a particular and politically significant way. The meaning of 'family' as it circulates in contemporary discourses cannot be reduced either to the definition of family or to particular family practices. That is, the goal is not to *define* 'a family', but to ask about the *function* of 'family' in discourse, to figure out its 'meaning' by looking for not only its definitions but also its uses, its implications, its resonances. Thus, I am treating 'family' as an object formed within specific discursive practices (Foucault 1972). 'Family' is not an object that *precedes* discourses *about* it; 'family' takes its shape and *comes to be within those discourses*. Most importantly, 'family' has numerous *effects* as it circulates in contemporary discourses, and these effects cannot be reduced to the merely linguistic. The discursive entailments of 'family' will prove just as much *material* as linguistic – concerned just as much with *power* as with 'meaning' in the narrow sense of defining a word (see Foucault 1972; cf. Chambers 2006).

This insistence on going beyond definitions does not preclude one from starting with the dictionary. Indeed, if we read dictionaries as another (but certainly not just any other) group of texts that participate in the circulation of meaning as I have described it above, then dictionaries themselves offer much more than definitions. If we reject the narrow notion that a dictionary simply contains a set of objective facts about the meanings of words, then we can interpret the dictionary as a place where conflicts of meaning are played out, and where changes in meanings (and therefore also changes in power relations within discursive practices) are both catalogued and, in their own way, fought over. In the case of 'family', I would argue, the dictionary definitions exceed all expectations. These definitions – despite any intentions of the authors – prove highly insightful; they reveal a great deal about not only the meaning of family but also the politics of family. In my reading of these definitions here I focus exclusively on the use of the word 'family' to apply to people, not to things, and I concern myself mainly with more modern definitions (e.g. I exclude the entries in which servants are considered family).

The *New Oxford American Dictionary* gives the following key definitions for 'family': 'a group consisting of parents and children living together in a household; a group of people related to one another by blood or marriage' (*New Oxford* 2007). These central definitions resonate well with the common usage of 'family' and with mainstream understandings. We typically take 'family' to refer to two broad categories of human relations: those that exist by way of blood and birth, and those brought about through marriage. The family starts with its nuclear core: parents related by marriage, and children related by blood. It then extends outward to 'extended family', a category that certainly 'counts' as family, but also remains consistently marked as outside or beyond the nuclear family. This grouping includes aunts, uncles, nephews, nieces, and cousins; indeed, 'cousins' is the liminal category of family, as at some point in the movement from first cousins to third cousins (depending on one's understanding) we move from family to non-family. Thus, the *New Oxford* definition points precisely to the nuclear family of the household, made up of blood and marriage relations, and the broader family relations constituted by the same.

In contrast both to this definition and to current dominant understandings of family, then, it proves quite significant to see what the *Oxford English Dictionary* leaves out of its entries on family: namely, marriage. The entry in the *OED*, which mirrors the second entry from above, reads as follows: 'any group of people connected by blood *or other relationship*' (*Shorter OED* 2002: 921, emphasis added). Thus, the *OED* listing still centres on blood relations, but it reaches out from that centre to the very broad and vague category of 'other relations'. Obviously, this 'other' is most commonly filled by marital relations, but nowhere in its definition does the *OED* specify or even mention marriage. This exclusion proves extremely significant, since it makes the borders of family much more porous. It also has a potentially powerful impact on the politics of the family, since it suggests other routes to family besides marriage.

Indeed, one might conjecture that in the space between the *OED* and the *New Oxford American Dictionary* definitions the politics of marriage and the family, particularly the US politics of so-called 'family values', has made its own 'entry'. That is, 'family' in the American dictionary explicitly includes marriage, as if 'marriage' were a core element in family values – whereas in the British dictionary marriage plays no role. The *OED* makes clear that 'family' starts with the household and with blood, and then expands outward in concentric circles to capture other relations. But the *New Oxford* listing names those 'other relations' and thereby places a limit on what those concentric circles might include: marriage. Has the politics of marriage successfully reshaped the meaning of family in the USA? Or, to rephrase in the form of a declaration: *marital relations are coming to stand for family relations by way of catachresis*. Marriage becomes the lynchpin of family in the *New Oxford* entries; to be 'family' means to be 'married'.[2] This catachrestic shift serves as the condition of possibility of a certain politics (just as it may well be the *result* of that very politics) since marriage rights now become the space to play out the politics of family.

Catachresis literally means to use a word improperly on purpose, but in such a way as to change its meaning. If it seems too strong a term here, or if it appears as if I am reading too much into the dictionary, then why not continue to pursue such a reading? Let me turn to a third and final dictionary entry for 'family'. The following *Random House* entry appears to mimic the *OED* but with an almost unbelievable twist: 'any group of persons closely related by blood, as parents, children, uncles, aunts, and cousins: *to marry into a socially prominent family*' (*Random House* 2006, emphasis added). This definition proves so fascinating and so analytically and politically important, first of all, because it appears to repeat the *OED* listing by making blood its focal point. Like the *OED*, and unlike the *New Oxford*, *Random House* specifies only blood relations as the core factor for determining family. Indeed, none of the *Random House* listings mentions marriage. But marriage does appear in the illustrative example within the particular listing I have quoted here. This appearance proves so significant, however, because *the example does not illustrate the given definition*. That is, this listing defines family as persons related by blood, but marriage is precisely – and almost always by both definition and legal requirements – a non-blood relation. (And perhaps it proves symbolically significant that some US states still require a blood test before marriage, although obviously the blood *test* does not check for blood *relations*.) Let me restate the problematic: the *Random House* definition stipulates family as something one only joins by way of blood. The example given of this definition refers to joining a family by way of marriage. But according to the definition itself, this would be impossible: if family relations are blood relations then relations by way of marriage would not count as 'family'. Here then, we have a catachrestic use of 'marry' within the very definition of family.

Of course, such usage would never be deemed catachrestic outside the dictionary. There can be little doubt that in everyday usage, 'family' refers precisely to relations of blood and marriage. Family includes the specific dictionary definitions of household and blood relations, but goes on to place marital relations into that core as well. Indeed, others doing what we might call definitional work on 'family' go so far as to make marriage more important than blood. In the words of US Catholic bishops, 'family' is: 'an intimate community of persons bound together by blood, marriage, or adoption, for the whole of life. In our Catholic tradition, the family proceeds from marriage – an intimate, exclusive, permanent, and faithful partnership of husband and wife'. Both this work and the particular definition tell us a great deal about the political contestation over the meaning of family (NCCB 1998: 17; cited in Locklin 2002: par. 17). To cite banal examples, no one would question whether the newly wed couple was 'family',[3] and when the nurse at the hospital says that the patient can have visitors from 'family only' we 'know' – that is, in everyday practices we always take the nurse to mean – that she or he is referring first and foremost to husbands and wives, and then to children and parents and other blood relations.

I propose to call this the *sanguinuptial* meaning of family since this neologism has the advantage of pulling together the two key ingredients that make up the very medium of the family: blood and marriage. The sanguinuptial understanding of family proves to be not only *dominant*, as the most common understanding, but also *hegemonic*, in that it crowds out, excludes, or positively rejects other meanings. Because of this hegemony, the sanguinuptial meaning of family proves politically significant: it colonises the very space of alternative renderings of the family, making them coextensive with the sanguinuptial meaning. In other words, even 'alternative' conceptions of family are still understood *in relation* to sanguinuptial family. Hence the need to move past alternatives; hence the need to challenge the sanguinuptial model itself. My goal in this chapter, by way of particular readings of *Buffy* as queer theory, is to build a radical and distinct conception of the family – one that cannot be hegemonised by the sanguinuptial understanding.

The foundation for this building is the observation that common usage, dictionary definitions, and political mobilisations all agree on a sanguinuptial rendering of family. This understanding of family starts with the nuclear family – forming the core of blood and marriage – but it seems crucial to note that the sanguinuptial thinking of family can easily extend outward. Beyond the nuclear family we have the further relations I listed above, but this 'extended family', while often taken as the most important alternative to the nuclear family – particularly in literature about African American extended families (see Hill *et al.* 1993 for an extensive list of citations) – turns out to be no alternative at all since the 'extended family' is really just the outer rings of family that confirm the nuclear core. From the left of the political spectrum, valorisations of extended family, however helpful they may be in certain contexts, offer almost none of the leverage needed to challenge a sanguinuptial understanding. And the arguments from the right – those that seek some sort of return to a 1950s model of the nuclear family – depend fundamentally on the sanguinuptial concept. That is, *the nuclear family is a particular configuration of the sanguinuptial family* – neither an alternative nor a critique.

I contend, then, that broader or subtly reframed definitions of family based on the same sanguinuptial conceptualisation do very little cultural or political work; they merely reify the sanguinuptial model, and this is the model *within which* most explicitly political battles over the family take place (even, as I will describe below, queer political battles). To rethink family we need not merely 'alternative' formulations – in the sense of ancillary conceptions that would serve only to augment, but not displace, the sanguinuptial meaning of family – but genuinely distinct and radical conceptions of family. That is, we require new ways of thinking of the linkage between people and new characterisations of the relationships that make them family in the first place. To carry out this task I turn to Joss Whedon's conception of family as a viable space for building a radical understanding of family that not only goes beyond blood and marriage but also rejects and replaces the sanguinuptial rendering of family.

BtVS AND ALTERNATIVE FAMILY

Buffy the Vampire Slayer ran for seven seasons, airing 144 episodes. However, the 'Buffyverse', as it is very frequently called, extends to the five seasons of the *Buffy* spinoff *Angel* (WB, 1999–2004), adding an additional 110 episodes to the list. 'Buffyverse' names that alternative universe created and developed by Joss Whedon – studied, fantastically lived-in, and adored by fans. It looks *very* similar to the universe that we all inhabit, populated by the same people, objects and places, and filled with the same cultural and political artefacts. But, in the Buffyverse, demons (vampires and other sorts) are tangible, physical creatures – though not all demons are wholly evil, just as not all humans are wholly good – as are the people who fight and kill those demons. *Buffy* is therefore a 'trespass story', but one that consistently subverts the rules of that genre (Westerfield 2003). The broad scope of the Buffyverse, the sheer length of the 'text' of *Buffy*, makes possible an almost limitless array of options for interpretive analysis. These options are multiplied by the self-referentiality of the episodes: the extended cross-referencing between and among episodes, the foreshadowing (sometimes *years* in advance) of what is to come, and the interaction between characters and plot-lines on *Angel* with those on *Buffy* (and vice versa), all mean that *Buffy* and *Angel* truly seek to construct a world. This fact helps to explain partially both the dedicated fan following of the shows and the, perhaps unexpected, creation of an academic subfield around the Buffyverse.[4]

Despite the almost limitless choices for interpretation and critique, one need not dig very deep to find a reading of *Buffy* that promulgates the theme of 'alternative' families. This interpretation can be found right on the surface, just by watching a show that consistently builds bonds of intimacy, trust, responsibility, and commitment between those who are not related by blood or marriage.[5] Or, if one somehow misses this trope, one need only turn to the literature on *BtVS* that makes this point consistently and repeatedly. That literature proves diverse in its treatment (choosing to read a variety of episodes through different lenses and with distinct applications) but thoroughly consistent in its themes. Two such themes repeatedly rise to prominence: the 'alternative' family and the family created by 'choice'. Scholars of *Buffy* see clearly that the show constructs families that look nothing like the 'traditional family' portrayed on television. The core characters on the show are: Buffy, her high-school (and after) friends, Willow and Xander, and her 'Watcher' (vampire slayer mentor), Giles. Xander's family is clearly dysfunctional; Giles, an English expat living in California appears not to have a family; Willow's family makes almost no appearances on the show at all (except when Willow's mother tries to burn her daughter at the stake ['Gingerbread', 3.11]); and Buffy lives with her single, divorced mother.

Viewers thereby recognise, almost immediately, that the most important family connections on the show are formed between these four main characters; here we find the nuclear core of 'family' on Buffy. 'The Scooby Gang' as they are called – both by fans of the show and by the characters themselves on the show – functions as an 'alternative' family. Extended family, in turn, gets created on Buffy whenever other characters form bonds of intimacy with someone in the core group, or when they somehow join the Scooby mission to fight evil – to kill demons. This list includes: Buffy's boyfriend, Riley; Willow's boyfriend, Oz, and later her girlfriend, Tara; Xander's girlfriends Cordelia and, later, Anya (an ex-demon); and, briefly, Giles's girlfriend, Jenny.[6]

Commentators can draw some obvious but nonetheless significant conclusions from analysing the basic structure of 'family' relations on the show. Many, particularly those concerned to explore other issues in more focused detail, simply take note of what they call an 'alternative vision' of the family (Locklin 2002; Jowett 2005; Burr 2006). Here the idea is that *Buffy* offers something 'other' than the traditional family; thus the language of alternative, which Jowett uses consistently, produces a dichotomous understanding of family by referring to the 'the real and the alternative family' (Jowett 2005: par. 5). When authors go on to provide an argument that fills in the content of that 'other' – i.e. that specifies how such alternatives are formed – they consistently hit upon the language of choice. Jean Lorrah calls this alternative form of family 'the self-made family' (Lorrah 2003: 167; see also Lorrah 2004: 58). In doing so she too implies a dichotomous thinking of the family: family as blood; family as choice. Lorrah suggests that the traditional family is not chosen, but based on blood. Thus, for her, what makes an alternative family 'alternative' is precisely the element of getting to choose them (or make them) for ourselves (cf. Burr and Jarvis 2005: 270; Burr 2006). Lorrah's reading of family in *Buffy* is both insightful and eloquent; however, and as I will argue below, her repeated returns to the language of 'chosen' and 'alternative' families only serves to weaken her otherwise powerful account of how (as both she and Whedon put it) the love of family can save the world (Lorrah 2003: 171).

Jennifer Stoy uses this very binary to frame her insightful essay on *Angel* and family: she titles it 'Blood and Choice'.[7] Stoy opens her piece by calling family '*the* pre-eminent concern in Joss Whedon's fictional universes' (Stoy 2004: 220, emphasis in original). I concur in her emphasis, but I depart from Stoy when she goes on to describe the Whedon family as 'chosen families' or as 'self-selected family units' (Stoy 2004: 220, 229). In making this move Stoy follows the same logic as Jowett in that both set up a binary between 'real' families, on the one hand, and alternative, other, non-blood, families of choice, on the other. Indeed, at one crucial point Stoy herself reveals this underlying logic by referring to these alternative families of choice as 'metaphorical families' (Stoy 2004: 229). But if the 'real' family is still the sanguinuptial family, and if families of 'choice' are merely the opposite side – the dichotomous 'other' to families of blood – then what power of cultural or political resistance do these 'families' offer us? I place families in inverted commas within my rhetorical question precisely because the commentary on 'alternative' families seems to suggest that these cannot *really* be families after all. These analyses lack critical force because they neither challenge directly nor seek to subvert the sanguinuptial family; they leave it standing as it is, and go on to build alternatives elsewhere. Thus, while they pose alternative forms of 'family', they do not construct alternative 'political rationalities' for grasping the meaning of family (see Brown 2006b). Indeed, to posit the difference between *real* and alternative families, and/or to call the latter 'metaphorical', can only serve, ultimately, to strengthen the sanguinuptial conception by reifying its status as the core meaning of family.

In setting out on a different tack, I wish to insist that while *Buffy* frequently uses metaphors to express human desires, emotions, dangers, and temptations, we must nevertheless reject the idea that the families on *Buffy* are metaphorical. *The monsters are metaphors; the families are real.*[8] In order to prove this point one must first of all take Stoy's claim about the importance of family quite seriously. However, this means following through to see family in *Buffy* as more than metaphorical: more important than an alternative and something more significant than a choice. Indeed, writ large, Joss Whedon's entire project can be read as a radical reconstruction of the family. His is a consistent effort to produce and sustain a family that exceeds the terms of blood and marriage relations.[9] Whedon says as much himself. First, when he refers to the idea of family as 'the mission statement of the show' (Whedon 2002; also quoted in Lorrah 2003: 167), and later when he further explains: 'I really want to get this message out, that it's not about blood' (Whedon 2001).[10] As suggested above, all of the main characters in the Buffyverse form their primary bonds with individuals outside the sanguinuptial family. Again, Whedon describes this in productive terms when he tells the story of the original production of *BtVS*: 'When we created the show, they said, "Do you want [Buffy's] family?" And I said, "Well, mom and whatnot, but basically, she has a family. Her father is Giles, her sister is Willow, and it's already in place"' (Whedon 2001). Finally, the sanguinuptial family itself, when addressed, almost always proves to be thoroughly dysfunctional, the source of conflict, strife, darkness – and often even evil (Busse 2002; Siemann 2002; Williams 2002; cf. Burr and Jarvis 2005).[11]

Of course, to interpret Whedon's larger family project would require a book in itself (see Lavery forthcoming). Thus, while gesturing toward some of the broader configurations of the Buffyverse that lend themselves toward a reworking of the sanguinuptial family, I maintain a different focus. The title of this chapter expresses that focus: to explore and analyse the *meaning* of family, specifically within cultural and political discourse. Again, such a project must be distinguished from anthropological cataloguing of family practices, through identification of 'alternative' family forms for example.

Consistent with my reading of television throughout this book, I study the family primarily from a *textual* angle. Hence, my narrower question: how does one particular episode of *Buffy* participate in the politics of the family? This question differs from 'what forms of family are practised over the course of the entire show, or within the entire Buffyverse?' Thus, I remain concerned to see the ways in which *Buffy*, particularly the episode 'Family', articulates a different meaning of family and does so *in relation to* the dominant discourses. My goal is to explore this episode for the conceptual resources needed to build not merely an 'alternative' to the sanguinuptial family, but a critique and rejection of it. The politics of *Buffy* therefore prove rather different for my strategy than for the more typical approach within *BtVS* studies. I look less for 'alternative arrangements' or 'countercultural moments' and more at specific elements of political resistance and mobilisation. With these strategies of reading in mind, I turn to the episode itself.

READING 'FAMILY'

'Family' is the sixth episode of season five of *Buffy*, one of only six episodes (out of 66) in the last three seasons written and directed by Joss Whedon.[12] The other five include celebrated and award-winning episodes ('The Body', 5.16; 'Once More, With Feeling', 6.7) and season and series finales ('The Gift', 5.22; 'Chosen', 7.22). As creator and executive producer, Whedon wielded enormous influence on the entirety of the show over the course of its seven seasons; his was the ultimate responsibility for the finished product, and especially for season story arcs and dialogue. This explains why the Buffyverse frequently is also called the 'Whedonverse'. Indeed, episode writers comment that often the best bits of dialogue in 'their' episodes were written by Whedon (e.g. Petrie 2002). Nonetheless, Whedon's own episodes clearly provide the space for him to leave his most indelible marks upon the show. 'Family' epitomises this practice, as Whedon takes a central theme of the entirety of the Whedonverse and uses it for the title of one particular episode. And Whedon himself minces no words about the importance of the episode: '"Family" is as much

of a didactic message show as I've ever done.' Moreover, it is specifically in reference to this episode that Whedon asserts, as quoted
above, 'it's not about blood' (Whedon 2001).

The theme of family proves not just central to the episode, but,
in fact, quite dominant. Indeed, the beginning story arc for the fifth
season serves to set up the exploration of family in this episode – especially in the form of the bizarre, and absolutely unexplained, appearance of Buffy's sister, Dawn. To be clear, for the first four seasons
Buffy had no sister, but in the final scene of the premiere of season
five Dawn suddenly emerges – literally out of nowhere. She is just
there. For the next three episodes no clarification of the situation is
forthcoming for viewers, and all of the characters on the show simply
seem to recognise Dawn as the sister Buffy has always had. Only in
episode 5 ('No Place Like Home', 5.5) does Buffy, along with viewers,
learn that Dawn is actually the human form given by monks to an
ancient and powerful energy that serves as an all-important 'Key' – a
Key central to saving the world in some as-yet-unknown way. These
monks gave the Key the human form of Dawn, created the memories that would make Dawn Buffy's sister, and finally sent the Key
into Buffy's family so that 'it' – now Dawn, an innocent teenage girl
– would be protected by the Slayer.

In the *Buffy* timeline, the episode of 'Family' begins on the very
same night during which Buffy has discovered that Dawn is the Key.
Both of the first two scenes take us away from the site of Buffy's
recent battle and place us in safe, softly lit, quiet domestic spheres
– the space of *family*. The first scene opens with the shot of a kitten
playing with string. We hear the voices of Tara and Willow as they
talk playfully to each other about saving the little kitty by bringing
her home from the pound. The scene quickly establishes their intimacy: from the pet they have adopted together, to the single dorm
room that they clearly share, to their flirting in bed. The scene also
spells out Tara's fear that her link to Willow does not prevent her
from being an outsider in relation to the others. Willow wants to
snuggle, but Tara says she needs to study more spells. When Willow
asks why, Tara explains: 'I just like to be useful. You know, to the
gang?' ('Family', 5.6). Thus, even as the scene declares the connec-

tion between Willow and Tara, it simultaneously places Tara's familial status in question.

From Willow and Tara's bed we cut to Buffy's living room, where
she explains to Giles that Dawn is the Key, even though, 'she thinks
she's my kid sister' ('Family', 5.6). Yet Giles insists, and Buffy readily
agrees, that Buffy must protect Dawn. They also concur in not telling
any of the others about Dawn's status as the Key; this means that
to everyone else, Dawn will still be Buffy's sister. Even to Giles and
Buffy, who now know more of the story, the memories of Dawn still
feel very real, as Buffy explains to Giles through the telling of a story
from childhood. Dawn's family status, too, remains undetermined.
Together these two scenes establish the centrality of the theme of
family, but they also readily undermine the notion that family can be
pre-determined – either by blood, by marriage, or by anything else.
Family status will need to be *worked out* – the meaning of family must
be produced – in ways that one cannot decide in advance. Already,
then, the episode shifts us outside the terms of the sanguinuptial
family. It proves crucial to note, however, that this is not merely a
move 'beyond' the nuclear core of the sanguinuptial family (i.e. to
some sort of 'extended' family). With Tara, Dawn and Willow make
up their own core unit (hence the importance of opening the episode
on them in their own domestic, family sphere). More forcefully, with
Dawn, what is at stake is blood relations themselves. If Tara is family it cannot be because of extension. If Dawn is family it cannot be
because of blood.

Season five plays out Dawn's family status decisively,[13] but this
episode centres on the struggle over the meaning of family with respect to Tara. Whedon raises the stakes of Tara's family status by
bringing Tara's sanguinuptial family (her father, her brother, and a
cousin) to town for a visit. Inevitably, with them comes conflict. As
Willow puts it, finishing Tara's incomplete sentence after the first
appearance of the latter's family: 'they make you crazy' ('Family',
5.6). Soon thereafter, Tara's father confronts her back in Tara and
Willow's dorm room. He has let himself in – literally invading Willow and Tara's domestic space, and, metaphorically, seeking to break
the bond that ties Tara to Willow. Tara's father insists that with her

twentieth birthday approaching Tara must leave her life in Sunnydale and return 'home'. He reveals the belief, apparently shared (though with less certainty) by Tara, that she has some sort of demon inside her, and that as she turns twenty the demon will come out – as it did in her mother. For Mr Maclay the choice is stark. Indeed, there really is no choice at all. He implicitly calls forth the power of the sanguinuptial family to frame the decision as that between family, on the one hand, and friends, on the other – between family and *not* family. He says, 'Your family loves you, Tara, no matter what. How do you think your friends are going to feel when they see your true face?' Cousin Beth later echoes this framing. First by calling Tara a 'selfish bitch' and then saying: 'You don't care the slightest bitty bit about your *family*, do you? ... I can't wait 'til *your little friends* find out the truth about you' ('Family', 5.6, emphasis added).

Their words play on Tara's fears about being excluded from the non-sanguinuptial family of Willow, Buffy, Giles, Xander, and Anya. Mr Maclay's revelations help explain to the viewer both these anxieties and the motivations for some of Tara's previous actions: in season four she mysteriously sabotaged a demon-locator spell ('Goodbye Iowa', 4.14). In her panicked state, Tara goes farther this time: she casts a spell over the entire non-sanguinuptial *Buffy* family that makes it impossible for them to see demons. Tara hopes to prevent them from seeing the demon in her, but her spell serves to put them at great risk. The entire group is attacked by Lei-ach demons in Giles's magic shop, and no one can see the demons. Tara arrives just in time to reverse the spell, but in so doing she reveals herself as having cast the original spell. Tara's father, brother, and cousin arrive moments later, just as Buffy and the others come to the realisation that it was Tara who put them in danger in the first place. Tara does not try to hide it. She admits: 'I didn't want you to see ... what I am' ('Family', 5.6). Mr Maclay explains that Tara has a demon in her, before going on to insist that she must leave with them immediately. But Willow intervenes, asking Tara if she *wants* to leave; through tears, Tara clearly says no. Mr Maclay takes umbrage not merely at Willow's discussion with Tara, but clearly with the intimacy they share; he insists that Willow have no role in this conversation.

Everything in the episode up to this point has set the stage for one grand confrontation between Mr Maclay and Buffy. Maclay has repeatedly asserted his role as patriarch of the family to which, from his perspective, Tara fully belongs. It does not occur to him that Buffy heads a radically different family, of which Tara may also be a member. The confrontation between Buffy and Maclay will be played out in two acts, in precisely such a way as to mobilise a powerful and rich resignification of family.

First, in response to Willow, and in a clear rejection of any relationship she might share with Tara, Mr Maclay reasserts himself as the family patriarch by making what he intends to be the definitive statement on the matter: 'The girl belongs with her family. I hope that's clear to the rest of you' ('Family', 5.6). With this claim Maclay draws on all the power and energy that the sanguinuptial conception of the family can muster. He plays 'family' as the trump card, just as he and Cousin Beth had used it with Tara to make her choice of staying or going a non-choice (a 'choice' of family or its other). Hence his posture and tone, both of which suggest that the conversation is over: family must go unquestioned and must override all other considerations. By insisting so clearly on the pre-eminence of the sanguinuptial family, Maclay's claim frames a potential conflict with that conception of the family – a conception that may either be avoided (e.g. by choosing 'friends' rather than family) or contested (by resignifying family itself).

In other words, Buffy would appear to have only two possible responses to Maclay's decisive appeal to family as the ultimate authority, '*the girl belongs with her family*':

1) Accept this claim, and let Tara leave.

   It is essential to emphasise here the appeal of this first option. Buffy has built almost no direct relationship of any kind with Tara; as she said herself earlier in the episode, Buffy does not even know Tara very well. In addition, Tara has, just moments before, freely admitted to taking actions that placed in mortal danger the lives of Buffy, Willow, Xander, Giles, and Anya. And finally, it has also just been revealed that Tara is part demon.

2) Reject the claim.

This means insisting that Tara belong not with her family but with Buffy and the others: with Willow, her lover; with her quasi-friends; with her allies in fighting evil.

Buffy answers the rhetorical question 'I hope that's clear to the rest of you?' by seeming to choose the first option. Buffy says succinctly, 'It is.' The camera then cuts to a shot of Tara, looking sad-but-understanding, followed by a shot of Mr Maclay, looking smug. Buffy appears to have acquiesced to the claim of family, when she says, 'You want her, Mr Maclay? You can go ahead and take her.' But then, she continues: '*You just gotta go through me*' ('Family', 5.6). With this statement Buffy suggests something quite distinct: that she has rejected *both* of the above options. Buffy's statement accepts that Tara belongs with her family, but simultaneously proposes to prevent Maclay from taking Tara away. Buffy backs up her words with her own posture of defiance (hands on hips). One by one, Dawn, Giles, Xander, and Anya all fall into position beside and behind Buffy, forming the appearance of both a family unit and military ranks – both of which stand in support of Tara and in opposition to Maclay.

This moves us to the second act of the confrontation between Maclay and Buffy, and to the second stage of the resignification of family. Buffy's first response, 'it is', makes the family status ambiguous: is she accepting that Maclay, brother Donny, and Cousin Beth are Tara's family? Or is she suggesting something more? Maclay reacts to the group lined up behind Tara with pure disgust and outrage. But what can he do? He has already played the trump card of family. Thus, he first tries to invoke the prerogative of physical force that belongs to the patriarch, saying 'I'm not gonna be threatened by two little girls [i.e. Buffy and Dawn]' ('Family', 5.6). It quickly becomes apparent, however, that the advantage of force lies decidedly with his opponents. Thus, with no other options, he turns back to family status. This time, however, he is forced to call on the sanguinuptial family *explicitly*. Thus, he drops the trope of 'family' in general, and turns specifically to blood. He asserts: 'This is insane. You people have no right to interfere with Tara's affairs. *We ...* are her blood kin! Who the hell are you?' ('Family', 5.6).

Maclay again ends his declaration with a rhetorical question. It goes without saying that a rhetorical question is not meant to be answered; the answer should be too obvious to speak. In this case, the answer should be 'no one', since only blood relations (and marital relations, but Tara is a lesbian and therefore cannot marry) count as family. Only '*blood kin*' count. To *answer* a rhetorical question, however, is to challenge the status quo – to refuse the given that the rhetorical question implies. In this case, the answer could involve the resignification of family. Here, then is Maclay's final, final word, followed by Buffy's response:

Mr Maclay:	This is insane. You people have no right to interfere with Tara's affairs. *We ...* are her blood kin! Who the hell are you?
Buffy:	We're family.[14]

The climactic battle of the episode is fought without weapons or blows, and this statement marks Maclay's defeat in this struggle of words with Buffy. It also marks the completion of the resignification of family. Throughout the episode, the statement 'we're family' has been circulated by the Maclays as a reiteration of the sanguinuptial conception of family and a proper claim on Tara as 'their own'. In the first stage of the conflict, Buffy refuses to let that claim stand, she resists the sanguinuptial understanding and places the status of family in question. In the second stage she takes the further step of resignifying family altogether. That is, Buffy now defines family in such a way that Tara, Willow, and Buffy *et al.* form a family while Tara, her father, and her brother do not.

Crucially, Buffy does not say to Maclay, 'We're family *too*'; instead, she rejects his claim to family and substitutes her own. Thus, I wish to stress that this resignification of family must be taken as a thoroughgoing rejection of the sanguinuptial model; it ought not be reduced to a mere extension of the sanguinuptial conception so as to include alternative and extended arrangements.

RECONSTRUCTING THE MEANING OF FAMILY: NEITHER BLOOD NOR CHOICE

My reading of this scene differs fundamentally from interpretations offered by others. Burr and Jarvis (2005) cite at length an excerpted version of the entire two-act confrontation between Buffy and Maclay. Consistent with other *BtVS* literature on the family, they emphasise *choice* as central to this conception of family. They conclude: 'the family is no longer the place where they *have* to take you in. It's the place *you choose to be* if they choose to have you' (Burr and Jarvis 2005: 275, second emphasis added). But this scene does not illustrate the *choosing* of families; rather, it stages a confrontation of sanguinuptial and non-sanguinuptial meanings of family. And, in doing so, it offers a possible resignification of the hegemonic meaning of family *away* from the sanguinuptial conception. That is, Tara does not choose Buffy's family, and Buffy does not choose to make Tara a part of it. Rather, both of them recognise and articulate that *they are already family* in a way that far exceeds the individual agency of either of them. I wish to foreground this point: even a non-sanguinuptial conception of family must insist that families are not something we simply choose. In other words, even if we wish to think of family as being outside blood and marriage, *family is not a choice*. Family is a commitment and an obligation that will always far outstrip choice.

Let me clarify the stakes of this argument. First of all, within the actual practices and history of the sanguinuptial family, one finds a large role for choice. Certain romantic and conservative renderings of the sanguinuptial conception of family would tempt us to think of family as destiny or fate, that is, to take family as some sort of *given* or to consider family as only about blood. But this temptation leads to an ill-conceived understanding of family, *even under sanguinuptial terms*. Thus, in rejection of sanguinuptial idealisations of family as somehow permanent and beyond choice, one must always remember that marital choice (for some) is an intrinsic part of the sanguinuptial conception. Moreover, if we are willing to pay the price to do so, we can always choose to leave our family. In other words, the sanguinuptial rendering of family has pretensions to an ideal conception of family that cannot be maintained on its own terms.[15] No-fault divorce makes the exit from marital family a mere legal (and emotional) hurdle. This is precisely why some conservative commentators wish to prop up a notion of sanguinuptial family as if it were permanent. Their rhetoric, however, seems to do nothing to stem the tide of rising divorce rates. Even the ties of blood family can be severed: by custody decisions, adoption, and the sheer force of will that leads family members to 'disown' one another – or simply to stop seeing and speaking to each other. In other words, marriage is a choice, divorce is a choice, and sometimes our family members no longer choose us. Thus, it will not do to construe family as a sphere beyond or outside choice.

Second, arguing from the other side of the dichotomy, I insist that even the most engaged and thoroughgoing critique of the sanguinuptial family should not lead us to the model of a 'chosen family'. We cannot *will* our family into being. Family relations do not come about – nor, especially, are they sustained – by pure choice. Even if, as I am here urging, we refuse to confine our understanding of family to blood and marriage, we cannot lazily conclude that 'family' is made and unmade through liberal contract and consent. Whatever else we may finally say about family, we must declare the following: *family* necessarily entails bonds of intimacy, relations of dependence, and unquestioned responsibilities and required commitments that far exceed any simple or singular 'choice'.

Thus, the blood/choice dichotomy proves false, almost from the start. The sanguinuptial conception of family has choice built right into it (through marriage), and any critique of the sanguinuptial family must still maintain a prominent space for family relations that far exceed mere choice. To read family as 'chosen family' therefore proves misguided. And analyses of *Buffy* that refer to the Whedonverse conception of family simply as 'chosen' lack the critical vocabulary and conceptual analysis needed to push past the hegemony of the sanguinuptial family.

The limitations of the concept of 'chosen families' come clearly to light even within the very *Buffy* episodes that authors cite for their evidence of chosen families. For example, let us take Buffy herself at her word, as she gives Whedon's carefully crafted climactic line, *'We're family'*. That is, let us stipulate that at the end of the episode 'Family' Buffy and Tara *are family*. Then we can ask: is this a 'chosen family'? Certainly it is not a blood family, but the previous work to deconstruct the blood/choice dichotomy opens up the space for us to ask whether *choice* is what holds Buffy and Tara together as 'family'. We might say that Willow chooses Tara, and that this choice brings her into the family. (Though some will insist that love itself is beyond choice, but I put this romantic critique to the side.) Thus, choice has a role to play. However, *Buffy never chooses* to make Tara a part of her family (nor does Tara choose Buffy). Tara becomes a part of Buffy's family (and Buffy of Tara's) through actions and decisions that never even involved Buffy. True, Buffy does choose to keep Tara in her family, to insist that she stay. However, Buffy is given the choice to defend Tara *as part of her family* only after Tara has already *become* a member of that family. And Buffy might say that she herself has very little choice in the matter: she and Tara are family and therefore Buffy defends her – simple as that.

Family are precisely those whom we support before finding out all the facts: Buffy backs Tara as family without asking any questions concerning Tara's demonic tendencies. We defend family despite what they have done. Thus, we could only say that we 'choose' family if we then go on to admit that these are choices we make based on very little information. That is, if they were choices, they would be bad choices.

A QUEER THINKING OF FAMILY

My project here calls not for a new definition of family, but for a re-signification of family. Even as I insist on this distinction, however, it raises thorny problems for this endeavour. Definitions are easy to produce; one just writes them up. But resignification proves to be a broad cultural and political phenomenon; its realisation lies far outside the scope of any particular writer, any particular politician, or any particular activist. To explain this point it will help to elaborate on the nascent theory of resignification.

'Resignification' names both a theory of language and a political strategy. Its resources are diverse, but its shape emerges sharply in the work of Judith Butler, particularly in her book *Excitable Speech* (1997). There she presents resignification specifically as an alternative to an earlier language theory that had called forth an attendant political strategy. That earlier theory of language is 'speech act theory'. It calls our attention to those facets of language that do more than describe a certain reality or reflect the world, and it refutes earlier theories that took language to be a reflection or mirror of reality (correspondence theories). Speech act theory asks instead about *How to Do Things With Words* – also the title of the book by John Austin (1962) that created the field of speech act theory. In other words, speech act theory points out the way in which speech can be *action*: from the action of *christening* a ship or *marrying* a couple (Austin's famous examples) to more everyday actions like 'warning', 'threatening', or 'consoling'. In the 1980s, critical race theorists and feminists appropriated this theory of language to support a political strategy of legislating against certain types of speech. If speech is action, they reasoned, then speech can do harm. Completing the logic, this would mean that the speaking of racial epithets that demean, threaten, or emotionally assault minorities should be made illegal and punishable by law through the creation of speech codes (Matsuda *et al.* 1993). It would mean that pornography that degrades women (by portraying them *as degraded*) should be banned (MacKinnon 1996). Speech act theory, as one can clearly see, opened up a very large gap in the defence of free speech, and it mobilised a series of political tactics to limit speech based on the harm that it can do.

Butler responds to the arguments of those who would regulate against hate speech and pornography *not* by returning to a classic, liberal defence of free speech. Nor does she reject the insight that speech can be action (she dismisses the correspondence theory of language as pointedly as speech act theorists do). But Butler asks instead whether the prohibition and censorship of putatively injurious speech actually serves as the best political strategy. Butler is particularly concerned that the legal efforts to regulate hateful and harmful speech seem to be caught up in a cycle of repeating such speech (Butler 1997: 14). And she critically questions the notion that one can eliminate the harm of speech by making particular words illegal to use. Thus, she asks: does not the effort to instantiate certain words as harmful *in the law* and through *the power of the state* serve only to augment their potential force and power? That is, do we limit the harm of speech by legislating against it (as those before her claimed), or do we instead unwittingly increase that power? Butler does not deny that speech can injure, but she refuses to conclude from this that we should respond to such injury by banning speech.

Instead, she suggests 'resignification' as an alternative political strategy. The core of the theory of resignification rests on the insight that it may be possible to defuse the power of an injurious word not by banning it but rather by reworking its meaning. The theory suggests 'how words might, through time, become disjoined from their power to injure and recontextualized in more affirmative modes' (Butler 1997: 15). What if one refuses the very hold that a word or phrase might have upon one (as the putatively injured party) and instead redirects it back at the sender? What if a stigmatised group takes up an epithet used to describe them, and uses that word as a badge of pride? This is not merely a hypothetical strategy, of course. As I sketched in the introduction to this book, over the past 25 years the word queer has been *resignified*. The meanings of the word have moved in a series of stages from:

1) a term of derision, an epithet used to describe lesbians and gay men; to

2) a term of pride used by certain lesbian and gay activist groups and LGBT communities, and a theoretical term appropriated to articulate a radical understanding of identity; to

3) a rather neutral term to describe lesbians and gay men, one that now appears frequently in popular culture, including within the titles of television shows.

As a theory of language, resignification recognises that meaning can never be permanently fixed in place: meanings change for reasons outside the control of any single author, or even of any legislative body (Butler 1997: 15). No matter how hard one tries, one cannot legislate against this process. Meanings cannot be unilaterally imposed, and changes in meanings cannot be stopped (Chambers 2003a). As a political strategy, then, resignification proves much less tidy and neat than the regulation of hate speech. There is no magic bullet to resignification because changes in meanings cannot be controlled or manipulated. *If* resignification occurs it happens for a wide variety of reasons, some intentional and some not. And resignification can only be fully grasped, fully understood, after the fact. With the word 'queer' we have an example of a rather successful resignification. But certainly a word like 'nigger' has not been fully resignified (although there have been some efforts within certain Black communities to do so), since many, including this author, are trepidatious about even using the word in writing. Few are willing to speak it aloud.

In the case of the project to resignify family, all of this explains why *resignification cannot be engineered and it cannot be predicted in advance*.[16] I can urge the resignification of family; I can call for it. I can suggest mechanisms for its success. But I cannot 'fully resignify family' if by that we mean to change the *meanings of family* as they circulate broadly in social, literary, cultural, and political discourses. In calling for such a resignification I can only do some of the crucial conceptual work needed to make such a broader project possible. In this final section, then, I turn to that work, seeking to lay out what I see as some of the necessary parameters and conceptual requirements of a radical rethinking of family. I seek not only an alternative to the sanguinuptial thinking of family, but also a critique of that thinking. Thus I eschew the choice to provide merely 'another' definition of family designed to sit alongside the sanguinuptial definition; instead, I provide a critical challenge and subversion of the sanguinuptial family. And the goal of that subversion, as Butler helpfully puts it, is to make life possible – to make life livable (Butler 2004). Here we see one reason to consider this a queer thinking of family.

Before trying to fill in some of the positive content in my account of family, let me first do a bit of ground-clearing by indicating the edges of my conception:

1) Family cannot be reduced to blood relations.
2) Family cannot be confined to the terms of marriage or other legal arrangements.
3) Family cannot be constituted only by choice.

As conceptualisations of family, blood and choice both make family out to be stark, clear, and simple. But we all know too well that if family is anything at all, it is *complicated*. Blood and choice obviously prove overly narrow and constrictive as accounts of family. Family will always serve to undermine and rework the narrow dichotomy of chosen/determined. It is not just that family is sometimes one, sometimes the other; family is *always* both. This critical insight provides me with one of the primary elements of a distinct definition of family, one that resists hegemonisation by sanguinuptial conceptions.

I propose to think of family as a complex temporal product of agency on both our part and on that of others. Family always proves to be partially chosen and partially unchosen, but this does not constitute a limitation or weakness of family. Indeed, the *unchosen* quality of family *makes family*. Being 'beyond choice' is an essential and constitutive element of family. To put this in informal terms, one might say: no one *chooses* the crazy uncle, the obnoxious sister-in-law, or the screaming nieces and nephews.

Family, then, must be understood to denote broad relations of intimacy, responsibility, support and commitment. Family is the place of home. It 'is a site in which certain needs are met' (Eisenstein 1981, cited in Lehr 1999: 41). 'Family' connotes a relation somehow both above and beyond all other relations. Furthermore, to grasp family one must understand these relations as developing over time; they become ingrained in the thought patterns and daily practices of family members. Family forms within and through such patterns; family is the imprint that these relations leave. Undoubtedly, love – however difficult to conceptualise – must play a role in this rendering of family, since ultimately these relations of family must somehow be grasped as relations of love – itself 'above and beyond' other connections between humans. The family produces love and love produces the family. And whatever shape of love makes the bonds of family, it cannot be solely romantic love and it cannot be all that fickle. Lorrah suggests we think of love in the *Buffy* family as *agape*, which she calls 'true friendship' (Lorrah 2003: 172). I believe we might do better to turn away from the dominant, Christian conception of *agape* as divine love, and instead return to the rarely used ancient understanding of *agape* as familial love. In ancient Greek, *agape* refers to the love of family members, and stands in contrast both to love as friendship (*philia*) and love as desire (*eros*).

Moreover, a family relation must somehow be established as a relation putatively beyond critique. Family relations must, in the first analysis, become both unquestioned and unquestionable. I say 'putatively' and 'in the first instance', since, as I have indicated above, ultimately all relations, even family relations, prove subject to choice (including the choice to end or annul the relation itself) without being wholly determined by choice. Nevertheless, I contend that we must maintain a clear distinction between 'family' and other relations that do not attain this ostensibly unquestioned status. Trying to state the point lucidly, and bearing in mind that no vision of family proves beyond choice, one might frame it thus: *family is not something you choose, but something you cannot deny*. Indeed, I read the final climactic scenes of the episode 'Family' in this way: Buffy does not choose Tara *as family*. Such action is not required given that Tara has already become Buffy's family; therefore Buffy merely accepts and positively asserts that Tara *is family*.

The conceptual work to this point begs a crucial question: what makes this a 'queer thinking of family'? Let me develop responses along a few different lines of reasoning. First, it cannot be forgotten that the sanguinuptial understanding of family plays a powerful role in support of heteronormativity. Heteronormativity depends upon the sanguinuptial family. Particularly in light of the dominant and now thoroughly politicised definition of marriage as 'the union of one man and one woman as husband and wife', family through marriage means family as heterosexual. And it goes without saying that family through blood remains wrapped up in heterosexual notions of reproduction (see Edelman 2004 and my discussion in Chapter 6).

Thus, the conceptualisation I lay out here proves queer at least to the extent that it challenges the heteronormative conceptualisation of family (i.e. the sanguinuptial definition).

Moreover, the project to construct a radical, non-sanguinuptial rendering of family will require not only more theoretical work along the lines laid out here, but also cultural and political work. In other words, one must explore and elaborate this conception of family in daily lives and practices, and there can be no doubt that queer communities offer an excellent site to begin such work. Lesbians and gay men have had no choice but to develop and sustain non-sanguinuptial families. As Valerie Lehr puts it: 'although the conservative story of family indicates that if family is functioning well then the best thing that political life can do is to protect the sanctity of the private sphere, the story of the private life and ethical decision making ... of many gays, lesbians, and bisexuals' suggests something completely distinct (Lehr 1999: 68–9). Queer families develop along a diverse array of paths and for a wide variety of compound reasons, but I would point to at least four central factors.

1. Non-normative sexual practices

Non-normative sexual practices give rise to non-normative family structures. Some would wish to argue that the nuclear family proves to be an unhealthy environment for modern sexuality in general, but, in any case, it obviously provides an inhospitable habitat for non-heterosexual, non-procreative, non-monogamous sexual practices (Warner 1999). I do not imply that queer sexualities can be easily summarised under, or contained within, those headings. Nonetheless, anyone whose sex life deviates from the heterosexual norm will also find the sanguinuptial family sphere to be off-limits, unlivable, or enervating. One may still try to live within, or at least within the *terms* of, the sanguinuptial family (such as the case of individuals simultaneously married and closeted), but many people will instead turn to other practices and understandings of family. Non-normative sexual practices provide enormous impetus for taking up the difficult, scary, and sometimes dangerous task of forming non-sanguinuptial families. At the very least, in these relationships sex is usually separated from procreation, and therefore the relationships cannot be justified by the assumed 'natural' drive to make and rear babies.

2. Family support systems

The AIDS pandemic has created an emergency situation, one which makes the non-sanguinuptial family more than *an* option; it becomes the *only* option for survival. One can obviously define the family as the space and the people who care for you when you are most in need, and AIDS creates desperate need for family. Family is a support system, and AIDS produces families that include lovers, friends, co-workers, distant, extended sanguinuptial family, and a long list of others (cf. Calhoun 2005). When the people whom one loves are dying, *they are family in an undeniable way*. Here we witness one reason why the plight of those living with HIV and/or suffering from the effects of AIDS first brought to light the hegemony of sanguinuptial family. Not only lifelong partners but also numerous others from the list above find themselves frequently and routinely prevented from having a say in the care of their family members. They are barred from making medical decisions, excluded from insurance coverage, eliminated from inheritance, and often physically denied access to their loved ones in the hospital (the example most commonly cited by writers on the subject and the one most frequently represented in film and television).

Moreover, this point goes well beyond the specific example of AIDS, since so many gays and lesbians find themselves rejected by their sanguinuptial family. They thereby lose access to that space of family as a primary support system. As a colleague put it to me: 'they *must* look to others for survival; otherwise, *they have no family*'. Not every gay person is kicked out of their home, of course, but for many of them, this always remains a possibility, 'if only in their minds'. This risk, even if only imagined,

> makes one aware of the importance of family outside of the sanguinuptial [family] from which they come: when one thinks 'what would I do? What are my options?', then one is working to consider, if temporarily, the meaning of family [outside the sanguinuptial model].
> (Williford 2007)

Another way of developing this argument lies in the straightforward point that the gay community, as a framework of support itself, lacks 'generations'. Most gay people do not have gay parents, nor, if they have children, are those children likely to be gay. In this context, family simply cannot be assumed as sanguinuptial.

3. Reproduction

To choose to have a baby and/or to raise children outside the model of 'making a baby' – where this connotes the culmination of heterosexual desire within the sanctified institution of marriage – means to queer oneself with respect to the norm. Lesbian and gay couples who want kids find themselves necessarily engaged in the practice of creating the non-sanguinuptial family. Children who have 'two mommies' (or perhaps even *three*) find themselves part of a queer family in a way that has little to do with 'sexual orientation' (Newman 1989; ALA 2007). As reproductive technologies continue to develop, the sanguinuptial family loses its hold on reproduction. These technological changes clearly drive the anxieties of those who wish to maintain the hegemony of the sanguinuptial family, but this queering of the family proceeds without any political efforts by, or inherently for, the queer community.

4. Queer households

What sort of families could form, and what shape would they take, within the terms of a non-sanguinuptial account of family? The primary emphasis on relations of love, responsibility, obligation, intimacy, and commitment means that the family as a 'household unit' (always the first dictionary entry for 'family') will take a variety of new shapes and forms. In other words, my conceptualisation of family allows us to imagine (or to observe) families thought of as 'households' such as the following: gay couples, unmarried straight couples, households of more than two lovers, child-free households, asexual households, households with adopted children or a neighbour's children. All of these household arrangements can be family, and they are all queer with respect to the dominant norms of both sex and family (Weeks *et al.* 1999).

As a final point, I want to return to my own production of this conception of family, particular to the theory of resignification. In a certain sense the notion of resignifying family may be considered queer. One must not overstate this point: the theory of resignification develops out of a confluence of analytic and continental philosophy of language. In and of itself, there is nothing necessarily queer about it. However, the work of queer theorists has advanced the theory of resignification in recent years and given it prominence. Furthermore, the best practical example of a (debatably) successful case of cultural and political resignification appears in the form of the word 'queer' itself.

One way to cash out on a queer thinking of family is to reconsider the difference between 'alternative' understandings of family and the articulation of *queer family*. This brings me back to the text of *Buffy* and the various readings of it. It comes as somewhat of a surprise to discover how rarely the vast literature on *Buffy* engages with or calls on the resources of queer theory. Key texts in the field of queer theory simply are not cited, despite the fact that the notion of a 'queer reading' crops up in numerous places. In a well-known and well-cited example, Farah Mendelsohn explores what she calls a 'queer reading' of *Buffy* in an article that fails to cite even a single piece of work in queer theory. And it offers a definition of 'queer reading' – again, uncited – that is anything but (Mendelsohn 2002; see also Beirne 2004; cf. Jowett 2002, Bartlem 2003, Battis 2003, Wilcox 2005: 85).

Moreover, those articles that deal with lesbian or so-called queer dimensions of *Buffy*, while they often refer to 'surrogate' (Battis 2003) or 'alternative' (Bartlem 2003) families, all fail to discuss or even cite the episode 'Family'. And, on the other hand, the numerous readings of the episode 'Family' that one does find in the *BtVS* literature all consistently fail to focus on the queer dimensions of the episode. These are not hard to spot: the episode begins and ends with Willow and Tara. Like my reading above, most interpretations of the episode stop with the climax: the confrontation between Buffy and Mr Maclay. But the episode itself continues to a crucial coda: Tara's birthday party. In it, all the Buffy family members (even 'extended' family) join in the celebration of the birth of one of their own. The final scene captures Willow and Tara on the dance floor, holding each other tight during a slow dance. The final dialogue reads as follows:

Willow: I still can't believe you didn't tell me about your family and all that.

Tara: I was just afraid if you saw the kind of people I came from, you wouldn't wanna be anywhere near me.

Willow: See ... that's where you're a dummy. I think about ... what you grew up with, and ... then I look at what you are ... it makes me proud. It makes me love you more.

Tara: [...]even when I'm at my worst ... you always make me feel special. How do you do that?

Willow: Magic.

From this point the camera pans back and we discover that as the couple dances they slowly levitate off the dance floor, clinging to one another in mid-air.

The overriding theme of the episode along with the arc of the story told within it both place a lesbian relationship at the very core of its effort to resignify family. Hence my surprise that interpretations of the episode place so little emphasis on the queer dimension of family that emerges here. Buffy's conflict with Maclay establishes the Buffy–Tara family relationship, but clearly such a relationship would not be possible without the Willow–Tara relationship, that is, without the family love that holds them together first. Thus, at the heart of the *Buffy* family, especially in this process of resignification, lies lesbian desire and the love of two women for one another. Whedon manages to resignify family without calling much explicit attention to this fact, but he certainly does not wish to deny it. And as viewers will see in episodes to come, Willow and Tara will become the 'heads' of the family for a time, particularly after Buffy's death at the end of season five (see Lorrah 2003).

SUBVERSION, RESIGNIFICATION, CULTURAL POLITICS

In completing my own reading of 'Family', I note that the queer dimension of the episode goes well beyond the lesbian relationship between Willow and Tara. One can easily see that the so-called 'demon' inside Tara symbolises her queer desire for women. In other words 'what she is' is a lesbian, and her marginalisation comes about because she remains queer with respect to the dominant sexual norms that her 'traditional' and sanguinuptial family would impose upon her. In other words, one must resist the temptation to read the conflict (and its resolution) in the episode as a narrow individual choice – as a question of 'who chooses Tara' or who loves her more. Heteronormativity here creates a world in which 'who Tara is' must be suppressed and thoroughly distorted. This is precisely the conflict, as I described it in Chapter 1, reflected in the relationship between David and Keith in *Six Feet Under*. Keith's desire to 'be who he is' seems 'too political' for David; David's attempt to seek shelter from heteronormativity in the confines of the closet seems 'cowardly' to Keith. Turning back to 'Family', we can say that this episode stages the broader political conflict between that heteronormative world, on the one hand, and a resistance to, or subversion of, heteronormativity that supports queer relations, queer sexuality, and thereby builds queer family, on the other.

I have been consistently calling this practice of cultural politics *resignification*. I do so both because I think this concept best grasps the effort of this episode, and of the overall project of *Buffy*, to transform fundamentally the meaning of family. To put it simply, family becomes – in the love shown between Willow and Tara, in the commitments of the Scooby gang members to one another, and especially by way of the ultimate confrontation between Buffy and Maclay – something utterly distinct from what the sanguinuptial conception tells us it must be. To use Whedon's terms, family 'is not about blood'. But it is also not about marriage, and not about choice. I call this a resignification of family so as to highlight the connections between *this project* (i.e. Joss Whedon's project in making *Buffy*, but also my project in reading *Buffy*) and the work of queer theory and queer politics, which have placed resignification at the heart of their work.

Of course, to describe this project one might also use the older language of revolutionary politics that Whedon himself calls upon: *subversion* (Chambers 2007; see Chapter 4). Whedon tells viewers that his main goal in the creation of *Buffy* was to subvert the genre of horror (Whedon 2002). He wanted to take the common tale of the little blond girl who gets caught in a dark alley and attacked by monsters, and turn it around. The 'little blond' turns out to be much more than we expect; she is a hero. She does not scream and run; she turns around and fights. And, as viewers come to learn, she always wins. What Whedon does with family amounts to a subversion of the sanguinuptial family. Repeated subversion, however, eventually ceases to be subversive and becomes expected. This no longer gives us a subversion of one genre but instead provides for the creation of another. In the Buffyverse, viewers no longer expect the blond girl to be killed; they expect her to fight the forces of darkness and to prevail. Resignification is just another name for the subversive process of moving from one set of hegemonic meanings (one dominant genre) to another (a new genre). *Buffy* successfully subverts the horror genre.

Even so, one might still wonder whether a television show is capable of doing any more than this. What use is *Buffy* to my (one might argue, separate) project of conceptualising and challenging the sanguinuptial family? Is it a mere illustration of the theory? Does it simply add pop culture cachet to a project that could just as well do without the example? Or, to put it the other way round, perhaps the playful turn to popular culture only serves to undermine what would otherwise be a serious political project – a line of critique that would seemingly apply not only to this chapter but also to the book as a whole. And one has to admit, taking television seriously within the academy can still prove difficult – certainly more so in the case of a show entitled *Buffy the Vampire Slayer*.

Nevertheless, I insist that *Buffy* proves essential to this project. Sometimes one must turn to fictional narratives to see possibilities that are not otherwise available in life. This particular episode, while part of a popular science fiction narrative television drama, when unpacked, reworks the frame of family in a radical way. The theorisation of the family and the political work that I seek to accomplish here would not be possible without my reading of the episode 'Family'. I need *Buffy* because of the politics of resignification. The political work I wish to do on family cannot be limited to the idea of redefining family, nor for calling for more tolerance of diverse family forms, nor for the celebration of those forms when they crop up. I call for, and seek to contribute to, the resignification of family, and this means challenging the current discursive meanings of 'family'. It means trying to effect a shift in discourse in which *that* is no longer what 'family' means, no longer how it functions, but instead *this* is.

The episode 'Family' contributes directly to this process of resignification. *Buffy* resignifies family in a way that liberals have failed to do. Definitions of family prove centrally important to the politics of family; they are at the heart of countless social and legal issues. Yet liberals have yet to put forth a meaningful reconceptualisation that challenges family as the claimed domain of heterosexual, married, child-rearing social groups. This failure is the result of a lack of political imagination (see Zerilli 2005). It marks the failure of a political rhetoric that cannot see past 'alternative families'. At best, these 'alternatives' tacitly reify the sanguinuptial conception by appearing as marginal deviations from it; at worst, they actively mimic the sanguinuptial idea of family but without the support of social and legal benefits.

This episode of *Buffy* also resignifies family in a way that queer theory has yet to do. It offers a concrete example of what the resignification of family might look like. It gives us an answer to the question that queer theory and queer politics have often implicitly posed, but never directly answered: how could we think through a viable challenge to the heteronormative, sanguinuptial version of family that is not just the dominant option, but seemingly the only option? With *Buffy* we see that it is sometimes possible to look *within* popular culture to discover a cultural text that does something very significant – in this case, enacting a queer politics that shows a possible answer to the questions above. The reading of *Buffy*, then, contributes directly to queer theory, but it also provides direct alternatives for queer politics. And it does it in a way that all my conceptual work on the sanguinuptial family could never do by itself. *Buffy*, and my reading of it, begins the process of resignifying family: opening up the space for a radical reworking of the meaning of family that pushes us well beyond the dominant, sanguinuptial conception.

NOTES

1   Therefore, while I am perhaps implying that my reading of *Buffy* proves more subtle or nuanced than some previous interpretations, I am not suggesting that my work somehow marks a radical break from previous writings on *Buffy*. It is certainly the case that my argument here rests upon and draws from the wide body of literature on *Buffy*.

2   *Webster's* entries look almost identical to those in the *New Oxford American*; in a somewhat pithier presentation, *Webster's* gives blood and marriage as *the* definition of family (*Merriam-Webster's Dictionary of Law* 1996).

3   Although it is doubtless the case that married couples *with children* fit the definition best of all. As any twentysomething knows: after 'When are you going to get married?' comes the question 'When are you going to have children?' – or, better, 'When are you going to start a *family* of your own?'

4   As of this writing, the *Buffy* studies bibliography, maintained by Alysa Hornick, contained well over a thousand entries and was too long to count (Hornick 2007). And *Slayage*, the online, peer-reviewed journal of Buffy studies, had just published its 22nd issue.

5   In order to prove the banality of this argument – rather than in an effort to substantiate the argument itself – I cite the Wikipedia entry for Joss Whedon, which contains its own subheading for 'Family'. It reads: 'There is a strong theme that family is the people that you live your life with, and not the family that raised you as a child. This is a major theme for the main characters in all of his television series' ('Joss Whedon' 2007).

6   The Wikipedia entry actually tracks in minute detail, over the course of the seven seasons, who is in and out of the gang ('Scooby Gang' 2006). This reference to the television cartoon series *Scooby-Doo* (various incarnations, 1969–present) underscores both the intertextuality of *Buffy* and 'alternative' operations of family, as the original group on *Scooby-Doo* also represents a family without blood relations (see Introvigne 2008).

7   Jes Battis (2005) echoes the language of choice in the title to his book, *Blood Relations: Chosen Families in* Buffy the Vampire Slayer *and* Angel. The book itself puts little effort into making the argument for families as chosen, focusing chapter by chapter on particular family member roles, but like the works discussed in more detail in the text, it falls back on the language of 'chosen' and 'extended' families (for the latter, see Battis 2005: 56).

8   Obviously the universe itself is fictional. My point is that within the narrative, families are not metaphors that stand for something else.

9   This notion of a television family is not unique to Joss Whedon, of course. It can be traced back at least as far as *The Mary Tyler Moore Show* (CBS, 1970–7). And it is certainly what gave the early Aaron Sorkin shows their charm and spark. The characters on *Sports Night* and *The West Wing* work so hard and for such long hours that they simply fail to have what we typically call 'a family life'. This does not bother viewers of the show, however, because the characters form a family at work. Thus the workplace can become the entire universe for these characters without making them thin or uninteresting characters; 'family drama' can be played out between and among the characters because they form family bonds with their work-mates. And, as a side note, this 'family connection' may prove to be the missing link in Sorkin's latest show, *Studio 60* (NBC, 2006–07).

10   Comments like these may encourage the blood/choice dichotomy that appears in the *BtVS* literature, since Whedon explicitly rejects the idea of 'family as blood'. Nevertheless, Whedon himself does not use the language of 'alternative' families or families of 'choice'. Instead, he describes the family as something created (Whedon 2001; Whedon 2002). Whedon's own intentions are largely beside the point here, but I would note that as long as we think of creation in a complex fashion, this notion of the 'created family' fits well with my own rendering of family.

11   Whedon highlights the dysfunctional nature of sanguinuptial families repeatedly throughout the series (absent fathers, abusive spouses, crazy in-laws, and, in general, sanguinuptial family members that one cannot count on), but perhaps he drives the point home most clearly by way of reversal, as seen quite powerfully in the episode 'Normal Again'. In this episode Buffy hallucinates a reality in which she is reunited with her deceased mother and her divorced father; it is the hallucination of the perfect, restored, nuclear family. In this reality, Buffy also finds herself in a mental institution, informed by her parents and by the well intentioned doctors that the vampires and demons, Buffy's demon-fighting friends, and also her mystical non-blood 'sister' are all nothing but hallucinations themselves. Thus, the nuclear sanguinuptial family filled

with happiness and joy proves to be a project of fantasy; to maintain it one must reject those to whom one is bound by something other than blood or marriage. In her struggle to choose a reality, Buffy's temptation to be 'normal again' almost gets her real friends killed. In the end, she rejects the fantasy of the nuclear sanguinuptial family and returns to the 'real' world of demons – and of non-sanguinuptial family (cf. Burr and Jarvis 2005).

12   'Lessons', the premiere of season seven, was written by Whedon and directed by David Solomon. Some episode guides to *Buffy* list Solomon and Whedon as co-directors. However, the credits of the episode itself do not give Whedon a directing credit, and the DVD lists Solomon as the director. This makes 'Lessons' the only one of the only later season episodes that Whedon writes but does not direct.

13   In the full story arc of season five, Whedon goes so far as to resignify blood itself. Dawn and Buffy were obviously not born from the same parents; Dawn was never even born. When Dawn discovers that she is the Key and that the hell-god Glory is out to kill her, her teenage insecurities allow her to assume that Buffy will reject her. In the final scene of the episode 'Blood Ties', Buffy declares to Dawn that she will always protect Dawn because she loves her, because she is her sister. Dawn responds with typical teenage insolence borne of fear: 'no I'm not'. And Buffy answers her: 'Yes, you are'. Buffy then grabs Dawn's bleeding hand, saying 'Look, it's blood. It's Summers blood', and then clasping the hand inside Buffy's own (bloody from a shoulder wound). She states: 'It's just like mine. Doesn't matter where you came from or – or how you got here. You *are* my sister. There's no way you could annoy me so much if you weren't' ('Blood Ties', 5.13). This scene proves central to the entire season: in the finale Glory uses Dawn's blood to begin the process of opening the borders that separate our dimension from the countless hell dimensions. Buffy realises that only *more blood* can close the opening, but that because she and Dawn share 'Summers blood' Buffy can take Dawn's place. Buffy then sacrifices her own life to save the world. In the end, then, Whedon powerfully rejects the sanguinuptial family: Buffy gives up her own life to save someone who on sanguinuptial terms is nothing but a ball of energy. But he also resignifies family more thoroughly then this, since the story asserts that Dawn and Buffy are united by their blood, but certainly not in the way we typically mean by 'blood relations'. Buffy can save the world because she and Dawn are truly family, yet this is neither the sanguinuptial family nor an expansion of it.

14   Joss Whedon comments on this scene, describing it as the entire point of the episode, before saying, 'hopefully you cried, if I did it right' (Whedon 2001).

15   I am suggesting here that the logic of the sanguinuptial family does not always prove consistent. On the one hand, it includes marital choice as a constitutive element of family; on the other hand, it evokes notions of permanence, destiny, and blood relations that appear to be beyond choice. Perhaps we see this best in an interesting exception to the literal meaning of sanguinuptial: adoption. Technically, adopted children are related to their parents neither by blood or marriage; instead, they become a part of the family through liberal contract. Nevertheless, adopted children are usually folded into the sanguinuptial understanding; they are considered real family – usually redeemed as such by the power of love. However, this is no simple exception to the sanguinuptial rules; instead, it is a rare and *highly policed* exception. Adoption rules are almost always complex and politically fraught and they often explicitly exclude gay couples. And I would suggest that the two phenomena are very much related: it is precisely adoption as an exception to the sanguinuptial conception that explains the political importance placed upon adoption rules and processes. Only through heavy regulation of adoption can the sanguinuptial model be preserved. My thanks to Columba Peoples for drawing my attention to the important case of adoption.

16   'Resignification alone', Butler writes, 'is not a politics' (2004: 223). Rather, resignification is a political strategy, available to anyone who would put it to work. Indeed, many would argue that the right has done a much better job than the left of resignifying family over the past 25 years (Lehr 1999: 103). Therefore, resignification must always occur within a context that provides its political meanings. In the text here I wish to show that my efforts toward the resignification of family must come about within a queer context. Obviously the effort to resignify family beyond the sanguinuptial conception goes on concomitantly with conservative efforts to revive an even more constraining understanding of family than currently offered by the sanguinuptial model.

6

Marriage and the Queer Family

D espite the unprecedented critical acclaim they have garnered and the untarnished aesthetic status they have maintained, HBO's original series have not necessarily been all that daring in terms of subject matter. Shows about the Mafia (*The Sopranos*), sexy successful Manhattan women (*Sex and the City*), or violent life on inner-city streets (*The Wire*, HBO, 2002–08) prove rather obvious choices for television. And while *Deadwood* (HBO, 2004–06) and *Six Feet Under* may deviate more from a typical Hollywood 'pitch', as later HBO series they also fit very well with the previously established 'quality TV' branding and style that HBO so carefully and so successfully cultivates. *Big Love* breaks this mould by taking up subject matter not only utterly unheard of for television but also thoroughly taboo for society – *polygamy*.

Big Love's televisual portrayal of polygamous marriage, along with the non-normative (but still rather vanilla) sexual practices it entails, raises crucial, complicated, yet rarely considered questions about the politics of marriage and the family. The show provides a powerful lens through which to view the contemporary political debates over marriage, and it resituates the problem of 'queer families' outside the dominant context of a potentially conservative call for gay marriage. The show therefore offers fertile ground for exploring key dimensions of queer theory and cultural politics.

This chapter will pull together key strands from all three major sections of the book in order to make the case for a particularly potent and particularly queer politics of *Big Love.* I will specify that politics below, but first let me delineate the ways in which this chapter synthesises and supplements previous arguments of the book. First, it will build directly on my conceptual work on the sanguinuptial conception of family in the preceding chapter and it will further the exploration of the contemporary (queer) politics of the family. I will argue that *Big Love* unsettles the sanguinuptial model. It accomplishes subversion's critical 'erosion from within', as detailed in Chapter 4, by starting with what at first glance appears to be the most conservative, suburban, 'nuclear' family imaginable. It then leverages this opening position through the obvious fact that the 'wives' in the *Big Love* family are not really 'wives' at all according to legal status and sanguinuptial conceptions. Rather than resignifying family as something radically new, along the lines suggested by my reading of *Buffy*, *Big Love* instead *subverts* the sanguinuptial family.

This interpretation can be fleshed out by drawing on a second strand from the book as a whole, the conception of subversion first articulated in Chapter 4. *Big Love* has the potential to subvert the sanguinuptial family because it works deeply from within the confines of a God-fearing, child-rearing, hard-working, family-values, middle-American family. This is not the 'alternative lifestyle' of gay families; neither is it the imaginary construct of science fiction, wherein 'anything' might be possible. The *Big Love* family can neither be thought (conceptually) nor displaced (politically) outside a certain Judeo-Christian tradition devoted precisely to the values of family and children. These facets come together to make its significant departure from the sanguinuptial family – and its resistance to that model's hegemony – all the more formidable. Perhaps this explains the notable discomfiture of the political right over *Big Love* (see for example Kurtz 2006; Schultz 2006). Polygamy explodes the sanguinuptial model. It does so almost literally – that is, by expanding the 'family' beyond recognisable sanguinuptial bounds – by destroying the concentric circle model of nuclear/extended family. And it does so in a way that a conservative call for gay marriage never could. This fact is reflected in the marginalised and abjected place of polygamy within the gay marriage debate: figured as a key spot which most viewers are well versed. Polygamous families are another story entirely. This likely explains why, in terms of genre, the first half-season of *Big Love* reads, as John Leonard puts it, 'more soapy than salacious' (Leonard 2006; see also Neary 2006). The episodes focus inward on the Henrickson family, not only to establish the characters but also to provide the needed exposition that will give audiences a working understanding of various polygamous practices.

To put it simply, one might describe *Big Love* as a straightforward family drama in which the 'family' is polygamous (cf. Sevigny 2006). Set in the suburbs of Salt Lake City, Utah, the show follows the lives of Bill Henrickson, his three wives (Barb, Nicky, and Margene) and their seven children. The creators of the show carefully situate the *Big Love* family between two better-known poles. On one side we have the Mormon Church (The Church of Jesus Christ of Latter-Day Saints, or LDS), which, under unprecedented pressure from the US Federal government, officially banned polygamy in 1890.[1] On the other side we have those splinter groups created as a result of the LDS's decision to ban polygamy: 'Mormon fundamentalists' who have continued the practice of 'plural marriage' to this day.[2] Most current estimates place the number of practising polygamists in North America at 50,000 plus or minus perhaps 20,000 (Lee 2006; Krakauer 2003) and the vast majority of them reside in Mormon fundamentalist communities or compounds. The Henricksons are neither LDS nor fundamentalists. Both Bill and his second wife Nicky come from fundamentalist families who live on a nearby compound, but Bill was thrown out (as young boys often are, so that more wives are available for marriage to the older men of the community) and Nicky married out.[3]

Big Love thereby dissociates the Henrickson family both from mainstream Mormonism and from the typical image of polygamy as a practice confined to backwards communities and bound up with child abuse, patriarchy, ignorance, and corruption. The first distancing move helps HBO to deal with the controversy caused by the show, as it was denounced loudly by the LDS. The second move encourages the viewer to see the Henricksons in a more sympathetic light. The viewer witnesses the potential abuses of fundamentalist polygamy in some abundance on the compound, but such scenes stand in marked contrast to the clean, tidy, utterly suburban-American home of the Henricksons. Indeed, were it not for their non-normative marital and sexual practices – they have *three homes* connected by a joint back yard – the Henricksons would probably be the most genuinely conservative and dull family on television. Some reviewers find the show boring despite the subject matter (Leonard 2006), while others remain convinced that the subject matter itself portends a serious step downward for civilisation as we know it (Kurtz 2006). That the show can elicit such dramatically divergent readings probably says something about the creators' success in self-consciously positioning *Big Love* somewhere in the political middle (Lee 2006).

CONTEXT 1: QUEER POLITICS AND THE MARRIAGE DEBATE

Big Love also finds itself placed in the middle of a much larger political conflict – the battle of cultural politics in which 'marriage' is a front line. As mentioned above, *Big Love* caused a bit of a stir when it raised the ire of the LDS. HBO's response – that is, aside from enjoying the free publicity – involved ending the pilot episode with a disclaimer noting the LDS renouncement of polygamy in 1890, and also indicating (probably to the LDS's displeasure) that 20,000 to 40,000 people currently practise polygamy in the USA (a rather conservative estimate, as I have indicated above). However, the internal politics of Mormonism prove much less significant than the politics of marriage, and even if only indirectly, *Big Love* must be understood to speak to the debate over gay marriage (especially in the USA, but also more broadly).

Taking a quick step back, it seems worth noting that the politics of the family is as old as political thought itself. In order to build his ideal regime, Plato famously obliterated the structure of the Athenian domestic family and the organisation of the household (*oikonomia*, the original root of the word 'economics'). Instead, he called for a 'community of women and children' for the ruling classes. For Plato, politics proved *inextricably* linked to family; to rethink and rebuild one necessarily meant to reshape the other. The weight of Plato's argument meant that Aristotle, in his turn, was forced to do 'family politics' as a central component of his political philosophy; for Aristotle, this meant *distinguishing* the household (*oikos*) and its organisation from the *polis* and its system of rule (*arche*). Nevertheless, for Aristotle the broad relations of politics and the political regime (*politea*) must still be considered in connection to family. Therefore, we can safely say that in an important sense the contemporary politics of family is not unique, and the fact that today's politicians spend more time talking about marriage, family life, and, most of all, 'the children' should not necessarily surprise us (see Shapiro 2001).

This background situates today's family politics; it demonstrates that in one sense there is little new about such politics. What is new is the central role played in today's family politics by the institution of marriage. In the previous chapter I argued that we must be able to articulate a conception of family beyond the limits of blood and marriage, because 'family' itself will always (at least for the foreseeable future) carry a certain cultural and political weight, a weight which far exceeds that of any potential 'alternative' conceptualisations of sexual, intimate, and other relations. Within this political context, abdicating the conceptual battle over family, that is, merely allowing the term to signify the nuclear family of blood and marital relations, would mean ceding an enormous swathe of political terrain.

Here I augment that argument by demanding that it join the political conflict over marriage (see Strasser 2002). In other words, it is essential to conceptualise family beyond marriage for reasons that cut through, in powerful and incisive fashion, the debate over 'gay' or 'same-sex' marriage. This makes *Big Love* an ideal candidate for interpretation since it offers us, or so I will suggest below, a queer family that is not merely a gay couple mimicking a heterosexual couple. The image of marriage and family in *Big Love* proves extremely helpful from my theoretical and political perspective to the extent that it broadens our understanding of the politics at stake in gay marriage. In other words, a queer reading of *Big Love* proves timely precisely because these stakes have been so successfully narrowed by both supporters and critics of gay marriage.

To take just one prominent example, the title itself of Andrew Sullivan's edited volume on the gay marriage debate speaks precisely to this problem: *Same-Sex Marriage: Pro and Con* (2004 [1997]). Like many other supporters of gay marriage, Sullivan suggests that the politics of the issue boil down to inclusion vs. exclusion: the extension of the civil right of marriage to lesbian and gay citizens on the grounds of equality, or the refusal to extend that right on the shaky ground of 'tradition' or the state's interest in procreation. But as Michael Warner's polemical-yet-rigorous attack on Sullivan shows, there proves to be a great deal more at stake here. Thus, rather than summarise the legislative history or work through the complicated court rulings, rather than re-hash the 'defence' of heterosexual marriage from the right, or replay the liberal claim for gay marriage as an equal right, I will give an overview of the politics of the marriage debate by looking at two perspectives (rarely are there only two 'sides' to a debate, and certainly not on this issue) from *within* lesbian, gay, and queer communities (see Warner 1999; Eskridge 2001; Wolfson 2005).

While it must be remembered that the debate within the gay and queer communities over the struggle for gay marriage covers a variety of concerns and issues, it can still safely be captured by the question of 'family'. Both sides of this debate find themselves, initially, struggling against the current – so-called 'traditional' – definition of family. The mainstream gay movement seeks gay marriage as a goal, as *the* goal, precisely because that traditional definition of marriage excludes gays and lesbians. Moreover, and most importantly, since 'family' status can only be conferred by way of marriage, lesbian and gay relations can never be recognised either by society (in terms of status) or by the state (in terms of privileges and benefits) unless gay marriage is made legal. Gay marriage makes it possible for gay and lesbian citizens to create the 'families' that they are currently denied (Sullivan 1996; Wolfson 2005).

However, those queer theorists and activists who resist the call to gay marriage as the ultimate goal of gay politics recognise another dimension to this problematic – again, one made clear when viewed through the lens of a conception of 'family' beyond marriage. These critics grasp the fact that if the battle for gay marriage does not *challenge the terms* of the traditional family, but instead, and for obvious strategic reasons, chooses only to *include* lesbians and gay citizens *within* the ambit of marriage, then such a tactical move produces its own significant political problems (even as it clearly expands the civil rights of certain gay and lesbian citizens). In terms of both the theory and practice of the family, this drive for 'gay marriage' renders all those other relations of intimacy and commitment that fall outside marriage (and will continue to do so even if gay marriage is made legal) unrecognisable, illegitimate, or, in many cases, simply invisible. Warner formulates this point in stark terms: 'as long as people marry, the state will continue to regulate the sexual lives of those who do not' (Warner 1999: 96). Warner's work must be seen as a signal contribution, because it grasps the *politics* of marriage more lucidly than most writings on the debate. He articulates this politics with a salient and succinct formulation: 'Marriage sanctifies some couples at the expense of others. It is selective legitimacy. This is a necessary implication of the institution ... Marriage, in short, discriminates' (Warner 1999: 82).

Put in the language I have been developing over the past two chapters, one might say the following: as long as being 'family' requires being married, then all of those who cannot marry will be stigmatised, at best, or rendered unintelligible, at worst. Moreover, anyone who does not *wish* to marry (a rather large and growing group, despite the social and legal pressures to marry) will find themselves excluded from the domain of 'family'. The 'choice' to marry is never simply a choice, and thus the argument that gay men and lesbians should have this choice made available to them is also not as simple as it appears. Judith Butler nicely describes the genuine complexity of the issue over the 'option' of marriage as follows:

> [I]t may be that one not only opposes [marriage] for oneself, but for everybody, and that the task at hand is to rework and revise the social organization of friendship, sexual contacts, and community to produce non-state-centered forms of support and alliance, since marriage, given its historical weight, only becomes an 'option' by extending itself as a norm (and thus foreclosing options), one which also extends property relations and renders the social forms for sexuality more conservative. (Butler 2002: 21)

All of this means, again translating into my own language, that anyone with 'queer' family (i.e. non-family in relation to dominant norms and laws) will find their relations taken as somehow of lesser status and significance than those of a drunk straight couple who decided to take 15 minutes out of their life to do the drive-through marriage ceremony in Vegas. My project here takes up this 'task of reworking' named by Butler.

Butler, however, leaves one crucial item off her list: namely, *family*. This may be because she urges her readers to resist the reduction of kinship to 'family' (2002: 40). I sympathise with this position, but in response I make one argument and one suggestion. First, I argue that to cede the language of 'family' to those who would defend the 'sanctity' of marriage and its support for heteronormativity is to grant them a significant political victory. Queer theory can rework 'friendship, sexual contacts, and community' to the maximum degree, but as long as the family/non-family distinction remains operative then heteronormativity will maintain its hegemony. Unless and until those who are queer with respect to the heterosexual norm can *be family*, it will matter little how much those 'other relations' have been refigured. To paraphrase Warner: as long as family connotes status and standing, both the state and social norms will discriminate against those who do not count as family. Therefore the battle against those norms must include not only the reworking of community and friendship but also the subversion of the sanguinuptial family and its further resignification. Thus my suggestion, in response to Butler's worry, that if we transfigure the meaning of family itself then we avoid the problem of reducing kinship to family; it will no longer be a 'reduction'.

Turning away from Butler and looking again at vocal advocates of gay marriage, we can also see that as long as family centres on blood and marriage relations, and as long as the politics of the family privileges and protects those relations deemed 'family relations', then any such politics of the family will remain conservative at its core, no matter how radical it seems on the surface. Gay marriage does not promise a radical challenge to sexual or family politics; it merely seeks a broadening, and very much legitimate *inclusion* of lesbian and gay citizens into the traditional definition of family. Indeed, the compulsion to marry – already felt by most straight people at some point in their twenties, and experienced most poignantly in the form of questions from parents about when the *inevitable* marriage ceremony might occur (followed by the 'inevitable' birth of a grandchild) – may prove much stronger for gay people, should marriage be granted as the universal right that most competent readers of the US Constitution would suggest it is. Put differently, given the power of heteronormativity to shape social expectations, straight people can strive to maintain semi-recognisable, semi-legitimate non-marital relations of intimacy (at least up to a point). But gay men and lesbians, in order to circumvent the power of heteronormativity, may wish (or feel compelled) to quickly jump the line from illegitimate to legitimate (or at least to legal and recognised by the law) by marrying. It is a sign of the resistance to marriage within lesbian and gay communities that so many gay couples have chosen not to travel to the US state of Massachusetts for a legal wedding ceremony.

In making this case, I am merely trying to demonstrate the following: at the centre of the debate over gay marriage lies a debate about the meaning of family. Those who argue vociferously for gay marriage as the ultimate goal, and perhaps ultimate end (in its fullest sense[4]), of lesbian and gay politics tend to elide this point. Or, they pretend that the potential legal inclusion of gays and lesbians into the sanguinuptial conception of the family – as I have described it in the previous chapter – will utterly transform that conception of family. Advocates of gay marriage maintain the hope that gay marriage will somehow, all on its own, fundamentally change the meaning of family. But my preceding analysis should make clear that if family currently means relations between individuals by blood or by marriage, then gay marriage does nothing inherently to alter that understanding. Indeed, some of the loudest proponents of gay marriage, like Sullivan and William Eskridge, not only realise this point fully but also articulate it clearly. Thus, they call theirs the 'conservative case' for gay marriage because marriage, they say, will *civilise* gays.

On the other hand, a broad effort to resignify 'family' – to make that word resound in such a way that it includes people related to one another neither by blood nor by a marriage certificate, but by way of bonds forged through friendship, commitment, caring, intimacy, support, and sex – such an effort would necessarily include a radical challenge to the very forces of exclusion (forces that rest precisely on the sanguinuptial definition of family) that gay marriage advocates seek to overcome. I have already initiated this project in the preceding chapter by putting forth a reading of *Buffy* as resignifying family. Here I turn to *Big Love* as a televisual artefact that can *subvert* the sanguinuptial family and in its place propose a possible model of queer family. To carry through on this set of claims I must first clarify the terms of queer family and queer politics that undergird them. I do so by entering into a recent debate as it has been proposed (though not necessarily joined) by one of today's foremost queer theorists, Lee Edelman.

Context 2: Queer Theory and the Politics of 'Reproductive Futurism'

Is the *Big Love* family queer? There are a number of reasons to think so. Before placing it to the side, we might start with 'authorial intention', noting that both creators of the show are out gay men, who themselves see an important connection between the Henrickson family and the lives of many gays and lesbians (Moylan 2006). They echo this external description of the show within one particular episode. When talking to the media about the Juniper Creek compound, its leader, Roman Grant (known as a true prophet by those who live within the compound), argues for a direct link between gay rights and the rights of polygamists: 'If the Supreme Court says yes to the privacy rights of homosexual persons, surely it's time to recognise our rights to live in peace too' ('Home Invasion', 1.3). Roman herein makes the very connection between gay marriage and polygamous marriage that most advocates of gay marriage strenuously disavow. This move almost certainly proves purely strategic on Roman's part, but through it he recognises the queerness of polygamous family.

Much more importantly, and as I have been suggesting since the opening of this chapter, *Big Love* illuminates the gap between the heterosexual norm and the lives and daily practices of a polygamous family. Something about this family clearly does not fit with heteronormativity, even though each of its members is transparently heterosexual. The reason is obvious: heteronormativity prescribes not just opposite-sex attraction and desire for each individual, it also calls for monogamy (even if in serial form) and it strictly requires that the marriage bond apply only to groups of two. Thus, if one takes the succinct definition of queer offered in Chapter 2 as a guide – that is, marginalised from the dominant norms by their sexual practices – then the Henrickson family somehow proves queer. In this context it may help to recall David Halperin's now well-known definition of queer, which I also quoted in Chapter 2:

> As the very word implies, 'queer' does not name some natural kind or refer to some determinate object; it acquires its meaning from its oppositional relation to the norm. Queer is by definition whatever is at odds with the normal, the legitimate, the dominant. *There is nothing in particular to which it necessarily refers*. It is an identity without an essence. 'Queer,' then, demarcates not a positivity but a positionality vis-à-vis the normative – a positionality that is not restricted to lesbians and gay men but is in fact available to anyone who is or feels marginalized because of his or her sexual practices: it could include some married couples without children, or even (who knows?) some married couples with children... (Halperin 1995: 62, emphasis in original)

It logically follows from this definition that 'families of one husband, three wives and seven children' would also be included in that which is 'at odds with the normal'.

Lee Edelman's recent rendering of queer complicates matters. In his powerful polemic, *No Future: Queer Theory and the Death Drive*, Edelman appears, at times, to endorse Halperin's precise thinking of queer. For example, when Edelman writes, 'queer can never define an identity, it can only ever disturb one', it sounds as though he means to echo Halperin's notion of queer as 'an identity without an essence' (Edelman 2004: 17). However, the slightly different wording betrays a radically distinct approach to queer, as becomes evident when Edelman makes his case against 'reproductive futurism' and the hegemony of 'the figure of the child'.

Despite its sophisticated and complex reading of psychoanalytic theories and texts, Edelman's argument obeys a surprisingly straightforward binary logic. Let me briefly reconstruct that logic here. Edelman begins with the Freudian death drive, which, he says, 'holds a privileged place in this book'. The death drive names 'the negativity opposed to every form of social viability' (Edelman 2004: 9). It is the job of politics, according to Edelman, to oppose the death drive, to stand *for* social viability (and thus to always stand against the death drive). In doing so, politics 'gives us history as the continuous staging of our dream of eventual self-realization by endlessly reconstructing, in the mirror of desire, what we take to be reality itself' (Edelman 2004: 10). Put simply, for Edelman we cannot imagine 'a politics without a fantasy of the future'; politics, in opposing the death drive, *is* the fantasy of a viable future (Edelman 2004: 11). Thus Edelman lays out the foundation of his argument in the form of the struggle between politics and the death drive.

Edelman then makes two crucial linkages to build up this basic structure. First, he links politics to the figure of the child. If politics points relentlessly toward a future, then it can only do so through a celebration of the child who is that future. The child becomes 'the telos of the social order', and 'the image of the child ... serves to regulate political discourse' (Edelman 2004: 11). Politics is always a politics of the future, and is therefore always a politics of the child: it cannot 'conceive of a future without the figure of the child' (Edelman 2004: 11; cf. 21). When we bring into consideration the power of heteronormativity, we witness another crucial linkage: that between the figure of the queer and the death drive. Queerness comes to stand for everything that rejects the future and the child; queerness is that which ruptures a faith in the future and a (political) commitment to the child. Thus, we move from the opposition of death drive/politics to that of queerness/child.

At this point Edelman makes his boldest and most unfashionable claims. He refuses merely to reject the heteronormative linkage between the death drive and the figure of the queer. Instead, he says that 'we might do better to consider *accepting* and even *embracing* ... this ascription of negativity to the queer' (Edelman 2004: 4, emphasis added; cf. 5, 6, 16, 17). This claim cannot be taken as a mere matter of political moderation, that is, a tactical choice to accept the terms of the struggle as they are given. Instead, Edelman here makes a much more radical move, by repeatedly asserting that '*queerness* names the side of those *not* "fighting for the children"' (Edelman 2004: 3). Moreover, 'queerness *should* and *must* redefine' the social contract and the conception of civil order; it must 'rupture' faith in reproductive futurism. Here Edelman insists that sometimes the political right, even in their homophobia, grasps the radical implications (i.e. the implosion of the social order) of queerness more clearly than the liberal left who seek only to domesticate that radical threat through 'tolerance'. As he puts it, 'the left would eliminate queerness by shining the cool light of reason upon it' (Edelman 2004: 28). Given this, Edelman insists that his call to embrace negativity cannot be grasped under the terms of reason: it has 'no justification' and it promises 'absolutely nothing' (Edelman 2004: 6, 5).

Adding these elements together leads Edelman to propose a thinking of queer as that, and only that, which stands in opposition and resistance to the powerful and dominant trope of reproductive futurism, located in the figure of the child. We can now return to Edelman's earlier formulation of queer in order to distinguish it from Halperin's approach. After the passage I quoted earlier concerning queerness as oppositional, Edelman continues (and I comment in square brackets): 'the burden of queerness [Halperin would not call it a burden] is to be located less in the assertion of an oppositional political identity [Halperin's definition] than in *an opposition to politics*' (Edelman 2004: 17, emphasis added). Edelman therefore produces a politics/queer theory binary. As he explains, 'queer theory as I construe it marks the "other" side of politics' (Edelman 2004: 7). Most significantly, this means that the task of queer theory is not to resist the move by which heteronormativity projects all threats to society onto queers. Instead, queer theory must 'uncannily return' this projection to the heteronormative order that produces it; queers must no longer disown but must rather 'assume' their negative association with the death drive (Edelman 2004: 24). Therefore, Edelman concludes, only by taking up the figural location given them through the heteronormative order can queers and queer theory offer a radical challenge to reproductive futurism and the figure of the child.

One must applaud Edelman for the bravery of his argument, for his willingness to take on perhaps the ultimate taboo (particularly in US culture and politics): the figure of the child. And Edelman is undoubtedly right to question the hegemony of this figure and its serious impact on political discourse. Nevertheless, one wonders if there is a space between, on the one hand, a liberal demand for tolerance that, as Edelman rightly says, would seek to eliminate queerness by finding a structured space for it within the liberal order of interest group politics and minority rights, and, on the other, what looks like a wholesale rejection of politics. Edelman seems to seek such utter purity in his theory that he must conflate all other challenges to heteronormativity with liberalism itself. Hence his implicit rejection of Halperin's conception of queer, as too focused on identity. Hence also his explicit critique of Butler's work on (un)intelligibility, which Edelman claims 'seems all too familiarly liberal' (Edelman 2004: 103).

With respect to my project here, Edelman implies that culture cannot be reworked radically by queerness; queerness can only be the constitutive other to culture, to reproductive futurism. What might be lost in Edelman's effort to cling to a radical conception of queer as absolutely other to politics? While Edelman criticises Butler for being too liberal, she herself, writing before Edelman, seems both to describe his theoretical project and to pose a question very appropriate to it:

> there is always the possibility of savoring the status of unthinkability ... as the most critical, the most radical, the most valuable. As the sexually unrepresentable, such sexual possibilities can figure the sublime within the contemporary field of sexuality, a site of pure resistance, a site uncoopted by normativity. *But how does one think politics from such a site of unrepresentability?* (Butler 2002: 18, emphasis added)

Within the terms of Edelman's theoretical framework, 'queer politics' turns out to be nothing more than a contradiction in terms. As John Brenkman puts it, 'The true queer politics is therefore beyond politics' (Brenkman 2002: 177). Because Edelman so tightly connects politics with the teleological drive of reproductive futurism, with a fixation on the figure of the child who will lead us into that future, he therefore reserves (and, as Butler might say, savours) a space for queer as everything that stands outside politics. In response to Brenkman, Edelman maintains that politics be thought of 'as the social elaboration of reality', and queerness thought of as that which 'necessarily destroys' politics (Edelman 2002: 185). But this means that there can be no politics that is not teleologically driven toward the future. Worse, it means that there can be no queer politics, since the figural function of queer must be to oppose politics as such. In other words, in taking up as his own the connection between the queer and social negativity, Edelman also eschews the chance to resist the totalising reduction of all politics to futurism, and he fails to see how this linkage itself may be a partial effect of heteronormativity.

In other words, Edelman's account can imagine no queer project in which politics itself were reworked. He therefore demands that queer theory and queerness stand opposed to politics. But what if the politics of reproductive futurism is not the exhaustion of politics' possibility, but rather one particular form that politics takes under the hegemony of heteronormativity? Is it not possible to conceive of cultural and even political challenges to heteronormativity that would themselves transform politics? Could we not imagine a politics that rejects teleology, that refuses to conceive of temporality on a linear model in which the future is a fixed point of destiny? This would be a politics that avoids the trap of reproductive futurism – understood exactly as a trap because the future is always an unrealisable fantasy. As I have argued previously, this would be an *untimely* politics: a politics of an open future-to-come that can never be predicted or controlled in advance (Chambers 2003a; see also Brown 2005, and Connolly 2005). It is a rather ghostly politics, attuned to the problems of (un)intelligibility.[5] It might even be a queer politics, but only if we continue to theorise queer in such a way that queer politics remains a possibility.

READING *BIG LOVE*:
QUEER FAMILY AND SUBVERSION

Let there be no doubts: the Henricksons consistently evince a complete and abiding commitment to both reproductive futurism and the figure of the child. As a family with seven children that, during the course of the first season, enthusiastically decides (on two different occasions) to have an eighth, their commitment to the child and to reproduction appears to far outstrip that of the average American heterosexual family. Throughout the season various members of the Henrickson family call on the idea of 'living the principle' of plural marriage, and this always means a commitment to children and to the future – both a future on this earth and one in the afterlife. Indeed, Joseph Smith's description of and support for plural marriage focused on the creation of a viable future for the fledging Mormon community and it linked this future on earth with a future in heaven only for those that 'lived the principle' (Krakauer 2003: 6; see also Smith and Pratt 1948, sec. 132). 'The principle' is the only thing that ties the Henricksons to those who live on the Juniper Creek Compound. In each case this makes Edelman's two critical targets – reproductive futurism and the figure of the child – the primary goals of polygamy.

These are not merely background conditions for the *Big Love* family. The characters themselves make their commitments explicit. At the end of episode 5, when Nicky claims (falsely, as it will later turn out[6]) that she is pregnant, she announces the news in the following language:

> There's something I want to say to everyone: I want to bring another soul into the family. It's time. We've been holding off for this reason or that. But it's time now. We've let worldly concerns come before what we're here for, what our purpose is. ('Affair', 1.5)

Their purpose is the future. Their purpose is the child. 'Worldly concerns' must be put aside to achieve these ends. The teleological language used here resonates with the narrow conception of politics (*as* teleology) that Edelman uses. And Nicky's announcement echoes an earlier conversation between Margene and Bill, which had already spelled out, and in the most lucid language possible, the family's position on children and the future. Bill comes home to apologise to Margene over an earlier indiscretion. To do so, he explains her central role in the family, as the member that makes them all 'complete'. And this wholeness of the family unit remains intertwined with the future and the unborn souls that will populate it. Bill says, 'we are links to eternity. Ahead of us, family yet to come, souls to be born' ('Viagra Blue', 1.2). Edelman probably could not have said it better himself.

Working within the terms of Edelman's conception, then, would force us to declare the Henrickson family utterly *unqueer*. How, then, to reconcile the Henricksons' devotion to the future and the child with the notion that their construction of the family and their sexual practices express and exemplify 'queer family'? To answer the challenge of this question will necessarily require displacing Edelman's theory of queer and rejecting his stark opposition between queerness and politics. And it will mean refusing to allow the binaries that Edelman constructs to stand. Finally, it will entail showing how the Henricksons subvert the sanguinuptial model: their queerness emerges not merely through a representation of marginalised or deviant family, but through an illustration of the conflict and contestation between their family practices and heteronormativity. It is precisely the *agonism* here that makes their family queer.

As noted in my first section, aside from this portrayal of the family as a locus of reproductive futurism, and also as a space to witness the conflict and drama of everyday life, the first six episodes of *Big Love* move slowly and with great care. These episodes introduce viewers to the characters, expose them to the family dynamic, and reveal the complex relation between the Henrickson family and Bill Henrickson's sanguinuptial family (mother, father, and brother) – along with the necessary entanglements (both familial and political) with the fundamentalists of the Juniper Creek compound. Once we move past the fact, presented by the show as more banal than we might expect, that Bill has three wives, and sleeps in the bed of a different one every night (though by no means has sex with one every night), then it quickly becomes apparent that there is little risqué or controversial in *Big Love*.

Thus, the so-called 'scandal' over the show is probably better thought of as a media-constructed quarrel. In any event, that controversy reached its peak *before* the airing of the very first episode, and the so-called controversy itself focused on the sheer fact of the show's existence, more than anything that went on within the episodes themselves. Most critics praised the show when they watched advance screenings of the first half of the season, but even those who were critical tended to damn the show for being unexciting. The *New York Times* published a wide-ranging piece that tries overtly to present responses to the show from a diversity of perspectives, but even the harshest comments hardly sound condemnatory. For example: 'Vicky Prunty, the head of [a] leading anti-polygamy group ... and herself a former polygamist, dismisses [*Big Love*] as a Hollywood fantasy for men' (Lee 2006: 1). Yet comments like this must surely be based on a reaction to the very *idea* of the show, and certainly not on a viewing of the pilot episode, or the five episodes that follow it.

Indeed, the *Big Love* pilot effects a reversal in the phenomenon we witnessed in the pilot of *The L Word*. Each pilot episode introduces viewers to a set of sexual practices that, when thought *within* the terms of heteronormativity, are simultaneously, first, stigmatised as deviant and, second, projected as objects of male sexual fantasy. As we saw in Chapter 3, *The L Word* pilot plays out precisely such a straight male fantasy in its portrayal of lesbian sexuality. However, and contrary to Prunty's comments above, the *Big Love* pilot thwarts, undermines, and disappoints any such fantasy at every turn. The pilot centres on the situation of the *Big Love* husband, Bill Henrickson, but it insists that his is not the glamorous life of getting the privilege to have sex with a different woman every night. His is the very dull, very typical, and extremely *difficult* life of being a husband – in this case a husband to three wives. This means serving as their partner in the toils of daily life (running three times as many errands, listening to three times as many family-related voicemails) while trying to service them sexually at night. From the perspective of the pilot, we see that the former tasks are enormous, and Bill is simply not up to the latter tasks – he has to turn to medical-technological aids in the form of Viagra in order to meet the collective sex drive of his three wives. If *The L Word* pilot says that lesbianism is acceptable because straight guys find it hot, the *Big Love* pilot warns the very same straight male to stay away from polygamy – it is just too much work.

In focusing on the relative drudgery of everyday life, the pilot sets the stage for the first six episodes (exactly half the season) of *Big Love*. Collectively, these episodes might appear to vindicate Edelman's articulation of queer, since there seems no reason to include the family portrayed in those episodes as queer. Would this not just be a watering down of the conception of queer – much as occurs, from a different angle, through the use of queer as a simple synonym for 'gay' in shows like *Queer Eye for the Straight Guy*? In other words, would calling the Henricksons queer not amount to a return to the narrow politics of representation and the associated identity politics from which I have been distancing my own project since Chapter 2 (a distancing articulated most explicitly in Chapter 4)?

Yes, in many ways perhaps it would. But that is why we cannot arrest our reading of *Big Love* halfway through the first season. In the last half of the first season we see a profound shift in the trajectory of the show: a move away from a vision of the family itself to relations between the family and the outside world. In these later episodes we witness the hegemony of the sanguinuptial model of family thrown into stark relief; we see the power of a norm revealed. This norm is not quite equivalent to heteronormativity but it still serves to render the Henrickson family *queer*. Indeed, the significance of *Big Love* lies in its capacity to expose this power of the sanguinuptial family from a different perspective – to cast it in a different light and let us see it from an angle that cannot be compressed to that of lesbian and gay identity. *Big Love* offers a potential subversion of the sanguinuptial family precisely because it breaks with that model in an unanticipated manner and to an unexpected degree.

This shift is marked most clearly by episode 7, making it the crucial episode for my reading of *Big Love*. This episode denotes a significant break in the show's trajectory as it turns away from the portrayal of the internal life of the Henrickson family while it also, and more importantly, signifies the move *outward* into a world dominated by heteronormativity and the sanguinuptial conception of family. In the first six episodes the viewer gets to know the Henricksons; in the last six episodes the viewer follows the Henricksons through their encounters with the world. Not surprisingly, the interaction between a polygamous family, on the one hand, and a heteronormative society, on the other, is riven with complications, complexities, and dangers. Most of all, however, this interaction is marked by *power*, that is, by conflict, domination, resistance, and perhaps ultimately (I suggest) subversion. Indeed, the very title of episode 7, 'Eviction', signals the importance of this confrontational engagement between the inner, private world of (polygamous) family and the broader world of heteronormativity outside it.

Eviction can easily be defined as the act of dispossessing someone of their home or property, and this happens literally in the episode when Roman forcibly removes the families of both Bill's father and brother from their respective homes on the Juniper Creek Compound. Furthermore, the word 'evict' also means to *expel*: 'to eject (persons) forcibly from any position' (OED 2007). Eviction can thus connote a much broader phenomenon: a general *displacement* from a space of safety, comfort, or home. In my reading of this episode, and of the last half of the first season generally, 'eviction' names a crucial process of movement across internal/external barriers. Eviction calls attention to the friction created in that crossing; it identifies the space in which conflict occurs through a clash between family practices and societal norms. The episode 'Eviction' includes an impressively long list of these crossings and powerful illustrations of their attendant friction.

After a morning scene with the family at home, the episode opens with Bill and his business partner, Don Embry (also a practising, non-compound polygamist), listening to an advertising pitch for their Home Plus stores. The advertising company wants to launch a massive campaign that will associate Home Plus with Utah, with home, and with family, by using Bill's 'competitive edge' of being 'home grown' and based in Salt Lake. The core hook of the campaign is to use subliminal messaging that associates Home Plus with Mormonism. As the ad exec says: the message is 'you're one of us; they're not'. Although they never say it directly, the advertisers want to convey this message by signalling subtly that the people in the Home Plus advertisements are LDS. Bill and Don are shown two nearly identical pictures of the same woman, but in one photograph she is wearing her Mormon undergarment (barely noticeable through her outer shirt) and in the other she is not. The message (again declared by the ad exec): 'I'm one of you.' The goal: to brand Home Plus as 'Utah's family superstore', with the added tag line: 'Home Plus is Us' ('Eviction', 1.7).

Bill is persuaded by the pitch, convinced that it can give him the leverage he needs to expand his stores and realise his business dreams. Don, however, remains sceptical, and becomes more uncomfortable through his tacit realisation that as he and Bill take in the pitch, the two of them are interpellated by the advertising salespeople as LDS members themselves. Their LDS status is simply *assumed*. Call it presumptive Mormonism. This is the simple-but-serious problem of 'passing', well known both to racial minorities and to gay men and lesbians (see for example Robinson 1994). 'Passing' occurs whenever one is passively assumed, or actively pretends, to be someone one is not. The possibility of passing gives those who deviate *from* the norm an opportunity to participate in the power and privilege *of* the norm, but it also poses the difficult question of whether to maintain the pretence. Don sees starkly that the advertisers think he and Bill are LDS (and passing worries him). Bill only sees the potential success that could result from this false presumption (so passing is not a concern for him). But the problem extends beyond this meeting with the advertisers, since not only do Bill and Don have to pretend, at least tacitly, to be LDS in front of the advertisers, but also they must actively project themselves into the world as something they are not through the advertising campaign. This is the problem of passing writ large, which stages an important conflict with the norm.

The tension that passing and the conflict it entails create within the Henrickson family will prove to be a central trope for the last half of the season. Every time one family member interacts with the world as a non-polygamist, his or her actions and choices place greater pressure on everyone else. Here again we see an echo of the epistemology of the closet explored in Chapter 1 through the text of *Six Feet Under*: David's self-closeting always strained his relationship with Keith as it got in the way of Keith's own efforts to be an out and proud gay man. In *Big Love* this pressure is often registered and measured by interactions between Bill and other characters: Bill's desire to be a successful businessman leads him to greater acceptance of passing as a monogamous family man (even an LDS member). But Don, at the office, and Nicky (even sometimes Barb), at home, frequently remind Bill that passing is never a simple act. Don points out to Bill that their office manager, Judy, has decided of her own accord that she will no longer take up membership in any association that rejects polygamy. Nicky explains to Bill that when he appears in public with Barb as 'his wife' it hurts both her and Margene. Barb herself says 'it feels like living a lie' ('Where There's a Will', 1.11). As the most visible public face of the Henrickson family, Bill experiences serious internal conflict over the broad choice either to protect his family's secret or to gain power, money, or security by passing.

As I discuss below, this tension will eventually burst in the season finale when the effort to pass finally fails. Before exploring that climax, I first need to lay out more of the strands of inner/outer conflict that are established by 'Eviction'. In addition to the general theme of socio-cultural 'passing', the viewer also glimpses the potential of this conflict to occur at other levels. On the legal plane, we see the threat of exposing 'private practices' to the outside world. Bill and Roman remain in dispute over business dealings throughout the season, and in this episode Bill blackmails Roman through a threatened call to the Attorney General that would expose to legal investigation some of the seedier elements of compound dealings. This exposure of secret knowledge echoes the secret of polygamy itself, which is illegal throughout the USA. This means that the practice of polygamy requires a furtiveness and protectiveness more intense than that required by gay people who are either closeted or 'discreet'. There is no genuine option to be an 'out' polygamist (compound members are the exception that prove this rule).

Given this crucial fact about polygamy's relation to both cultural norms and the law, simply telling the truth never really appears as an option for members of the Henrickson family. Even when one is found out, one still cannot 'come out'. The only 'out polygamists' are fundamentalist (compound) polygamists – a thoroughly stigmatised and denigrated group not merely marginalised in respect to the norm, but thoroughly displaced to the margins of society. The Henricksons, in contrast, have no desire to live outside society. They love the trappings of American culture and commodities just like any 'average' American family: this includes their suburban home with swimming pool, the kids with their iPods, the gigantic SUV that Bill drives, and 'movie theaters with the chairs that go all the way back', as Margene poetically describes the American strip-mall cinema ('Eviction', 1.7). Viewers see a stark example of the impossibility of coming out when Margene's new friend (and neighbour from across the street), Pam, makes an unannounced visit to Margene's. Barb interrupts them when she enters Margene's house through the backyard and must then hastily make up a set of lies to cover for her casual familiarity with Margene (a mere 'neighbour'). Luckily, Pam seems to accept the story: in terms of secrecy, polygamy has the advantage among queer forms of family of being so taboo as to be both unexpected and unlooked-for. Although this generalisation perhaps proves weaker in Utah than elsewhere, later in the season Pam will come to suspect Nicky is a polygamist. She identifies Nicky not by her living arrangements but by her dress and demeanour. Her compound background, not her current practices, 'give her away'.

In any event, this brief scene shows just how marginalised polygamy is in relation to the dominant norms: so much so that one cannot even *mark* oneself in relation to that norm. This helps explain the logic detailed above, and gives a sense of why Margene and Barb do not recognise 'outing themselves' as members of the same family to be a viable choice. Instead, all members of the family must constantly lie to maintain their facade of normality. This tension is exacerbated in later episodes, first as Margene and Pam become closer ('A Barbecue for Betty', 1.9), and then when Pam decides that Nicky is a danger to the neighbourhood and must be watched closely. To maintain the friendship Margene plays along with Pam at first, but she soon comes to an important and life-changing realisation. Margene recognises that she herself is exactly what Pam hates, a polygamist. For the first time in her life she sees the extent to which her choice to marry into a polygamous family makes her 'queer'. In other words, in this interaction with Pam, Margene comes to understand that she will always be outside the norms to which Pam adheres. She therefore tells Pam that she cannot be friends with her, that Nicky 'is a good person', and that Margene would never help to harm her in any way ('The Baptism', 1.10). Still, Margene never declares to Pam her identity as a polygamist (although she does finally declare it to herself); she never reveals the extent and nature of her family. These options appear unavailable, showing how the Henrickson family is, in certain respects, much more queer than we first expected them to be – more queer then an average gay man or lesbian woman, who might at least have the option of coming out (even with its attendant repercussions, dangers, and implications). This explains the Henricksons' favoured tactic when negotiating the friction between their internal lives and external norms: to hide, to keep their secret, to always 'be careful' – a phrase used frequently by all the family members ('A Barbecue for Betty', 1.9).

Nonetheless, as I argue in the first two chapters of this book, you can never be completely in or out of the closet. That the Henricksons never attempt to come out does not alter the fact that they can never be completely secure inside the protective space of the closet. Therefore, no matter how *careful* the Henricksons are, someone, somewhere will always discover the secret. And some know the secret already. In other words, the encounter with the norm will also be marked by a passage from outside to inside. 'Eviction' stages one form of this encounter when the eldest Henrickson daughter, Sarah, brings an unplanned and unannounced visitor home to dinner. Heather, Sarah's friend from work, has already found out that Sarah's family is polygamous. She has also, over the course of the first half of the season, shown herself to be both fiercely protective of Sarah and relentlessly interested in polygamy. While LDS herself, Heather claims to be extremely tolerant – noting that she volunteers for a gay, lesbian, and transgender teen group, though failing to understand what 'transgender' means ('Viagra Blue', 1.2). Sarah has therefore revealed the truth about her family, and simultaneously sworn Heather to secrecy ('Eclipse', 1.4). Nonetheless, even Sarah does not come out: she admits that her family is polygamous while claiming that she herself is not ('Viagra Blue', 1.2). In bringing Heather home with her, Sarah literally brings the encounter between polygamy and the dominant norms to the dinner table. Heather's genuine tolerance – she truly believes in the Christian principle of unconditional love – coupled with her utter fascination with polygamy leads her to ask a number of awkward questions. At the end of the evening, she thanks Barb and Bill kindly for the food, and then says 'You know, I really have some strong opinions about polygamy and would love to sit down and talk to you about it one day'. All Barb can do is smile and say, 'Well, we should do that some time' ('Eviction', 1.7).

In this episode, finally, the conflict with the norm also appears both more starkly and with more potential force. The conflict comes about through the figure of LDS missionaries: they literally come from outside, knocking on Nicky's door to bring to bear the power of their own beliefs and values, which, while not necessarily mainstream, at least have the sanction of heteronormativity in the form of disavowing and rejecting polygamy. Nicky repeats a line that Bill had earlier used when defending Don against an employee's charges of suspected polygamy ('Affair', 1.5). Nicky says to the missionaries, 'I am not what you think I am' ('Eviction', 1.7). This line could be read as an attempt to disavow the power of the norm, to avoid *any* relation to the closet. That is, Nicky neither comes out as polygamous nor tries to pass as LDS (or any other religion). The missionaries, however, remain unconvinced. In their first encounter Nicky cites *Doctrine and Covenants*, one of the holy books of Mormon scripture. The missionaries use this as evidence against Nicky. The first missionary states, 'You quote Mormon scripture, yet, you're not LDS' and then the second takes this up with, 'We understand now; the polygamist lifestyle is wrong' ('Eviction', 1.7). Nicky tries to resist their claim to know her identity, but she is reduced to shouting at them as they ride away on their bicycles. Despite her defiance, she still cannot proclaim proudly any identity.

She gets a second chance later in the season, when another 'external force' appears outside her door, this time in the form of Barb's sister, Cindy. For this encounter, a bit of the back-story proves essential. Barb and Bill were happily married monogamists for many years. They became polygamists after Barb was diagnosed with cancer and was nursed back to health by Nicky.[7] Since her recovery and conversion to living the principle of plural marriage, Barb's sanguinuptial family has largely disowned her: she has hardly spoken to her mother and only occasionally made contact with her sister over the past seven years. Here we see the role of choice within the sanguinuptial family, as discussed in the previous chapter. In this context, Cindy appears late in the season, wanting to take Barb's three bloodchildren to visit their grandmother. Barb agrees, hoping this will be the chance to reconcile with her mother. But Nicky rightly suspects that Cindy is up to no good, saying to Barb: 'She's judgemental and she only makes you feel bad about yourself' ('The Baptism', 1.10). Nicky goes further than this, when Cindy comes round to pick up the kids. Inviting Cindy into their 'homes' (and then insisting she accept), Nicky gives Cindy a tour, designed precisely to force Cindy to confront the realities of polygamy – designed, that is, to bring to light the conflict between two different practices of family. Nicky not only calls out Cindy's negative judgements against polygamy but also conducts a reversal of expectations on this front by using Cindy's conservative 'family values' to effect an unexpected twist. Witness this exchange:

Nicky: You should really come around more often. Family is so important. Don't you agree?

Cindy: Certainly.

Nicky: It must be so hard on your kids when you travel.

Cindy: Oh, we have a terrific nanny.

Nicky: I can't imagine not raising my own kids!

('The Baptism', 1.10)

This sets the stage for the final confrontation, when Cindy returns later in the episode and condemns Barb's decision to baptise their daughter in the family swimming pool. Cindy tries to draw a line between Barb's adult choice to choose a polygamous lifestyle, on the one hand, and a certain corruption of the children by 'involving' them in this lifestyle when 'they are innocent', on the other. Nicky interrupts with a fierce defence of both Barb and of polygamy. She confronts Cindy directly, 'Not staying for my punch? Then please leave our house.' Cindy tries, unsuccessfully, to interrupt. Nicky continues:

> ...there's nothing wrong with our children. They are perfectly strong-minded, independent, works of art – much like their mothers. Our children are at least three times as cared-for, and Barb is ten times the mother. Where are your children when you skip off every week on business? Family first, right? Then how about you go home to yours and leave us to our own! ('The Baptism', 1.10)

In the opening episodes, Nicky is by far the least likeable character and the one most clearly associated with the stereotypical image of polygamy – backwards, ignorant, out of touch with the world, and associated with violence – that most viewers are likely to have in their heads before watching *Big Love*. She also seems to be the most possessive, jealous, and judgemental of the three wives – the source of more conflict within the family. Her consistent reference to Barb, especially in the first few episodes, as 'boss lady', signals the power dynamic between the three wives. Finally, Nicky appears to be the character with the biggest weaknesses herself: a compulsive online shopper, she has racked up $60,000 in credit card debt and hidden it from the rest of the family. Whether despite or because of all this, Nicky proves to be one of the most compelling and important characters on the show. And Nicky's voice speaks most forcefully over the last half of the season for a defence of polygamous family and a subversion of the sanguinuptial, heteronormative model. It is Nicky who challenges Cindy's heteronormative judgement. It is Nicky who calls Bill back to himself when he is considering joining a league of conservative (read: LDS) business leaders. It is Nicky who defends the family houses with the promise of force when threatened by Roman's hands from the compound.

Taken as a whole, the entire last half of the first season of *Big Love* stages the encounter between a deviant, marginalised and/or abjected form of family, on the one hand, and the power of hetero-normativity or the sanguinuptial model of family, on the other. At the end of the episode 'Eviction', Bill's dad, Frank, says, 'We have been thrown out of our lives' ('Eviction', 1.7). It is a curious and ellip-tical line, but I would like to read it in the terms already established by this book, by asking: is that not what happens to people when the stigmatising and denigrating power of heteronormativity makes its force felt? To be thrown, not merely out of your house or even your home, but out of your very *life*, is to be displaced more fundamental-ly than any legal eviction from a physical place could hope to effect. To be queer is to be subject to such displacement. It is to be subject to the power of a norm that can render one's very life unintelligible (see Carver and Chambers 2007). The exploration of these inner/outer conflicts over the last half of the first *Big Love* season gives viewers a glimpse of this process.

Of course, in many cases the encounter with the norm serves only to discipline the queer family – to force either a conformity with the norm, or a secretive hiding of those practices that would deviate from it. Therefore, to call this process to light does not automati-cally translate into subversion of the norm, and I would not wish to suggest as much. I cannot stress enough, however, the point made in Chapter 4: one step in challenging the norm lies in revealing its very operation. Norms function best when they are least seen. *Big Love* accomplishes this task of revealing the operation of the norm in countless ways, some of which have been delineated here. But it often takes the further step – and commonly does so through the character of Nicky – of actively challenging or subverting the norm. It sometimes goes so far as to expose to light the internal inconsis-tencies of the norm, and to call into question its status, its function, its purpose, or its legitimacy.

In doing this, *Big Love* raises some very serious questions for the queer politics of the family. Is the sanguinuptial family built upon heteronormativity even the best model for supporting the figure of the child? Edelman's polemic may unwittingly serve to shore up the link between heteronormativity and the child – to lend credence to the conservative claim that children should be brought up in two-par-ent, monogamous, heterosexual families. Considered from the other side of the equation, we might also ask: is a commitment to children and family necessarily incompatible with queerness? By taking the side of 'those *not* "fighting for the children"', Edelman makes it too easy to presume that queerness cannot be located in the same space as children (Edelman 2004: 3). Finally, is there anything inherently offensive, violent, or dangerous about polygamous family arrangements? *Big Love* raises all of these questions and suggests a number of paths of thought along which we may find answers. Ultimately, *Big Love* subverts the sanguinuptial model by exploring alternatives to it that prove to be both more radical (i.e. polygamous and therefore taboo) and less radical (i.e. conservative and heterosexual) than heteronormativity would lead us to believe.

THE QUEER POLITICS OF PLURAL MARRIAGE

It would be easy to transform this careful attention to the exploration of polygamous family forms in visual culture into a demand for the extension of liberal rights. Indeed, my final question in the section above seems to point toward a defence of the individual rights of the polygamist. While the logic of such an argument would prove relatively straightforward – as it claims a mere extension of sexual privacy rights – it would nevertheless amount to a bold set of political demands. Despite the massive literature and strong political support (in some quarters) for the defence of gay marriage, there has been almost no case made in favour of polygamy. Quite the contrary, in fact: most supporters of gay marriage actively disavow any links to polygamy. They refuse to recognise it as potentially another queer practice of marriage and sexuality; they insist on *mis-recognising* it as simply unimaginable or as simply abuse. It is the conservative critics of gay marriage – those threatening us with descriptions of the end of society as we know it – who consistently call up the image of the slippery slope from gay marriage, to polygamy, to paedophilia, to bestiality, and so on (Kurtz 2006).

Cheshire Calhoun's work on polygamy and the same-sex marriage debate must therefore be noted for its bravery, a bravery found in her willingness to take up this undesirable political work (Calhoun 2005; cf. Turley 2004). Calhoun shows that gender inequality has no *necessary* role to play in polygamy: historically women in polygamous marriages in the USA often had more rights, freedoms, and relative power than other women (Calhoun 2005: 1038–9). And Calhoun goes on to argue persuasively that, far from weakening the case for same-sex marriage, close analysis of the actual history and practice of polygamy may provide firm grounds of support for the advancement of rights to same-sex marriage (Calhoun 2005: 1042). Nevertheless, mine is not a liberal project, and I insist that the queer politics of plural marriage on *Big Love* exceeds the terms of liberal tolerance and liberal rights. Here, as I have been throughout the book, I remain interested in the politics of norms. As I demonstrate in this final section, when considered in terms of the cultural politics of norms, *Big Love*'s polygamous family turns out to be queer. And the show itself proves politically significant in a way that leaves behind the narrow (though certainly important) debate over rights.

To see why this is the case, I would like to turn to the season finale. This episode marks the culmination of the key storylines opened up in episode 7, as it centres on a ceremony to be held at the Governor's mansion that will honour Barb and two others as nominees for 'Mother of the Year'. Tancy, Barb's youngest daughter, nominated Barb through an essay contest, and since being named a finalist Barb's excitement over the process has continued to grow while tensions in the houses have steadily risen. As many theorists have shown, the idea of 'the normal' produces a desire for that very idea – a desire to be normal, to fit into the statistical average (Warner 1999). The reality of her nomination as 'Mother of the Year' brings out in Barb a longing to be 'normal'; or, at least it produces in her a set of incentives for performing the norm. But, just as with the discussion of passing, above, Barb's efforts to put on a performance of the normal husband/wife/daughter/son family creates conflict and produces tensions for the other two wives (and their children) – those who cannot be made to fit this pattern.

The tensions reach an apogee on the day of the ceremony: to carry out a proper performance of the normal, Barb wants Nicky to dress differently, saying to Margene that with Nicky's typical outfits, 'it's like walking into the governor's mansion with a sign that says "practising polygamist"' ('The Ceremony', 1.12). Nicky overhears this exchange and later confronts Barb with her own feelings on the issue, telling Barb not to accept the award. Barb wants to enjoy this one-off performance of the normal, but Nicky reveals to her what might be lost when the norm is aped in this fashion. Nicky pleads with Barb as follows: 'Either we are what we say we are, or we're not. You accepting this award feels like we're not what we say we are – *a family* – and that hurts me' ('The Ceremony', 1.12). Both Barb's desire for the normal and the performance of the norm serve to undermine the queer model of family that Nicky lives and loves. Not surprisingly, then, when Barb insists on attending the ceremony, Nicky decides not to go.

This conflict finds little resolution in the end, showing once again the impossibility of ever fully evading the power of the norm. It cannot be hidden from; it cannot be overcome. When the time comes to leave for the ceremony, Nicky makes a surprise appearance: wearing a dress and with her hair down (no longer in its standard braid); her last-minute choice to attend the ceremony moves Barb to tears. The soft background piano music encourages the viewer to share in one of the most powerful and intimate moments of family over the entire season. But just before the viewer is also brought to tears, the music comes to an abrupt halt: they have been given only enough tickets for Barb, Bill, and their three children (the sanguinuptial family of blood and legal marriage). The extra tickets requested for Barb's 'sisters' (i.e. her sister-wives, Nicky and Margene) never showed up.

So the putatively traditional family heads off to the ceremony, and Margene and Nicky go to dinner by themselves. This concluding episode thereby refuses to draw closure to the inner/outer struggle that runs throughout the last half of the season. Moreover, the climax of the season occurs at the ceremony itself, where the Henricksons discover that, even at the very moment when they are trying their hardest to pass as a happy, nuclear, monogamous family, outside forces can expose their queerness. Bill and Roman have continued to escalate their battle over business matters, with Bill making a hostile takeover, in this episode, of a seat on the Board that runs both the Compound and Roman's business. Roman retaliates: minutes before the ceremony begins, he calls the Governor's mansion and 'outs' Barb. She, along with Bill and the kids, must make a painful and embarrassing exit from the ceremony as the Governor's wife announces that one of the contestants has had to drop out 'for personal reasons' ('The Ceremony', 1.12). Back at the houses, the piano music returns, but in a scary and disturbing minor key. Barb flees to the bedroom in great distress, Bill contacts Don Embry to say 'we've been exposed', and Nicky is reduced to complete hysterics. She races through the house pulling closed the curtains. Bill asks her what she is doing; Nicky screams, 'Protecting us! They could come for us; they could burn us down. You could be arrested – you could be taken.' Bill tries his best to console her, whispering 'That doesn't happen any more', but Nicky's fear is palpable. The episode, the season, ends with the three wives in Barb's bedroom. Barb looks into Nicky's eyes and says with conviction, 'I got what I deserved.' With tears starting to run down her face, Nicky says in a whisper, and with great tenderness, 'Oh, boss lady' ('The Ceremony', 1.12).

This episode, and particularly these final scenes, dramatises the power of the norm: it demonstrates the very real, utterly tangible threat that the norm poses to the Henricksons and their form of family. This power is mobilised not necessarily from outside the Henricskon family, nor from mainstream, heteronormative society. Roman is, after all, Bill's father in law, and a practising polygamist of the highest order. But because Roman already occupies the most stigmatised and denigrated space within the heteronormative order, because he is already 'out' in a way that Bill's family never could be, he attains a perverse access to the power of heteronormativity. He can call on its force against the Henrickson family.

Big Love both illustrates and participates in a cultural politics, a queer politics, whose repercussions reach beyond Edelman's project to make queer the unassailable other to politics. Contrary to Edelman's rendering of queer, the Henricksons do not stand outside or opposed to the future, to the child, or even to politics. But by consistently going against what a heteronormative world wants family to be, by resisting both accommodation to that norm or utter opposition against it, the Henricksons subvert the sanguinuptial conception of family. When Nicky insists that true family values *mean* polygamy she offers viewers a glimpse of what it would take to transform the sanguinuptial model from the inside out. This view is amplified over the course of the season's 12 episodes through the daily lives of the characters and their routine practices of family – practices that can never be made to fit the sanguinuptial model, but which also cannot be transformed into an oppositional rejection of society as we know it (*à la* Edelman).

This is why the practice of family on *Big Love* is truly queer in the sense articulated by Halperin and Warner: both *marginal* in relation to the median point on the normal curve and *resistant* to the hegemony of the norm. The cultural politics of the show come to light when one emphasises this queerness vis-à-vis the dominant norms of family, sexuality, and marriage. Thus, polygamy per se is not the crucial variable, just as 'gay identity' has not been a central conceptual component of my broader arguments in the book concerning the queer politics of television. With *Big Love*, like *Desperate Housewives*, we continue to work outside the domain of a politics of representation. The significance of the show should not, indeed cannot, be reduced to a positive representation of 'polygamists', as if the latter were simply another fixed identity label that we might attach to people – in the same manner that identity politics seeks always to return to and to start with labels such as 'woman', 'minority', and 'gay'.

What we find on *Big Love* is not 'polygamists' who are normal and therefore likeable and loveable. We might take something like this (something positive, no doubt) away from a show such as *Will and Grace*, a show that says implicitly to its viewers, 'Look, there is a gay person and he seems normal and nice.' But *Will and Grace* spends almost none of its airtime showing viewers what it means to be gay. *Big Love*, in stark contrast, spends most of its time showing viewers what family life looks like. And, of course, it does so within a family that practises polygamy. *Big Love* lets viewers glimpse the daily life and experiences of all the members of a polygamous family, but the emphasis always remains on those practices and those experiences, not on fixed individual identities.

In this context it may be very helpful to stress that, for the Henrickons at least, polygamy cannot be properly understood as one husband *having* or being married to multiple (in this case, three) wives. The sanguinuptial model of family encourages one to take this sort of approach to understanding polygamy. That is, the sanguinuptial conception – based as it is on the heteronormative presumption of straight, binary couples in pairs – tempts us to think of polygamy as a relation of domination by one husband over multiple women. It suggests that polygamy could be nothing more than a variant on patriarchy, with a strong tendency toward spouse abuse. Within this framework, it is as if the husband has three separate marriages, and each wife is married only to one man. But this conception is fatally flawed, and not only because polygamy includes the possibility of polyandry. Putting aside semantics, we can admit that the form of marriage described above surely has been practised historically, both within and without the Mormon tradition of plural marriage. Nonetheless, and whatever else we wish to say about polygamy, we must declare that polygamy proves to be an utterly distinct model of family, unassimilable to the sanguinuptial conception. To think of polygamy as nothing more than a perverse and perhaps violent extension of the nuclear family is to misunderstand the radically different bases on which polygamy founds family.

Heteronormativity insists on the two-ness of marriage, while polygamy allows conceptually (and sometimes in practice) for the possibility of a marriage based on something more. The name plural marriage can evoke something very different from serial patriarchy. In the case of *Big Love*, that is, in the case of the Henricksons, I emphasise that their marriage is truly *plural*. The marriage and the family it produces cannot be grasped as Bill's singular relationships with three different women. Instead, as the characters themselves repeatedly remind the viewer over the last half of the season: *they are all married to one another*. In an apparently banal disagreement between Barb and Bill, Bill criticises Barb for keeping a secret of Nicky's from him. He asks, seemingly rhetorically, 'I'm your husband aren't I?' To which Barb replies: 'Yes, but I'm married to two other people' ('Barbecue for Betty', 1.9). The next episode brings this point home with much greater clarity, as Margene grapples with what it means to be a polygamist. The episode concludes with the baptism of Tancy in the family's backyard pool. In the midst of the ceremony, Margene jumps into the pool and with the words 'me next' asks Bill to baptise her also. She explains:

> Bill, when I married into this family, I guess I must have thought I was just marrying you. [Margene turns to Barb and Nicky] And now I realise I was marrying all of you. I was marrying sisters – my sisters. That was my choice, and I'd make that choice all over again. ('The Baptism', 1.10)

Thinking of polygamy as the practice of one husband having many wives makes it easy to dismiss. There is nothing novel or politically significant about such an idea, and both liberals and conservatives can find safe ground on which to base their rejection of it. However, if we grasp plural marriage as potentially the marriage of more than two people to one another, then we move to an understanding of polygamous family as queer family. Effecting this shift also makes it much harder to reject polygamy offhand. The idea of polygamy as plural marriage offers a powerful resistance to heteronormativity, played out by *Big Love* over the course of its first season. By coming at it from the inside, the marriage of Barb, Bill, Nicky, and Margene to one another serves to undermine the nuclear/extended conception that supports the sanguinuptial model of family. In tracking this process *Big Love* subverts sanguinuptial family and thereby does the crucial work of cultural politics.

NOTES

1   By 'unprecedented pressure' I refer to what others have called 'the so-called Utah War' waged by the US government against Mormons (Krakauer 2003: 8).

2   To clarify terms, 'plural marriage' was the name given by LDS founder Joseph Smith, Jr, to what he claimed was the divinely ordained practice of polygamy. 'Polygamy' refers to any form of marriage in which a person has more than one spouse simultaneously, whereas 'polygyny' specifically names the practice of a husband taking more than one wife and 'polyandry' names the practice of a wife taking more than one husband. Smith's plural marriages were mainly confined to polygyny but could also (and sometimes did) include polyandry. While most polygamous

Mormon sects that practise polygamy call themselves 'fundamentalists' and often include this word in the name of their church, the LDS insists that these sects are neither Mormon (a word reserved only for LDS members) nor fundamentalist.

3   Bill and Nicky's past and present ties to the compound create a series of conflicts and other sources of dramatic tension, particularly since Nicky's father, Roman, is the man responsible for ejecting Bill from the compound community and, years later, for agreeing to let Nicky leave (in order to become Bill's second wife).

4   Andrew Sullivan suggests that, 'following legalization of marriage and a couple of other things, I think we should have a party and close down the gay rights movement for good' (Groff 1997; quoted in Warner 1999: 60–1).

5   In her recent writings on (un)intelligibility, Butler herself works hard to occupy that space between liberalism and the outright rejection of politics. We can move beyond a framework of liberal tolerance while still remaining committed to politics. Butler does so through her concept of 'the unintelligible' – a category that cannot be reduced to that of an oppressed or abjected liberal subject. Edelman says that Butler 'sounds' liberal, but Butler *stresses* her distance from liberalism: 'to be oppressed you must first become intelligible' (Butler 2004: 30; see also Carver and Chambers 2007). And Butler would agree with Edelman that there will always be some degree of structural exclusion, some remainder of unintelligibility (Edelman 2004: 27; Butler 2004). However, the best response to this problem is not to embrace figural exclusion *tout court*; rather, one can strive to make the unintelligible intelligible, to render some lives more livable, while still refusing a vision of the social in which all could be included. This is why Butler's is not a liberal politics of inclusion, but a queer politics that resists and subverts heteronormativity (Chambers 2007; Chambers and Carver 2008).

6   As viewers discover in the very next episode, Nicky is still taking birth control pills. Her 'fake pregnancy' was merely a tactic, in her competition with Barb for Bill's time and affection. Barb and Bill had been meeting clandestinely in hotel rooms to have sex – an 'affair' between husband and wife. They both see this as a form of cheating, however, and soon call it off.

7   Some viewers of *Big Love* would interpret Nicky's inclusion into the marriage of Bill and Barb as brought about by their desire to have more children, coupled with Barb's infertility (a result of her cancer). Thus, Nicky joins the family to bear the children that Barb cannot. This reading makes a prior reproductive futurism the cause of polygamy. I resist

this reading. While living 'the principle' means having a commitment to bring new souls into the world, I would insist that first Nicky and then Margene are both included in the family because of the choice made by the current members. This reading jibes with the fact that all 'new wives' are voted on, and it resonates better with my reading of Margene, presented here.

EPISODE GUIDE

BIG LOVE

'Pilot' (1.1). 2006. Written by Mark V. Olsen and Will Scheffer. Directed by Rodrigo Garcia.

'Viagra Blue' (1.2). 2006. Written by Mark V. Olsen and Will Scheffer. Directed by Charles McDougall.

'Home Invasion' (1.3). 2006. Written by Mark V. Olsen and Will Scheffer. Directed by Charles McDougall.

'Eclipse' (1.4). 2006. Story by David Manson. Teleplay by Mark V. Olsen and Will Scheffer. Directed by Michael Spiller.

'Affair' (1.5). 2006. Story by Alexa Junge. Teleplay by Alexa Junge, Mark V. Olsen, and Will Scheffer. Directed by Alan Taylor.

'Eviction' (1.7). 2006. Written by Mimi Friedman and Jeanette Collins. Directed by Michael Spiller.

'A Barbecue for Betty' (1.9). 2006. Written by Jill Sprecher, Karen Sprecher, Mark V. Olsen, and Will Scheffer. Directed by Steve Shill.

'The Baptism' (1.10). 2006. Written by Dustin Lance Block. Directed by Michael Lehmann.

'Where There's a Will' (1.11). 2006. Story by Eileen Myers. Teleplay by Mimi Friedman and Jeanette Collins. Directed by Alan Poul.

'The Ceremony' (1.12). 2006. Written by Mark V. Olsen and Will Scheffer. Directed by Julian Farino.

BUFFY THE VAMPIRE SLAYER

'Hellmouth' (1.1). 1997. Written by Joss Whedon. Directed by Charles Martin Smith.

'Revelations' (3.7). 1998. Written by Douglas Petrie. Directed by James A. Contner.

'Gingerbread' (3.11). 1999. Written by Jane Espenson. Directed by James Whitmore, Jr.

'Goodbye Iowa' (4.14). 2000. Written by Marti Noxon. Directed by David Solomon.

'No Place Like Home' (5.5). 2000. Written by Joss Whedon and Douglas Petrie. Directed by David Solomon.

'Family' (5.6). 2000. Written and directed by Joss Whedon.

'Into the Woods' (5.10). 2000. Written and directed by Marti Noxon.

'Blood Ties' (5.13). 2001. Written by Steven DeKnight. Directed by Michael Gershman.

'The Body' (5.16). 2001. Written and directed by Joss Whedon.

'The Gift' (5.22). 2001. Written and directed by Joss Whedon.

'Once More, With Feeling' (6.7). 2002. Written and directed by Joss Whedon.

'Chosen' (7.22). 2003. Written and directed by Joss Whedon.

Desperate Housewives

'Pilot' (1.1). 2004. Written by Marc Cherry. Directed by Charles McDougall.

'Anything You Can Do' (1.7). 2004. Written by John Pardee and Joey Murphy. Directed by Larry Shaw.

'Suspicious Minds' (1.9). 2004. Written by Jenna Bans. Directed by Larry Shaw.

'Your Fault' (1.13). 2005. Written by Kevin Etten. Directed by Ariene Sanford.

'Impossible' (1.15). 2005. Written by Marc Cherry and Tom Spezialy. Directed by Larry Shaw.

'Children Will Listen' (1.18). 2005. Written by Kevin Murphy. Directed by Larry Shaw.

'Live Alone and Like It' (1.19). 2005. Written by Jenna Bans. Directed by Ariene Sanford.

My So-Called Life

'Pilot'. 1994. Written by Winne Holzman. Directed by Scott Winant.

QUEER AS FOLK

'Episode 5'. 2001. Written by Jonathan Tolins. Directed by Kari Skogland.

SIX FEET UNDER

'Pilot' (1.1). 2001. Written and directed by Alan Ball.

'The Will' (1.2). 2001. Written by Christian Williams. Directed by Miguel Arteta.

'The Foot' (1.3). 2001. Written by Bruce Eric Kaplan. Directed by John Patterson.

'Familia' (1.4). 2001. Written by Lawrence Andries. Directed by Lisa Cholodenko.

'An Open Book' (1.5). 2001. Written by Alan Ball. Directed by Kathy Bates.

'The New Person' (1.10). 2001. Written by Bruce Eric Kaplan. Directed by Kathy Bates.

'The Trip' (1.11). 2001. Written by Rick Cleveland. Directed by Michael Engler.

'Nobody Sleeps' (3.4). 2003. Written by Rick Cleveland and Alan Ball. Directed by Alan Poul.

'Making Love Work' (3.6). 2003. Written by Jill Soloway. Directed by Kathy Bates.

'Tears, Bones and Desire' (3.8). 2003. Written by Nancy Oliver. Directed by Dan Attias.

'The Opening' (3.9). 2003. Written by Kate Robin. Directed by Karen Moncrieff.

'Everyone Leaves' (3.10). 2003. Written by Scott Buck. Directed by Dan Minahan.

'The Dare' (4.7). 2004. Written by Bruce Eric Kaplan. Directed by Peter Webber.

THE L WORD

'Pilot' (1.1). 2004. Written by Ilene Chalken. Directed by Rose Troche.

'Pilot, Part 2' (1.2). 2004. Written by Ilene Chalken. Directed by Rose Troche.

'Let's Do It' (1.3). 2004. Written by Susan Miller. Directed by Rose Troche.

'Longing' (1.4). 2004. Written by Angela Robinson (III). Directed by Lynne Stopkewich.

'Lies, Lies, Lies' (1.5). 2004. Written by Josh Senter. Directed by Clément Virgo.

'Lawfully' (1.6). 2004. Written by Rose Troche. Directed by Daniel Minahan.

'Losing It' (1.7). 2004. Written by Guinevere Turner. Directed by Clément Virgo.

'Limb from Limb' (1.14). 2004. Written by Ilene Chalken. Directed by Tony Goldwyn.

WILL AND GRACE

'William, Tell' (1.6). 1998. Written by William Lucas Walker. Directed by James Burrows.

Cast List

Big Love

Barb Henrickson (Jeanne Tripplehorn)
Bill Henrickson (Bill Paxton)
Cindy (Judith Hoag)
Don Embry (Joel McKinnon Miller)
Heather Tuttle (Tina Majorino)
Margene Heffman (Ginnifer Goodwin)
Nicolette Grant (Chloë Sevigny)
Pam Martin (Audrey Wasilewski)
Roman Grant (Harry Dean Stanton)
Sarah Henrickson (Amanda Seyfried)
Tancy Hendrickson (Jolean Wejbe)

Buffy the Vampire Slayer

Anya (Emma Caulfield)
Buffy Summers (Sarah Michelle Gellar)
Cordelia Chase (Charisma Carpenter)
Cousin Beth (Amy Adams)
Dawn Summers (Michelle Trachtenberg)
Glory (Clare Kramer)
Jenny Calendar (Robia LaMorte)
Mr Maclay (Steve Rankin)
Oz (Seth Green)
Riley Finn (Marc Blucas)
Rupert Giles (Anthony Head)
Tara (Amber Benson)
Willow Rosenberg (Alyson Hannigan)
Xander Harris (Nicholas Brendon)

DESPERATE HOUSEWIVES

Andrew Van De Kamp (Shawn Pyfrom)
Bree Van De Kamp (Marcia Cross)
Carlos Solis (Ricardo Chavira)
Deirdre (Jolie Jenkins)
Edie Britt (Nicollette Sheridan)
Felicia Tilman (Harriet Sansom Harris)
Gabrielle Solis (Eva Longoria Parker)
John Rowland (Jesse Metcalfe)
Julie Mayer (Andrea Bowen)
Justin (Ryan Carnes)
Lynette Scavo (Felicity Huffman)
Mary Alice Young (Brenda Strong)
Mike Delfino (James Denton)
Paul Young (Mark Moses)
Rex Van De Kamp (Steven Culp)
Susan Mayer (Teri Hatcher)
Zach Young (Cody Kasch)

ELLEN

Ellen Morgan (Ellen DeGeneres)

QUEER AS FOLK

Brian Kinney (Gale Harold)
Justin Taylor (Randy Harrison)

SIX FEET UNDER

Billy Chenowith (Jeremy Sisto)
Brenda Chenowith (Rachel Griffiths)
Claire Fisher (Lauren Ambrose)
David Fisher (Michael C. Hall)
Federico 'Rico' Diaz (Freddy Rodriguez)
Keith Charles (Mathew St Patrick)
Kurt (Steven Pasquale)
Matthew Gilardi (Gary Hershberger)
Nate Fisher (Peter Krause)
Nathaniel Fisher (Richard Jenkins)
Olivier Castro-Staal (Peter Macdissi)
Russell Corwin (Ben Foster)
Ruth Fisher (Frances Conroy)

THE L WORD

Bette Porter (Jennifer Beals)
Dana Fairbanks (Erin Daniels)
Harrison (Landy Cannon)
Jenny Schecter (Mia Kirshner)
Lara Perkins (Lauren Lee Smith)
Marina Ferrer (Karina Lombard)
Tim Haspel (Eric Mabius)
Tina Kennard (Laurel Holloman)
Tonya (Meredith McGeachie)

THIS LIFE

Ferdy (Ramon Tikaram)

WILL AND GRACE

Grace Adler (Debra Messing)
Jack McFarland (Sean Hayes)
Will Truman (Eric McCormack)

Works Cited

American Library Association (ALA). 2007. 'Banned books', available online at *http://www.ala.org*, accessed 25 February 2007.

'And the plot thickens'. 2005. Zap2It, quoting TV Guide Online, 9 February, available online at *http://tvbb.zap2it.com/showflat.php?Cat=&Board=des perate&Number=181864&page=0&view=collapsed&sb=3&o=&fpart=2*, accessed 12 June 2005.

Arditi, Benjamin, and Jeremy Valentine. 1999. *Polemicization: The Contingency of the Commonplace*. Edinburgh and New York: Edinburgh University Press and New York University Press.

Atkinson, Ted. 2004. Correspondence with the author, 10 March.

Austin, John. 1962. *How to Do Things with Words*. Cambridge, MA: Harvard University Press.

'Baby Name Wizard'. 2005. Online at *http://babynamewizard.com/namevoyager/lnv0105.html*, accessed 25 June 2005.

Ball, Alan. 2001a. '*Six Feet Under*: Death takes a trip'. Interview by Sherri Sylvester, available online at *http://www.cnn.com/2001/SHOWBIZ/TV/06/01/six.feet.under*, accessed 1 June 2001.

Ball, Alan. 2001b. 'Alan Ball brings darkly funny *Six Feet Under* to HBO'. Interview by Christine Champagne, available online at *http://content.gay.com/channels/arts/gaywatch/six_feet_under.html*, accessed 10 July 2001.

Bartlem, Edwina. 2003. 'Coming out on a hell mouth', *Refractory: A Journal of Entertainment Media* 2, available online at *http://blogs.arts.unimelb.edu.au/refractory/2003/03/06/coming-out-on-a-hell-mouth-edwina-bartlem/*, accessed 15 March 2008.

Battis, Jess. 2003. '"She's not all grown yet": Willow as hybrid/hero in *Buffy the Vampire Slayer*', *Slayage: the Online International Journal of Buffy Studies* 2.4, available online at *http://slayageonline.com/essays/slayage8/Battis.htm*, accessed 1 November 2008.

Battis, Jess. 2005. *Blood Relations: Chosen Families in* Buffy the Vampire Slayer *and* Angel. Jefferson, NC: McFarland.

Battles, Kathleen, and Wendy Hilton-Morrow. 2002. 'Gay characters in conventional spaces: *Will and Grace* and the situation comedy genre', *Cultural Studies in Media Communication* 19.1: 87–105.

Beirne, Rebecca. 2004. 'Queering the Slayer-text: reading possibilities in *Buffy the Vampire Slayer*', *Refractory: a Journal of Entertainment Media* 5, available online at *http://blogs.arts.unimelb.edu.au/refractory/2004/02/03/ queering-the-slayer-text-reading-possibilities-in-buffy-the-vampire-slayer-rebecca-beirne/*, accessed 10 February 2008.

Berlant, Lauren, and Michael Warner. 1995. 'What does queer theory teach us about X?', *PMLA* 110.3: 343–9.

Bersani, Leo. 1995. *Homos*. Cambridge and London: Harvard University Press.

Boswell, John. 1982–3. 'Revolutions, universals, and sexual categories', *Salmagundi* 58/59: 89–113.

Brenkman, John. 2002. 'Queer post-politics', *Narrative* 10.2: 174–180.

Brown, Wendy. 2002. 'At the edge', *Political Theory* 30.4: 556–76.

Brown, Wendy. 2005. *Edgework: Critical Essays on Knowledge and Politics*. Princeton: Princeton University Press.

Brown, Wendy. 2006a. *Regulating Aversion: Tolerance in the Age of Identity and Empire*. Princeton: Princeton University Press.

Brown, Wendy. 2006b. 'American nightmare: neoliberalism, neoconservatism, and de-democratization', *Political Theory* 34.6: 690–714.

Brunsdon, Charlotte. 1996. 'Television studies', available online at *http:// www.museum.tv/archives/etv/T/htmlT/televisionst/televisionst.htm*, accessed 10 March 2008.

Burr, Vivien. 2006. '"Friends are the families we choose for ourselves": towards the democratisation of relationships', *BPS Psychology of Women Section Review* 8.2: 27–33.

Burr, Vivien, and Christine Jarvis. 2005. 'Friends are the family we choose for ourselves: young people and alternative families in *Buffy the Vampire Slayer*', *Young: Nordic Journal of Youth Research* 13.3: 269–83.

Bush, George, W. 2003. 'Marriage Protection Week', presidential proclamation, available online at *http://www.whitehouse.gov/news/releases/2003/10/20031003-12.html*, accessed 3 November 2003.

Bush, George W. 2006. 'President discusses marriage protection amendment', available online at *http://www.whitehouse.gov/news/releases/2006/06/20060605-2.html*, accessed 5 July 2006.

Busse, Katrina. 2002. 'Crossing the final taboo: family, sexuality, and incest in Buffyverse Fan Fiction', in Rhonda Wilcox and David Lavery (eds), *Fighting the Forces: What's at Stake in* Buffy the Vampire Slayer. Lanham, MD: Rowman Littlefield: 207–17.

Butler, Judith. 1993. *Bodies that Matter: On the Discursive Limits of 'Sex'*. New York: Routledge.

Butler, Judith. 1995. 'Contingent foundations: feminism and the question of "postmodernism"', in *Feminist Contentions: A Philosophical Exchange*. New York and London: Routledge: 35–58.

Butler, Judith. 1997. *Excitable Speech: A Politics of the Performative*. New York and London: Routledge.

Butler, Judith. 1999 [1990]. *Gender Trouble: Feminism and the Subversion of Identity*. 2nd edn. London and New York: Routledge.

Butler, Judith. 2000. *Antigone's Claim: Kinship Between Life and Death*. New York: Columbia University Press.

Butler, Judith. 2002. 'Is kinship always already heterosexual?', *differences* 15.1: 14–44.

Butler, Judith. 2004. *Undoing Gender*. New York and London: Routledge.

Calhoun, Cheshire. 2005. 'Who's afraid of polygamous marriage? Lessons for same-sex marriage advocacy from the history of polygamy', *San Diego Law Review* 42: 1023–42.

Capsuto, Steven. 2000. *Alternate Channels: The Uncensored Story of Gay and Lesbian Images on Radio and Television*. New York: Balantine.

Carter, David. 2004. *Stonewall: The Riots that Sparked the Gay Revolution*. New York: St Martin's Griffin.

Carver, Terrell. 2004. *Men in Political Theory*. Manchester and New York: Manchester University Press.

Carver, Terrell. 2007. '"Trans-Trouble"', in J. Browne (ed.), *The Future of Gender*. Cambridge: Cambridge University Press: 116–35.

Carver, Terrell, and Samuel A. Chambers. 2007. 'Kinship trouble', *Politics and Gender* 3.4: 427–49.

Chambers, Samuel A. 2003a. *Untimely Politics*. Edinburgh and New York: Edinburgh University Press and New York University Press.

Chambers, Samuel A. 2003b. 'Dialogue, deliberation, and discourse: the far-reaching politics of *The West Wing*', in Peter Rollins and John O'Connor (eds), *The West Wing: The American Presidency as Television Drama*. Syracuse, NY: Syracuse University Press: 83–100.

Chambers, Samuel A. 2006. 'Cultural politics and the practice of fugitive theory', *Contemporary Political Theory* 5.1: 9–32.

Chambers, Samuel A. 2007. '"An incalculable effect": subversions of hetero-normativity', *Political Studies* 55.3: 656–79.

Chambers, Samuel A., and Terrell Carver. 2008. *Judith Butler and Political Theory: Troubling Politics*. London and New York: Routledge.

Connolly, William. 2002. *Neuropolitics: Thinking, Culture, Speed*. Minneapolis: University of Minnesota Press.

Connolly, William. 2005. *Pluralism*. Durham: Duke University Press.

Connolly, William. 2007. Keynote address given at the conference 'Becoming Plural: The Political Thought of William E. Connolly'. Swansea University, 11–12 May.

de Lauretis, Teresa. 1991. 'Queer theory: lesbian and gay sexualities', *differences* 3.2: iii–xviii.

D'Emilio, John. 1983. *Sexual Politics, Sexual Communities: The Making of a Homosexual Minority in the United States, 1940–1970*. Chicago: University of Chicago Press.

D'Emilio, John. 1992. *Out of the Closets: Voices of Gay Liberation*. New York and London: New York University Press.

Dennis, Jeffery. 2003. 'Heteronormativity', in Michael Kimmel (ed.), *Men and Masculinities: A Social, Cultural, and Historical Encyclopedia*. New York: ABC–CLIO: 109–10.

Derrida, Jacques. 1982. *Margins of Philosophy*, trans. Alan Bass. Chicago: University of Chicago Press.

'*Desperate Housewives* Marcia Cross denies lesbian slur'. 10 February 2005. Available online at *http://femalefirst.co.uk/entertainment/28602004.htm*, accessed 15 August 2005.

Disch, Lisa. 2008. 'Representation as "spokespersonship": Bruno Latour's Political Theory', *Parallax* 14:3: 88–100.

Dover, Kenneth. 1989 [1978]. *Greek Homosexuality*. Cambridge, MA: Harvard University Press.

Dunlap, David. 1996. 'Gay parents ease into suburbia: for the first generation, car pools and soccer games', *New York Times*, 16 May.

Edelman, Lee. 1994. *Homographesis: Essays in Gay Literary and Cultural Theory*. New York and London: Routledge.

Edelman, Lee. 2002. 'Post-partum', *Narrative* 10.2: 181–5.

Edelman, Lee. 2004. *No Future: Queer Theory and the Death Drive*. Durham and London: Duke University Press.

Eisenstein, Zillah. 1981. *The Radical Future of Liberal Feminism*. London: Longman Books.

Eskridge, William. 2001. *Equality Practice: Civil Unions and the Future of Gay Rights*. New York: Routledge.

Fausto-Sterling, Anne. 2000. *Sexing the Body: Gender Politics and the Construction of Sexuality*. New York: Basic Books.

Ferguson, Kathy. 2008. 'This species which is not one: identity practice in *Star Trek: Deep Space Nine*', in Terrell Carver and Samuel A. Chambers (eds), *Judith Butler's Precarious Politics: Critical Encounters*. New York and London: Routledge: 173–87.

Feuer, Jane. 1984. 'The MTM style', in Jane Feuer, Paul Kerr, and Tise Vahimagi (eds), *MTM 'Quality' Television*. London: British Film Institute: 32–60.

Fiske, John, and John Hartley. 2003 [1978]. *Reading Television*. London: Routledge.

Foucault, Michel. 1972. *The Archaeology of Knowledge*, trans. M. Sheridan Smith. New York: Pantheon Books.

Foucault, Michel. 1978. *History of Sexuality, Vol. 1: An Introduction*, trans. Robert Hurley. New York: Vintage Books.

Freydkin, Donna. 2005. 'I'm single and straight, Cross says', *USA Today*, 9 February, available online at *http://www.usatoday.com/life/people/2005-02-09-cross_x.htm*, accessed 28 July 2005.

'Gay adoption row'. 2007. BBC, available online at *http://news.bbc.co.uk/1/hi/uk_politics/6298477.stm*, accessed 25 May 2007.

Giantis, Kat. 2005. 'Marcia Cross: Yep, I'm not gay', 9 February, available online, *http://entertainment.msn.com/celebs/article.aspx?news=181071*, accessed 16 August 2005.

Groff, David. 1997. *Out Facts: Just About Everything you Need to Know About Gay and Lesbian Culture*. New York: Universe Publishing.

Grossberg, Larry. 1992. *We Gotta Get Out of this Place*. New York: Routledge.

'Guide to literary and critical theory'. 2004. Available online at *http://www.sla.purdue.edu/academic/engl/theory/genderandsex/terms/heteronormativity.html*, accessed 26 February 2004.

Halberstam, Judith. 1998. *Female Masculinity*. Durham, NC: Duke University Press.

Hall, Stuart. 1973. *Encoding and Decoding in the Television Discourse*. Birmingham: Centre for Cultural Studies, University of Birmingham.

Halley, Janet. 1993. 'The construction of heterosexuality', in Michael Warner (ed.) *Fear of a Queer Planet*. Minneapolis: University of Minnesota Press.

Halperin, David. 1990. *One Hundred Years of Homosexuality: And Other Essays on Greek Love*. New York and London: Routledge.

Halperin, David. 1995. *Saint Foucault: Towards a Gay Hagiography*. Oxford: Oxford University Press.

Halperin, David. 2002. *How to Do the History of Homosexuality*. Chicago: University of Chicago Press.

Halperin, David. 2003. 'The normalization of queer theory', *Journal of Homosexuality* 45.2–4: 339–43.

Havrilesky, Heather. 2004. 'Land of the lipstick lesbians', available online at *http://www.salon.com/ent/tv/review/2004/02/11/l_word/index.html*, accessed 22 July 2005.

Herman, Didi. 2005. '"I'm gay": declarations, desire, and coming-out on prime-time television', *Sexualities* 8.1: 7–29.

'Heteronormativity'. 2004. Online entry at Wikipedia, available at *http://en.wikipedia.org/wiki/Heteronormativity*, accessed 22 February 2004.

Hill, Robert Bernard, with Andrew Billingsley, Eleanor Engram, Michelene R. Malson, Roger H. Rubin, Carol B. Stack, James B. Stewart, and James E. Teele. 1993. *Research on the African-American Family: A Holistic Perspective*. London: Auburn House.

Hornick, Alysa. 2007. 'Buffyology: an academic Buffy studies and Whedonverse bibliography', available online at *http://www.alysa316.com/Buffyology*, accessed 17 January 2007.

Hull, Kathleen. 2006. *Same-Sex Marriage: The Cultural Politics of Love and Law*. Cambridge: Cambridge University Press.

Huntington, Samuel. 1993. 'The clash of civilizations?', *Foreign Affairs* 72.3: 22–49.

Introvigne, Massimo. 2008. 'From *Scooby-Doo* to *Buffy the Vampire Slayer* and back', available online at *http://www.cesnur.org/recens/Halloween_99.htm*, accessed 24 March 2008.

Jagose, Annamare. 1996. *Queer Theory: An Introduction*. Melbourne: Melbourne University Press.

'Joss Whedon'. 2007. Online entry at Wikipedia, available at *http://en.wikipedia.org/wiki/Joss_Whedon*, accessed 7 January 2007.

Jowett, Lorna. 2002. 'Masculinity, monstrosity, and behaviour modification in *Buffy the Vampire Slayer*', *Foundation* 84: 59–73.

Jowett, Lorna. 2005. 'The Summers' house as domestic space in *Buffy the Vampire Slayer*', *Slayage: The Online International Journal of Buffy Studies*, 5.2, available online at *http://slayageonline.com/essays/slayage18/Jowett.htm*, accessed 1 November 2008.

KATC3. 2004. '*Desperate Housewives*: Insulting but Fun', available online at *http://www.katc.com/Global/story.asp?S=2380431&nav=EyAzRZoq*, accessed 12 July 2005.

Katz, Jonathan. 1993. *Gay/Lesbian Almanac: A New Documentary*. New York: Harper and Row.

Keck, William. 2004. 'Desperately seeking Metcalfe', *USA Today*, 18 November, available online at *http://www.usatoday.com/life/people/2004-11-18-desperate-metcalfe_x.htm*, accessed 3 July 2007.

Keith, Christie. 2006. 'Is a gay kiss on TV finally just a kiss?', available online at *http://www.afterelton.com/TV/2006/12/kissing.html*, accessed 12 December 2006.

Krakauer, Jon. 2003. *Under the Banner of Heaven*. New York: Anchor Books.

Kurtz, Stanley. 2006. '*Big Love*, from the set', *National Review Online*, 13 March, available online at *http://www.nationalreview.com/kurtz/kurtz200603130805.asp*, accessed 8 January 2007.

Lavery, David. 2005. '"It's not television, it's magic realism": the mundane, the grotesque and the fantastic in *Six Feet Under*', in Janet McCabe and Kim Akass (eds), *Reading* Six Feet Under. London: I.B.Tauris: 19–33.

Lavery, David. Forthcoming. *Joss: A Creative Portrait of the Creator of the Whedonverses*. London: I.B.Tauris.

Lawson, Mark. 2005. 'Foreword: Reading *Six Feet Under*', in Janet McCabe and Kim Akass (eds), *Reading* Six Feet Under. London: I.B.Tauris: xvii–xxii.

Lee, Patricia. 2006. '*Big Love*: Real polygamists look at HBO polygamists and find sex', *New York Times*, 28 March, available online at *http://www.nytimes.com/2006/03/28/arts/television/28poly.html?pagewanted=1&ei=5090&en=f5a8a1639b304daf&ex=1301202000&partner=rssuserland&emc=rss*, accessed 10 February 2007.

Lehr, Valerie. 1999. *Queer Family Values: Debunking the Myth of the Nuclear Family*. Philadelphia: Temple University Press.

Leonard, John. 2006. 'Polygamy for dummies', *New York Magazine*, 13 March, available online at *http://nymag.com/arts/tv/reviews/16328/*, accessed 12 February 2007.

Lo, Miranda. 2004a. 'Does *The L Word* represent? Viewer reactions vary on the premiere episode', available online at *http://www.afterellen.com/TV/thelword/reaction.html*, accessed 27 June 2005.

Lo, Miranda. 2004b. 'It's all about the hair: butch identity and drag on *The L Word*', available online at *http://www.afterellen.com/TV/thelword/butch.html*, accessed 27 June 2005.

Locklin, Reid. 2002. '*Buffy the Vampire Slayer* and the domestic church: revisioning family and the common good', *Slayage: the Online International Journal of Buffy Studies* 2.2, available online at *http://slayageonline.com/essays/slayage6/Locklin.htm*, accessed 1 November 2008.

'LOGO network blurb'. 2007. Available online through *iTunes*, at *http://www.logoonline.com/about/*, accessed 19 May 2007.

Lorrah, Jean. 2003. 'Love saves the world', in Glenn Yeffeth (ed.), *Seven Seasons of Buffy: Science Fiction and Fantasy Writers Discuss Their Favorite Television Show*. Dallas: Benbella: 167–75.

Lorrah, Jean. 2004. 'A world without love: the failure of family in Angel', in Glenn Yeffeth (ed.), *Five Seasons of Angel: Science Fiction and Fantasy Writers Discuss Their Favorite Vampire*. Dallas: Benbella: 57–63.

Lynch, Frederick. 1992. 'Nonghetto gays: an ethnography of suburban homosexuals', in Gilbert Herdt (ed.), *Gay Culture in America*. Boston: Beacon Press: 165–201.

MacKinnon, Catharine. 1996. *Only Words*. Harvard: Harvard University Press.

Mamdani, Mahmood. 2005. *Good Muslim, Bad Muslim: America, The Cold War, and the Roots of Terror*. New York: Pantheon.

Matsuda, Mari J., Charles R. Lawrence III, Richard Delgado, and Kimberlè Williams Crenshaw. 1993. *Words that Wound*. Boulder: Westview Press.

Mendelsohn, Farah. 2002. 'Surpassing the love of vampires: or, why (and how) a queer reading of the Buffy/Willow relationship is denied', in Rhonda Wilcox and David Lavery (eds), *Fighting the Forces: What's at Stake in* Buffy the Vampire Slayer. New York: Rowman and Littlefield: 45–60.

Merriam-Webster's Dictionary of Law. 1996. Springfield, MA: Merriam-Webster. Available online at *http://dictionary.reference.com*, accessed 8 January 2007.

Miller, D.A. 1991. 'Anal rope', in Diana Fuss (ed.), *Inside/Out: Lesbian Theories, Gay Theories*. New York: Routledge: 119–41.

'Movie/TV News'. 2005. IMDB update, 10 February, available online at *http://www.imdb.com/news/wenn/2005-02-10*, accessed 10 August 2005.

Moylan, Brian. 2006. 'Feeling the "love"', *Washington Blade*, 10 March, available online at *http://www.washblade.com/2006/3-10/arts/television/feeling.cfm*, accessed 14 February 2007.

Mulvey, Laura. 1989 [1973]. *Visual and Other Pleasures*. Bloomington: Indiana University Press.

National Conference of Catholic Bishops Committee on Marriage and Family (NCCB). 1998. *A Family Perspective in Church and Society: Tenth Anniversary Edition*. Washington, DC: United States Catholic Conference.

Neary, Lynn. 2006. 'HBO's *Big Love*: my three wives', 9 March, available online at *http://www.npr.org/templates/story/story.php?storyId=5254450*, accessed 10 February 2007.

New Oxford American Dictionary. 2006. New York: Oxford University Press. Available online at *http://www.oxfordamericandictionary.com*, accessed 8 January 2007.

Newcomb, Horace (ed.). 1997. *Encyclopedia of Television*. 3 vols. Chicago: Fitzroy Dearborn.

Newman, Leslea. 1989. *Heather Has Two Mommies*. New York: Alyson Publications.

Nietzsche, Friedrich. 1967 [1887]. *The Genealogy of Morals*. Trans. Walter Kaufmann. New York: Vintage Books.

Norton, Anne. 2004. *95 Theses on Politics, Culture, and Method*. New Haven: Yale University Press.

Oxford English Dictionary. 2007. 2nd edn. Oxford: Oxford University Press. Available online at *http://dictionary.oed.com/entrance.dtl*, accessed 25 March 2007.

Peterson, Karla. 2004. 'Typing in stereo: shows sound good to real housewives', available online at *http://www.signonsandiego.com/news/features/peterson/20041018-9999-1c18karla.html*, accessed 7 July 2005.

Petrie, Douglas. 2002. 'DVD Commentary on episode "Revelations"'. *Buffy the Vampire Slayer: The Complete Third Season*. 20th Century Fox.

Peyser, Mark, and David Jefferson. 2004. 'Sex and the suburbs', *Newsweek*, 29 November, available online at *http://www.msnbc.msn.com/id/6542185/site/newsweek/*, accessed 6 July 2005.

Potts, Kimberly. 2004. 'Advertisers not "desperate"', 20 October, available online at *http://www.eonline.com/News/Items/0,1,15181,00.html?tnews*, accessed 15 June 2005.

Random House Unabridged Dictionary. 2006. New York: Random House. Available online at *http://dictionary.reference.com*, accessed 8 January 2007.

Rehfeld, Andrew. 2006. 'Towards a general theory of representation', *Journal of Politics* 68.1: 1–21.

Rich, Adrienne. 1980. 'Compulsory heterosexuality and lesbian existence', *Signs: Journal of Women in Culture and Society* 5.4: 631–60.

Robinson, Amy. 1994. 'It takes one to know one: passing and communities of common interest', *Critical Inquiry* 20:4: 715–36.

'Row over mixed-sex hospital wards'. 2006. BBC, available online at *http:// news.bbc.co.uk/1/hi/health/6175642.stm*, accessed 25 May 2007.

Schultz, Gudrun. 2006. 'HBO promotes polygamy with *Big Love* series', 28 February, available online at *http://www.lifesite.net/ldn/2006/feb/0602 2805.html*, accessed 12 February 2007.

'Scooby Gang'. 2006. Wikipedia entry online at *http://en.wikipedia.org/wiki/ Scooby_Gang*, accessed 28 December 2006.

Searle, John. 1969. *Speech Acts: An Essay in the Philosophy of Language*. Cambridge: Cambridge University Press.

Sedgwick, Eve Kosofsky. 1990. *Epistemology of the Closet*. Berkeley: University of California Press.

Sevigny, Chloë. 2006. 'Stirring the pot', Home Box Office interview with Chloë Sevigny, available online at *http://www.hbo.com/biglove/interviews/chloe_sevigny.html*, 15 February 2007.

Shapiro, Michael. 2001. *For Moral Ambiguity: National Culture and the Politics of the Family*. Minneapolis: University of Minnesota Press.

Shorter Oxford English Dictionary. 2002. 5th edn, vol. 1. Oxford: Oxford University Press.

Siemann, Catherine. 2002. 'Darkness falls on the endless summer: Buffy as Gidget for the Fin de Siècle', in Rhonda Wilcox and David Lavery (eds), *Fighting the Forces: What's at Stake in* Buffy the Vampire Slayer. Lanham, MD: Rowman Littlefield: 120–29.

Slan, Heidi. 2005. 'Publicist's statement on behalf of Marcia Cross', quoted in the *Advocate*, 10 February, available online at *http://www.advocate. com/news_detail_ektid02779.asp*, accessed 20 July 2005.

Smith, Greg. 2003. 'The Left takes back the flag: the Steadicam, the snippet, and the song in *The West Wing*'s "In Excelsis Deo"', in Peter Rollins and John O'Connor (eds), The West Wing: *The American Presidency as Television Drama*. Syracuse, NY: Syracuse University Press.

Smith, Joseph, and Orson Pratt. 1948. *The Doctrine and Covenants of the Church of Jesus Christ of Latter-Day Saints*. Salt Lake: Church of Jesus Christ of Latter-Day Saints.

Stoy, Jennifer. 2004. 'Blood and choice: the theory and practice of family in *Angel*', in Roz Kaveney (ed.), *Reading the Vampire Slayer: An Unofficial Critical Companion to* Buffy *and* Angel, 2nd edn. New York: Tauris: 220–32.

Strasser, Mark. 2002. *On Same-Sex Marriage, Civil Unions, and the Rule of Law: Constitutional Interpretation at the Crossroads*. New York: Praeger.

Sullivan, Andrew. 1996. *Virtually Normal*. New York: Vintage.

Sullivan, Andrew (ed.). 2004 [1997]. *Same-Sex Marriage: Pro and Con*. New York: Vintage Books.

Susman, Gary. 2005. 'Cross words', *Entertainment Weekly*, 9 February, available online at *http://www.ew.com/ew/report/0,6115,1026117_3_0_,00.html*, accessed 12 July 2005.

Thompson, Robert. 1996. *Television's Second Golden Age: From* Hill Street Blues *to* ER. New York: Continuum.

Traister, Rebecca. 2005. 'Our favorite housewife', 23 April, available online at *http://www.salon.com/ent/feature/2005/04/23/huffman/index.html*, accessed 23 April 2005.

Turley, Jonathan. 2004. 'Polygamy laws expose our own hypocrisy', *USA Today*, 3 October, available online at *http://www.usatoday.com/news/opinion/columnist/2004-10-03-turley_x.htm*, accessed 15 February 2007.

Turner, Victor. 1967. *The Forest of Symbols: Aspects of Ndembu Ritual*. Ithaca: Cornell University Press.

Vary, Adam. 2005. 'Marcia Cross: desperate rumors', the *Advocate*, 15 March, available online at *http://www.findarticles.com/p/articles/mi_m1589/is_2005_March_15/ai_n13610510*, accessed 25 June 2005.

Walker, Dave. 2004. 'On the air', available online at *http://desperatehousewives.ahaava.com/articles092804.htm*, accessed 10 June 2004.

Warn, Sarah. 2002. 'Will *Earthlings* be the lesbian *Queer as Folk*?', available online at *http://www.afterellen.com/TV/lesbianqaf.html*, accessed 11 June 2005.

Warn, Sarah. 2003. 'Sex and *The L Word*', available online at *http://www.afterellen.com/TV/thelword-sex.html*, accessed 11 June 2005.

Warn, Sarah. 2004a. 'Too much otherness: femininity on *The L Word*', available online at *http://www.afterellen.com/TV/thelword/femininity.html*, accessed 14 June 2005.

Warn, Sarah. 2004b. 'Review of *The L Word*', available online at *http://www.afterellen.com/TV/thelword/review.html*, accessed 14 June 2005.

Warn, Sarah. 2005a. '*Desperate Housewives* outs gay teen with a kiss', 21 February, available online at *http://www.afterelton.com/TV/2005/2/housewives.html*, accessed 22 May 2005.

Warn, Sarah. 2005b. 'The outing of Marcia Cross', 8 February, available online at *http://www.afterellen.com/People/2005/2/marciacross.html*, accessed 31 May 2005.

Warn, Sarah. 2005c. '*The L Word* season 2 review', available online at *http://www.afterellen.com/TV/2005/2/thelword.html*, accessed 16 July 2005.

Warner, Michael. 1993. 'Introduction', in Michael Warner (ed.), *Fear of a Queer Planet*. Minneapolis: University of Minnesota Press.

Warner, Michael. 1999. *The Trouble with Normal: Sex, Politics, and the Ethics of Queer Life*. New York: Free Press.

Weeks, Jeffrey. 1981. *Sex, Politics and Society: The Regulation of Sexuality Since 1800*. New York: Longman.

Weeks, Jeffrey, Catherine Donovan, and Brian Heaphy. 1999. 'Everyday Experiments, Narratives of Non-Heterosexual Relationships' in Elizabeth Silva and Carol Smart (eds), *The New Family*. London: Sage: 83–100.

Westerfield, Scott. 2003. 'A slayer comes to town', in Glenn Yeffeth (ed.), *Seven Seasons of Buffy: Science Fiction and Fantasy Writers Discuss Their Favorite Television Show*. Dallas: Benbella, pp.30–40.

Whedon, Joss. 2001. Interview with SciFi IGN, available online at *http://uk.geocities.com/samleeloo/jossdancing.htm*, accessed 12 November 2006.

Whedon, Joss. 2002. 'DVD commentary on episode "Welcome to the Hellmouth"', *Buffy the Vampire Slayer: The Complete First Season*. 20th Century Fox.

Wilcox, Rhonda. 2005. *Why Buffy Matters: The Art of* Buffy the Vampire Slayer. London: I.B.Tauris.

Wilcox, Rhonda, and David Lavery. 2002. 'Introduction', in Rhonda Wilcox and David Lavery (eds), *Fighting the Forces: What's at Stake in* Buffy the Vampire Slayer. New York: Rowman and Littlefield: 1–16.

'Will and Grace: about the show'. 2001. Available online at *http://www.nbc.com/Will_&_Grace/about/index.html*, accessed 30 June 2001.

Williams, J.P. 2002. 'Choosing your own mother: mother–daughter conflicts in *Buffy*', in Rhonda Wilcox and David Lavery (eds), *Fighting the Forces: What's at Stake in* Buffy the Vampire Slayer. Lanham, MD: Rowman Littlefield: 61–72.

Williford, Daniel. 2004. Correspondence with the author, 5 March.

Williford, Daniel. 2007. Correspondence with the author, 10 January.

Wolfson, Evan. 2005. *Why Marriage Matters: America, Equality, and Gay People's Right to Marry*. New York: Simon & Schuster.

Zeman, Ned. 2005. 'Bed, burbs, and beyond', *Vanity Fair*, 537: 197–205, 264–6.

Zerilli, Linda. 2005. *Feminism and the Abyss of Freedom*. Chicago: University of Chicago Press.

INDEX